DOS 4.0: CUSTOMIZING THE SHELL

"DESIGN YOUR OWN WORKING ENVIRONMENT"

Thomas Goodell

COPYRIGHT

DEDICATION

This book is dedicated to my wife Barbara, whose patience and support made it possible.

ACKNOWLEDGMENTS

I would like to thank the following people for assistance and support in the writing of this book: Curt Blanchard, who provided valuable technical advice; Lily Lasker, who worked long evenings and weekends typing the manuscript; my wife Barbara and daughter Sarah, who spent many evenings and weekends without me; and the clients of Integrated Knowledge Systems, Inc., who continue to present me with challenging problems.

TABLE OF CONTENTS

NOTATIONS

The following notations are used throughout this book:

- Keys in square brackets indicate keys to be pressed on the keyboard. For example,

  [F9]

  means to press the F9 key.

- Keys separated by a slash indicate key combinations. For example,

  [Shift/F9]

  means to press and hold down the Shift key while simultaneously pressing the F9 key.

- Any commands to be typed in by the user appear in the following typeface:

  CHKDSK /V

- Any output or messages that would be displayed on the screen appear in the following typeface:

  `Press any key to continue...`

- The vertical line character (|) appears as a solid line in this book. It will appear as a split line on your computer screen (|).

- The Return key is the same as the Enter or ⏎ key.

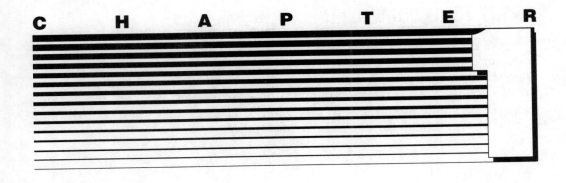

C H A P T E R

INTRODUCTION TO DOS AND DOS 4.0

ABOUT YOUR COMPUTER

To make the best use of DOS, you should understand a few basic concepts about how your computer works. The computer consists of five essential parts: a screen or monitor, a keyboard, a Central Processor Unit (CPU), memory, and disk storage systems. The computer contains other parts, but you must know about these parts to understand how to use DOS. It is also important to know about files, which contain all the computer's information.

The Monitor

There are several types of monitors, but for the purpose of understanding DOS, you only need distinguish between two monitor types: text monitors and graphics monitors. **Text monitors** can only display text and limited diagrams; **graphics monitors** can display graphic images as well as text. There are many different types of graphics monitors with varying degrees of image quality. Most monitors delivered with current PCs have graphic capabilities, even if they do not display color.

The Keyboard

There are two primary types of keyboards used with PCs: the standard keyboard included with the original PCs and the enhanced keyboard included with current PCs. The standard keyboard has 10 function keys at the left end of the main keyboard, and the cursor keys (Up, Down, Left, and Right Arrow keys) are combined with the numeric keypad on the right side of the keyboard. The enhanced keyboard includes 12 function keys across the top and a separate set of cursor keys between the main keyboard and the numeric keypad on the right.

The Central Processor Unit

The CPU (Central Processor Unit) is the "brains" of the computer — it reads and carries out instructions. It is an **integrated circuit** — also known as a **chip**. All your computer's actions are ultimately controlled by the CPU. The original IBM PC contained a CPU named the 8088. All subsequent IBM (and compatible) computers include either an 8088 or a CPU that has evolved from the 8088. The IBM AT, for example, has a CPU named the 80286, which can make use of more memory in your computer and can execute tasks faster than the 8088.

The most recent CPU in this line is the 80386 — the CPU used in the top-of-the-line PS/2 computers (models 70 and 80), the Compaq 386, and other high performance computers. These chips are manufactured by Intel Corporation, which is currently working on the next chip in the line — the 80486.

Each CPU in the line is **backward compatible**, which means that all software that runs on 8088 machines runs on machines with all types of CPUs, and all software that runs on 80286 machines runs on 80286 and subsequent machines. In other words, each chip in the line can run software designed for earlier chips. The CPUs are *not* **forward compatible**; software written to take advantage of the special features of the 80286 will not run on 8088 machines. Most software packages will run on any machine because they are written for the original 8088; however, more and more software is appearing that will run only on the 80286 and, in some cases, only on the 80386. Before you purchase a computer, it is important to make sure that the software you will want to run now (and in the near future) will run on the chip the machine contains.

Memory

Memory refers to electronic storage locations inside the computer. Memory is measured in **bytes**. One byte consists of 8 **bits**. A bit is a single electronic "switch"; it is either on or off, which means that it contains either a 1 or a 0. Information is stored in units of bytes. A computer requires a large number of bytes to do anything useful, so rather than refer to, say, "64000 bytes," most users refer to "64K," where the "K" means Kilo, or thousand.

When you purchase a computer, it comes with a predetermined amount of memory. You can choose to install additional memory later if necessary. First-generation IBM PCs included 64K of memory, which seemed like a lot of memory at the time. By today's standards, very little can be accomplished with 64K. Most PCs include 512K, 640K, or as much as 1 **megabyte** (1 million bytes), also referred to as a "meg."

The first PCs were limited to a maximum of 640K. Today, PCs can contain much more memory. DOS, however, can only make direct use of 640K — a built-in limitation of all DOS versions that is not likely to change. Consequently, three companies (Lotus, Intel, and Microsoft) developed a technique to allow certain programs to use memory beyond 640K. This technique is referred to as the **LIM standard**.

Remember, memory is electronic storage for information, and because it is electronic, information can be moved in and out of it very quickly. The CPU can only retrieve information (both program information and data) from memory. A program on disk must be read into memory before the CPU can execute it. The only drawback to electronic memory is that it is **volatile** — when the computer is turned off, for example, all information in memory is lost. This drawback is one reason why disk storage devices are used; also, disk storage units are much less expensive than electronic memory.

Disk Storage Systems

Disk drives store information on magnetic disks. Information on magnetic disks is **nonvolatile** — it is not lost when you turn off the computer. Also, floppy disks are easily removable; they can be used for transferring information and programs among different computers. When you purchase your copy of DOS 4.0, the program files are included on floppy disks.

Like memory, disk capacity is measured in kilobytes and megabytes. This occasionally causes confusion when computer users think that disk drives and memory are the same thing. It is important to remember that disk drives and memory serve very different purposes. Disk drives are for information *storage*; memory is for *action* on that information.

There are two types of disk drives: **floppy disks** and **fixed disks**. Floppy disks are inserted into disk drives on the front of your computer (or on the side of some models). There are two physical sizes of floppy disks: 3-1/2" and 5-1/4". For each size, there are two capacities: **low-density** and **high-density**. 5-1/4" disks are offered in 360K (low-density) and 1.2-meg (high-density) capacities; 3-1/2" disks are offered in 720K (low-density) and 1.44-meg (high-density) capacities. The disk drive being used must correspond to the disk capacity. Low-capacity drives cannot read from or write to high-capacity disks, but high-capacity drives can read from and write to both high-capacity and low-capacity disks.

Fixed disks (also referred to as **hard disks**) are permanently installed in your computer (they can be removed and replaced, but only with much effort). Fixed disks have two main advantages over floppy disks: they can hold much more information, and they can move information to and from memory much faster. An additional advantage is that if you have a fixed disk, you can install DOS on it in such a way that the computer **boots** (starts operation) from the fixed disk, so you don't need to insert a floppy disk each time you turn on the computer.

Fixed disks come in many sizes. The smallest is 10 megabytes, but 20 megabytes is becoming the common starting size. There is no theoretical limit on how large a fixed disk can be; you can purchase fixed disks with hundreds of megabytes of storage. Until the release of DOS 4.0, DOS could only access a maximum of 32 megabytes on one drive. If you had a drive with more than 32 megabytes, you were required to **partition** it so it appeared to DOS as two or more drives, each within the 32-meg limit. DOS 4.0 allows you to use fixed disks of any size as one drive.

Disk drives are referred to by letters of the alphabet. For example, if your computer contains two floppy drives, they are referred to as drive A and drive B. If your computer contains a fixed disk, that disk is referred to as drive C. Even if your computer includes only one floppy drive, the fixed drive is, by convention, referred to as drive C. Additional drives are then named D, E, F, etc.

Files

A computer **file** is where information is stored. All information your computer uses, whether it is instructional information that tells the computer what to do (such as a word processor program) or data information that the computer works on (such as a letter you write with your word processor), is stored in a file.

All files have names that allow people and computers to refer to them. On IBM and compatible personal computers, all filenames consist of two parts: a name and an extension, separated by a period. The name can include up to eight characters, and the extension can contain up to three characters. The extension is commonly used to indicate the type of file. Several extensions have special meaning to DOS: EXE, COM, BAT, MEU, and SYS. The first three extensions refer to files that DOS executes; MEU files are used by the DOS 4.0 Shell; and the last extension (SYS) refers to files that contain special commands used by DOS when you start your computer.

Some software packages automatically provide file extensions for your data files to identify files being used by the particular software. For example, R:BASE database files all have extensions of RBF. Following are some examples of filenames and extensions:

Filename	File Type
letter.fil	data file — perhaps created with your word processor
format.com	executable file — one of the programs that comprises DOS
business.bat	executable file — batch file written by the computer user
mydata.rbf	database file — created and used by the R:BASE database program

There are essentially two types of files: **executable files** and **data files**. An executable file instructs the computer to do something. All application software programs — word processors, database managers, spreadsheets, etc. — contain executable files. These files have EXE and COM extensions.

Files with BAT extensions (**batch files**) are files that you can write and then instruct DOS to execute. Batch files consist of one or more DOS commands, each of which is carried out in sequence when the batch file is executed. You can accomplish sophisticated tasks with batch files (see Chapter 5).

Files are discussed in detail in Chapter 2.

WHAT IS DOS?

DOS stands for **Disk Operating System**. DOS is a set of programs that instruct your computer how to perform the fundamental tasks it is required to carry out. Even when other software is running, such as your word processor or spreadsheet program, DOS remains in the background, helping the program carry out its tasks. That is why it is referred to as an operating system; it is the system by which your computer operates. It is referred to as a disk operating system because it resides on a disk rather than being "locked" into the hardware of your computer. Keeping the operating system on a disk is a wise design strategy; it allows different versions of the operating system to be distributed without requiring that any hardware be changed.

Because your computer performs many different tasks, DOS is not just one program but many programs. When you turn on your computer, some of these programs are read from the disk and stored in memory, and they remain in memory until you turn the computer off. On a floppy disk system, you can remove the DOS disk, and these programs remain available for use.

Other DOS programs are not loaded into memory when you boot (turn on) your computer. For example, on a floppy disk system, the DOS disk must remain in the computer for you to be able to use these programs. If your computer contains a fixed disk, the DOS directory must be available to use these programs.

The programs stored in memory are the programs used most often, including the COPY program, which copies files, and the DIR (DIRectory) program, which lists files on a disk. The programs not loaded into memory are only used occasionally, such as the FORMAT program, which prepares a new disk for use, and the BACKUP program, which is used for backing up files from a a fixed disk.

The programs included with DOS are, for the most part, used for managing the overall operation of your computer. You can copy and erase files, organize files into directories and subdirectories, and change the way the screen appears when you turn on the computer. You can also use DOS to make it easier and faster to start software programs such as word processors and database packages. DOS provides many such features; the extent to which you use them will depend on your own interests and needs.

WHY DOS 4.0 IS IMPORTANT TO YOU

Versions of DOS prior to DOS 4.0 were much more difficult to use because you were required to learn all of the commands and enter them on the keyboard, which led to a great deal of confusion and frustration. The single most important change from earlier DOS versions is that you are no longer required to remember and enter DOS commands. DOS 4.0 makes these programs available from **menus** that appear on the screen. All you must do is make your menu choices; DOS does the rest.

Even though it is easier to use, DOS 4.0 is more powerful than previous DOS versions. A number of new commands have been added, and many old commands have been enhanced.

A new command — MEM — displays the contents of the computer's memory, including all programs, system device drivers, and install device drivers, as well as a summary of all used and unused areas of memory.

The SWITCHES command has been added to cause an extended keyboard to emulate a conventional keyboard, which allows you to run software intended for a conventional keyboard even when using an extended keyboard.

DOS 4.0 is the first version of DOS to support fixed-disk volumes greater than 32 megabytes. Under previous DOS versions, if your computer contained a fixed disk larger than 32 megabytes, you were required to partition the disk so it would behave like two or more separate drives. With DOS 4.0 you can use fixed disks of any size as a single drive.

The National Language Support function now includes Japan, Korea, People's Republic of China, and Taiwan.

Previous versions of DOS occasionally used slightly different error messages when the same problem arose under different circumstances. This has been corrected for consistency.

Syntax is checked more tightly in DOS 4.0, which means that you must follow the syntax requirements for DOS commands more carefully than in the past because variations of commands that were not "legal" but were tolerated in earlier versions will now generate error messages.

DOS 4.0 provides support for the LIM expanded memory standard, which means that if your computer has more than 640K of memory, you can make use of the extra memory in more ways than were previously available.

The SELECT command has been expanded to provide a simple, menu-driven installation of DOS, complete with on-line help screens.

The ANSI.SYS device driver has been expanded to provide more power in replacing and modifying the keyboard and display input and output management.

The following commands have also been enhanced to increase their power in DOS 4.0: APPEND, BACKUP, BUFFERS, CHKDSK, COUNTRY, DEL, DISPLAY.SYS, FASTOPEN, FDISK, FORMAT, GRAFTABL, GRAPHICS, KEYB, MODE, PRINTER.SYS, REPLACE, SELECT, SYS, TIME, TREE, and VDISK.SYS.

INSTALLING DOS 4.0

Normally, when you install a new operating system on your computer, you replace the old one. You may, however, want the option of running the existing operating system sometimes and running DOS 4.0 other times. One reason for doing this might be that you have installed OS/2 on your computer but also want the option of running DOS 4.0. You may also want the option of running an earlier version of DOS. In these cases, you must follow a special installation procedure to prevent overwriting the existing operating system.

To install the DOS 4.0 Shell on your computer, you must first boot the computer with the DOS 4.0 Install disk. Insert the Install disk in drive A and turn on your computer. If the computer is already on, insert the Install disk in drive A and simultaneously press the Ctrl, Alt, and Del keys ([Ctrl/Alt/Del]), which will cause the computer to reboot.

After the computer has booted, you will be shown several screens that explain use of the Select program for installation, the different types of disk drives that you may be using, and the use of certain keys that have special functions during installation. After this introduction, you will see the screen in Figure 1.1.

```
                    Specify Function and Workspace

        SELECT sets up your computer to run DOS and your programs
        most efficiently based on the option you choose.

        Note:  You can review the results of your choice later
        in this program.

        Choose an option:


            1. Minimum DOS function; maximum program workspace

            2. Balance DOS function with program workspace

            3. Maximum DOS function; minimum program workspace




    _____

    Enter    Esc=Cancel    F1=Help
```

Figure 1.1   *SELECT program screen for allocating memory to DOS 4.0*

You are given three choices for configuring the use of memory during Shell operation. The appropriate choice depends on several factors, including your hardware configuration, your anticipated uses of the DOS 4.0 Shell, and other types of software you intend to run while using the Shell. The primary consideration is whether or not your computer contains a fixed disk. If your computer contains a fixed disk, you can choose option 3 — "Maximum DOS function; minimum program workspace" — because you can install the Shell in **transient mode**. Transient mode frees the memory used by the Shell when you run a program, so you do not suffer ill effects by using the maximum amount of memory for DOS during Shell operation. It is inconvenient, however, to run the Shell in transient mode if you do not have a fixed disk. If this is the case, you must carefully weigh each of the three options.

The difference between transient and resident mode and the use of memory by the Shell is discussed in detail in Chapter 3. For your initial installation, consider the following factors:

Option 1:   **Minimum DOS function; maximum program workspace**

This choice uses the least amount of space for DOS but may limit some functions. For example, the Shell File System may not be able to list and manipulate all of the files on your fixed disk. You may, however, have programs that will not run with any other configuration, in which case this is the best installation choice.

Option 2:   **Balance DOS function with program workspace**

This option is the most likely choice if you have a floppy disk system; it will leave enough memory for most applications without overly sacrificing the Shell's memory requirements.

Option 3:   **Maximum DOS function; minimum program workspace**

Choose this option if you are installing on a fixed disk because you can run in transient mode. This means that the DOS memory is freed for program use when you execute a program, so you can use the maximum memory available for the Shell. If you are installing on a floppy disk system, you should only choose this option if your other programs have minimal memory requirements.

The next screen you will see is used for specifying the country and keyboard layout you will be using. This screen appears in Figure 1.2.

```
                       Select Country and Keyboard


       Predefined country . . . . .: United States              (001)
       Predefined keyboard. . . . .: None




       Choose an option:

          1. Accept predefined country and keyboard

          2. Specify a different country and keyboard





    _____

   Enter    Esc=Cancel    F1=Help
```

Figure 1.2   *SELECT program screen for selecting country and keyboard*

The choice of country determines, among other things, the format in which the date and time are displayed; the choice of keyboard determines the language for which the keyboard codes are interpreted. Choosing Option 1 accepts the default values of the U.S. as the country and no special keyboard installed. These choices will be correct in most cases, but if you want to modify the country and/or keyboard, select Option 2, which will bring up a menu of country and keyboard (language) selections from which you can choose.

You will next be prompted for the drive on which you want to install DOS 4.0. This screen, which appears in Figure 1.3, lists all available drives on your system. To make your selection, press the number key of your choice.

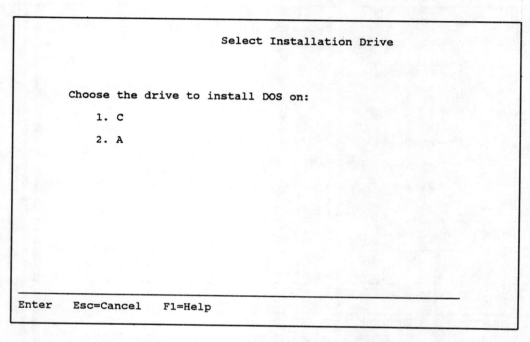

```
                          Select Installation Drive



         Choose the drive to install DOS on:

              1.  C

              2.  A
```

```
 Enter    Esc=Cancel    F1=Help
```

Figure 1.3   SELECT program screen for selecting install drive

The next screen, which appears in Figure 1.4, allows you to specify the directory on which you want to install DOS 4.0.

The drive you specified in the previous step (C: in Figures 1.3 and 1.4) is outside the brackets in which you enter the directory because you cannot change the drive on this screen.

If DOS 4.0 will be the only operating system on your fixed disk, you can select the default directory of DOS. However, if you are installing DOS 4.0 to coexist with a previous version of DOS on a fixed disk, you may already have a directory named DOS in which the previous version resides. You must not use this directory for installing DOS 4.0 because the DOS files for the previous version will be over-written with the DOS 4.0 files. You must therefore specify a new directory for DOS 4.0. "DOS4" would be a logical choice for the new directory's name. You can edit or replace the default DOS directory name on the DOS Directory line.

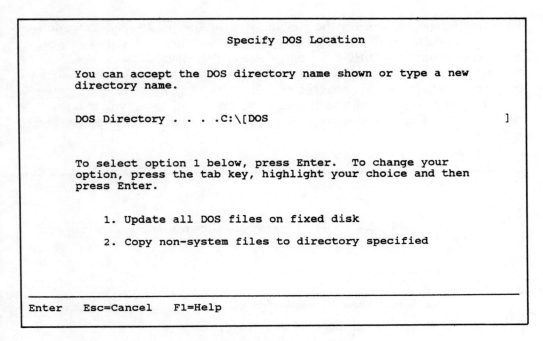

```
                    Specify DOS Location

      You can accept the DOS directory name shown or type a new
      directory name.


      DOS Directory . . . .C:\[DOS                                  ]



      To select option 1 below, press Enter.  To change your
      option, press the tab key, highlight your choice and then
      press Enter.

          1. Update all DOS files on fixed disk

          2. Copy non-system files to directory specified




   ────────────────────────────────────────────────────────────
    Enter    Esc=Cancel    F1=Help
```

Figure 1.4   Specifying directory for DOS 4.0 files

The screen in Figure 1.4 is also used to tell the SELECT program whether you want to install DOS 4.0 to coexist with another operating system or to be the only operating system on a fixed disk. If you want to make DOS 4.0 the only operating system on the disk, press the Return key after entering the directory name, which will cause the DOS system files on the fixed disk to be updated with the version 4.0 files. If you do not want DOS 4.0 to be the only operating system, use the Tab key to move the cursor to the bottom part of the screen and highlight Option 2—"Copy non-system files to directory specified"—before pressing the Return key. If this is your choice, when you want to use DOS 4.0 you will need to boot your computer with a special DOS 4.0 boot disk created at the end of the installation process.

The next screen asks you how many printers are attached to your computer. If you answer one or more, you will be shown a menu of printers. Your choice will inform the Shell which printer(s) you will be using. This menu listing will depend on the version of DOS 4.0 in use. The IBM menu lists only IBM printers and a single option each for "Other Parallel Printer" and "Other Serial Printer." The Microsoft version of DOS 4.0 supports a larger selection of printers. If you are installing printers, you will also be asked to enter the port(s) they are connected to.

Based on the choices made on the previous screens, the SELECT program defines a configuration for installing DOS 4.0. This configuration includes many options not specified on the SELECT screens; these options involve aspects of DOS 4.0 that are usually altered only for advanced technical purposes, so most users are better off not being asked about their preferences. It is, however, informative to see what they are. If you understand these aspects of DOS, you may want to modify them. The next screen you see is the Installation Options screen shown in Figure 1.5.

```
                          Installation Options

         SELECT defined a configuration based on the options
         you chose for DOS functions and program workspace.


         Choose an option:


            1. Accept configuration and continue with installation

            2. Review, change, or add installation choices




 _____
 Enter    Esc=Cancel    F1=Help
```

Figure 1.5   Option to modify default configuration

If you do not want to bother with the advanced options and are happy with the selections you made during the installation process, you should choose Option 1, which will complete the installation and allow you to continue with your work. If you would like to change one or more of the choices you made or would like to review the options not included in the installation process up to this point, you should choose Option 2, which brings up a series of screens, beginning with the Review Selections screen in Figure 1.6.

```
                        Review Selections

        SELECT made these selections for you.  You can accept
        these selections or change any of them.  If you change
        an item from No to Yes, it will increase the amount of
        memory DOS uses.

        To change a selection, use the up and down arrow keys to
        highlight your choice, then press the spacebar.  To accept
        all the selections, press the Enter key.
                                                        Choice:
            Code Page Switching                           No
            Expanded Memory support                       No
            Extended display support (ANSI.SYS)           Yes
            File performance enhancements (FASTOPEN)       Yes
            GRAFTABL display support                      No
            GRAPHICS PrtSc support                        Yes
            DOS SHARE support                             No
            DOS SHELL                                     Yes
            Virtual Disk support (VDISK.SYS)              No


    ─────────────────────────────────────────────────────────

     Enter    Esc=Cancel    F1=Help
```

Figure 1.6   *SELECT Program Review screen*

All of the options on this screen, with the exception of the DOS SHELL option, are advanced features of DOS. The DOS SHELL option determines whether the Shell will appear when you boot your computer. The alternative is to have the computer display the traditional DOS prompt when you boot and to require that you enter the DOSSHELL command to start the Shell.

None of these options are determined by your responses to the installation screens; they are all default values built into the SELECT program.

You can change any of these options by using the Up and Down Arrow keys to highlight the option to be changed and then pressing the Space bar, which toggles the options between Yes and No. If you change any of the No options to Yes, the amount of memory used by DOS 4.0 will be increased. When you have made the changes you want, press the Return key to accept the settings.

The next screen you see is the DOS Parameters screen shown in Figure 1.7.

```
                         DOS Parameters

     SELECT has set these values for you (if any).  Press
     Enter to accept these values or type in new values.


     DOS PATH . . . . . . [C:\DOS                                    >


     APPEND PARAMETERS  . [/E                                        ]
     APPEND PATH  . . . . [C:\DOS                                    >


     PROMPT . . . . . . . [$P$G                                      >




     _____

     Enter    Esc=Cancel    F1=Help
```

Figure 1.7   Screen for setting DOS parameters

The values that appear on the DOS Parameters screen for your computer may be different from those in the previous figures; they depend on both your hardware configuration and the responses made to some of the SELECT installation screens. Again, you can edit the settings as you see fit before pressing the Return key to accept them.

The DOS PATH, APPEND, and PROMPT commands are discussed in detail in Chapters 4 and 7. These commands, with the parameters specified on the DOS Parameters screen, will be entered into the AUTOEXEC.4xx file that SELECT creates upon completion of installation.

The next screen is the DOS SHELL Parameters screen shown in Figure 1.8. These are the parameters that appear on the @SHELLC line of the DOS-SHELL.BAT file, which is discussed in Chapter 3.

```
                    DOS SHELL Parameters


    SELECT has set these values for you (if any).  Press
    Enter to accept these values or type in new values.


    SHELL parameters . .          [/MOS:PCIBMDRV.MOS/TRAN/COLOR/DOS>
```

```
Enter    Esc=Cancel    F1=Help
```

Figure 1.8   Screen for setting Shell parameters

The area in which the parameters appear is marked at the left with a left square bracket ([) and at the right with a greater-than sign (>). The greater-than sign indicates that the text continues beyond the right edge of what is displayed on the screen. Using the Right Arrow key, you can move the cursor to the right edge. At that point, the text will begin to scroll to the left, displaying more parameters. You can also use the End key to jump to the end of the line and the Home key to return to the beginning of the line. You can edit these parameters to customize the way the Shell appears and behaves, as discussed in Chapter 3.

The next screen is the FASTOPEN Parameters screen shown in Figure 1.9. If you turned off the "File Performance Enhancements (FASTOPEN)" option in the Review Selections screen, this screen has no effect. The FASTOPEN option is explained in Chapter 7.

```
                        FASTOPEN Parameters

     SELECT has set these values for you (if any).  Press
     Enter to accept these values or type in new values.


     FASTOPEN parameters  . . .      [C:=(150,150)                    >




   ─────────────────────────────────────────────────────────────────
   Enter    Esc=Cancel    Fl=Help
```

Figure 1.9   Screen for setting FASTOPEN parameters

The GRAPHICS Parameters screen shown in Figure 1.10 appears next. This screen displays a graphics mode setting if your computer includes one. You can change this setting if you do not want to use the setting the SELECT program has chosen.

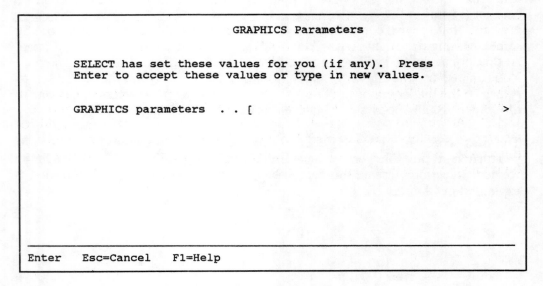

```
                        GRAPHICS Parameters

      SELECT has set these values for you (if any).  Press
      Enter to accept these values or type in new values.


      GRAPHICS parameters  . . [                                       >




   ─────────────────────────────────────────────────────────────────
   Enter    Esc=Cancel    Fl=Help
```

Figure 1.10   Screen for setting GRAPHICS parameters

The next screen is the Configuration Parameters screen shown in Figure 1.11. This screen affects the configuration commands that can be used in your CON-FIG.SYS file, which is discussed in Chapter 4. SELECT places these commands in the CONFIG.4xx file it creates upon completion of installation.

```
                      Configuration Parameters

       SELECT has set these values for you.  Press
       Enter to accept the values shown or type in
       new values.


       BREAK.  . . . . . [ON ]        (ON/OFF)
       BUFFERS  . . . . [25,8    ]    (1-99,1-8)
       FCBS . . . . . . [20,8    ]    (1-255,0-255)
       FILES  . . . . . [8   ]        (8-255)
       LASTDRIVE  . . . [E]           (A-Z)
       STACKS . . . . . [        ]    (8-64,32-512)
       VERIFY . . . . . [OFF]         (ON/OFF)




    Enter    Esc=Cancel    F1=Help
```

Figure 1.11   *Screen for setting CONFIGURATION parameters*

After the Configuration Parameters screen, you may see a screen like the one in Figure 1.12. This screen allows you to change the partitioning of your fixed disk. Unless you are thoroughly familiar with fixed disks and partitions, you should not attempt to use this screen. Select Option 1 ("Leave disk unchanged") and continue to the next screen. If you later decide you would like to modify the partitions on your fixed disk, you can do so.

```
                        Partition Fixed Disk


    Fixed Disk........ 1


    This fixed disk is not completely set up. The fixed disk has space
    that needs to be divided into areas called partitions.  You can
    leave the fixed disk as it is, or you can define your own
    partition sizes.


    Choose an option:

        1. Leave disk unchanged

        2. Define your own partition sizes




   ─────────────────────────────────────────────────────────────

    Enter    Esc=Cancel    F1=Help
```

Figure 1.12   Screen for partitioning a fixed disk

The installation is essentially complete at this point. The last screen will direct you to update your AUTOEXEC.BAT and CONFIG.SYS files and reboot your computer.

The AUTOEXEC.BAT and CONFIG.SYS files are read by DOS when you start your computer; they contain commands that initialize certain aspects of DOS. If you want the Shell to appear when you start your computer, you must include the DOSSHELL command in the AUTOEXEC.BAT file. The AUTOEXEC.BAT and CONFIG.SYS files are discussed in Chapter 4.

If your computer previously contained an earlier version of DOS, you almost certainly already have AUTOEXEC.BAT and CONFIG.SYS files that contain commands you will not want to lose, so SELECT does not replace those files when you install DOS 4.0. Instead, it produces two new files: AUTOEXEC.4xx and CONFIG.4xx. The xx represents the DOS version number (e.g., 00 for DOS 4.00, 01 for DOS 4.01, etc.).

If you are installing DOS 4.0 as the only operating system on your computer, you should use a text editor such as EDLIN or SIDEKICK to copy the commands from the AUTOEXEC.4xx file to your AUTOEXEC.BAT file and from the CON-FIG.4xx file to your CONFIG.SYS file. If you are installing DOS 4.0 to coexist with another operating system, you should leave your AUTOEXEC.BAT and CONFIG.SYS files unchanged and create new ones on your boot disk (discussed below).

If DOS 4.0 is the only operating system on your computer, you can reboot at this point. DOS 4.0 will begin operating, and you can go ahead with your work. If, on the other hand, you have installed DOS 4.0 to coexist with another operating system, you must prepare a boot disk that will cause DOS 4.0 to appear instead of the other operating system. This procedure is performed as follows:

1. Insert the INSTALL disk in drive A.

2. Reboot your computer by simultaneously pressing the Ctrl, Alt, and Del keys.

3. When the opening SELECT screen appears, press the Esc key to stop the installation process.

4. At the A> prompt, enter the following command:

FORMAT A: /S

5. When prompted to do so, insert a new disk in drive A.

6. When asked for a volume label, you can enter a name for the disk (up to eleven characters long), such as DOS4START, and press the Return key. (If you do not want to give your disk a volume label, you can press the Return key; the volume label simply helps you identify the disk.)

7. The disk is now formatted to allow you to use it for booting your computer with DOS 4.0. You should create AUTOEXEC.BAT and CONFIG.SYS files on the disk by using the commands in your old AUTOEXEC.BAT and CONFIG.SYS files as well as the new ones in the AUTOEXEC.4xx and CONFIG.4xx files created by the SELECT program during installation.

When you want to use DOS 4.0, insert this disk in drive A before starting your computer; it will boot with DOS 4.0 and use the AUTOEXEC.BAT and CONFIG.SYS commands you have specified.

Memory Requirements

Previous versions of DOS would run on any IBM or compatible computer, even if it had only 128K of memory. The DOS 4.0 Shell, however, requires at least 256K of memory, and taking full advantage of the Shell requires a minimum of 360K. Tailoring the Shell to your particular hardware setup is covered in detail in Chapter 3. If you do not use the Shell, you can use DOS 4.0 with less than 256K of memory.

It is important to understand that DOS 4.0 can be configured to use only the 256K-360K of memory when you are actually in the Shell. As soon as you run one of your application programs or leave the Shell to use the traditional DOS prompt, the memory used by the Shell can be freed. Consequently, for purposes of running your applications, DOS 4.0 only occupies about 8K more memory than DOS 3.3. Configuration of DOS 4.0 is discussed in Chapter 3.

WHAT IS A SHELL?

In previous versions of DOS, after booting your computer you were prompted to enter the date and time and were then presented with the DOS prompt, which is simply a letter indicating the disk drive from which the computer was booted, followed by a greater-than sign. For example, if you booted from your hard drive (drive C), after entering the date and time you would be presented with the following prompt:

```
C:>_
```

This prompt is not very helpful. If you are new to PCs, the next step would be to start searching through manuals to figure out what you could do from here or ask someone familiar with PCs for help. Even if you figured out what to do, the next time you turned on your computer, you would be required to remember the steps. Each time you needed to use a new command, you would be required to look it up and memorize it.

The concept of a Shell is to "cover" the command prompt and provide an easy interface to it. The DOS 4.0 Shell uses menus as this interface. If you have installed DOS 4.0 on your computer and made sure your AUTOEXEC.BAT file contains the proper commands, when you boot your computer, you will see the screen in Figure 1.13.

```
  01-24-89                     Start Programs                   10:20 am
  Program  Group  Exit                                       |  F1=Help
                               Main Group
              To select an item, use the up and down arrows.
           To start a program or display a new group, press Enter.

  Command Prompt
  File System
  Change Colors
  DOS Utilities...













      F10=Actions   Esc=Cancel   Shift+F9=Command Prompt
```

Figure 1.13   *Start Programs screen in DOS Shell*

The Command Prompt line is highlighted. Using the Arrow and Tab keys or a mouse, you can move the highlight bar around this screen. Maneuvering around the Shell is explained in detail in Chapter 2. If you boot your computer with DOS 4.0 and see a traditional DOS prompt (e.g., C:>), you should refer to Chapter 4 to learn how to set up your AUTOEXEC.BAT file so that you go directly to the Shell upon booting.

The Shell was designed to address the most common complaint about IBM and compatible computers: DOS was difficult to learn and use, which resulted in hours of lost user time. The DOS 4.0 Shell makes DOS accessible and easy to use without requiring that you memorize many commands. In addition, the Shell provides a convenient method for adding software packages that you purchase, such as your word processor or spreadsheet, to the menu so you can run them without entering commands.

The DOS 4.0 Shell also includes on-line help, which means that you are no longer required to look up common DOS commands in manuals to know how to use them —you simply press the Help key, and a screen appears explaining how the currently selected command works. Furthermore, when you add your own programs to the Shell menus, you can write custom Help screens to explain how to run those programs.

Moving Between the Traditional DOS Prompt and the Shell

There may be times when you prefer to work with the traditional DOS prompt rather than the Shell. If you are familiar with an earlier version of DOS, this technique may seem easier at first, but once you become familiar with the Shell, you will find that using it is usually faster and easier than entering commands.

Another reason for working at the DOS prompt is that some of the more advanced commands are not available through the Shell menus. These commands can only be executed by entering them at the DOS prompt unless you add your own menu options for them. Techniques for adding your own options are discussed in Chapter 3.

There are two methods for moving between the DOS prompt and the Shell. The first is to press the Return key when the Command Prompt choice on the Main Group menu is highlighted, which will clear the screen and display the DOS prompt. You can enter any DOS commands or run other software from this point. When you are done, simply enter

exit

and press the Return key to return to the Shell. Pressing

[Shift/F9]

from anywhere in the Shell has the same effect as selecting Command Prompt from the Main Group menu.

The only drawback to this method is that it leaves a small part of the Shell in memory. This part of the Shell continues to occupy about 6K that would otherwise be available to your applications. This is not much memory, but, in some critical situations, it may make the difference between being able to run an application and not being able to run it.

The other method for moving to the DOS prompt is to exit altogether from the Shell, which frees up the additional 6K of memory. To return to the Shell, you must enter the command DOSSHELL. You must either be in the DOS directory or have a PATH command that includes the DOS directory. The PATH command is discussed in Chapters 4 and 7.

If you choose to run an application directly from the Shell by selecting it from one of the Shell menus, when the application stops running, you will be returned directly to the Shell at the point from which the application was called.

This chapter provides a brief overview of DOS 4.0 and the new DOS Shell. The following chapters will present DOS and the Shell in more detail and will explain how to customize them to create a working environment that closely matches your own particular needs.

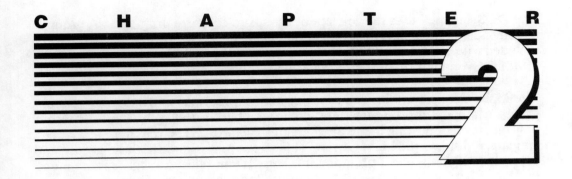

C H A P T E R

2

THE DOS 4.0 SHELL IN DETAIL

The DOS 4.0 Shell uses the concept of **groups** to organize programs. A group is a related set of programs that appear on one menu. Two groups of programs are included with DOS 4.0: the Main Group and the DOS Utilities Group. The DOS Utilities Group is a subgroup of the Main Group.

The Main Group contains two types of items: programs and subgroups. Subgroups can contain programs; they cannot contain further subgroups. There is only one level of nesting in the Shell menu structure. When the first Shell screen appears, it displays the Main Group. This screen may include both subgroups and programs. If you select a program, it is run. If you select a subgroup, the menu for that subgroup is displayed. All items on the subgroup menu are programs — you cannot have more than one level of subgroups.

A Shell program is a special kind of executable file. Commands for Shell programs are written in files with MEU extensions. This is a special extension that signals to DOS 4.0 that the file can be executed from within the Shell.

Adding subgroups and programs is discussed in detail in Chapter 3. For now, the discussion will focus on the programs and subgroups built into the Shell when you purchase it.

THE DOS 4.0 START PROGRAMS SCREEN

When you start the DOS 4.0 Shell, the Start Programs screen appears as in Figure 2.1.

You should note several items on this screen. At the top of the screen is its name — Start Programs. Beneath the screen name is the name of the group being displayed — in this case, the Main Group. Instructions appear immediately beneath the Main Group heading.

There are two areas of the screen from which you can make selections. Between the Start Programs line and the Main Group line is an area called the **Menu Bar**. The Menu Bar contains three choices: Program, Group, and Exit. On the left side of the screen, beneath the Main Group heading and instructions, is the Group Contents area.

```
01-24-89                    Start Programs                10:20 am
Program  Group  Exit                                    | F1=Help
                            Main Group
              To select an item, use the up and down arrows.
            To start a program or display a new group, press Enter.

Command Prompt
File System
Change Colors
DOS Utilities...








F10=Actions   Esc=Cancel   Shift+F9=Command Prompt
```

Figure 2.1   *Start Programs screen*

The Group Contents Area

The Group Contents area displays the contents of the currently selected group.
In Figure 2.1, the currently selected group is the Main Group. Again, a group
consists of a list of the programs that can be run. In the case of the Main Group,
the contents may also include subgroups. The contents of the Main Group are as
follows:

- a program named "Command Prompt"
- a program named "File System"
- a program named "Change Colors"
- a subgroup named "DOS Utilities"

You can identify DOS Utilities as a subgroup because it is followed by ellipses
(...), which indicate that another menu follows this one.

A highlight bar indicates the position of the cursor on this screen. When the screen first appears, the Command Prompt line is highlighted, which means that if you press the Return key, the computer will run the program named Command Prompt.

You can change the position of the cursor to select other choices in the Group Contents by pressing the Up and Down Arrow keys; the highlight bar will scroll through the choices. If you are at the top of the menu, you can go immediately to the bottom by pressing the Up Arrow key. You can go from the bottom of the menu to the top by pressing the Down Arrow key. As your menu grows, you will find this feature provides a useful shortcut.

The Menu Bar

To move from the Group Contents area to the Menu Bar, press the F10 key. The Program selection in the Menu Bar becomes highlighted. Note that whatever item was highlighted in the Group Contents area remains highlighted. Pressing F10 again returns you to the Group Contents area. The Program selection in the Menu Bar is no longer highlighted.

Whenever anything in the Menu Bar is highlighted, the Menu Bar is active. Pressing the Return key will cause the highlighted Menu Bar item to appear. When there is no item highlighted in the Menu Bar, the Group Contents area is active, and pressing the Return key will execute the highlighted program or bring up the next menu if a subgroup is highlighted.

The Menu Bar choices are used primarily to modify the menu system, so their functions are discussed in detail in Chapter 3. One action is relevant here, however; if you highlight the Program choice on the Menu Bar, the following menu appears:

```
Program   Group   Exit
┌─────────────────────────┐
│  Start                  │
│                         │
│  Add...                 │
│  Change...              │
│  Delete...              │
│  Copy...                │
└─────────────────────────┘
```

If the name of a program is highlighted on the menu displayed in the Group Contents area, selecting Start will run that program. If a subgroup name is highlighted, the S in Start will be replaced with an asterisk if you are in text mode or will be blurred if you are in graphics mode, both of which indicate that Start is not available for the currently highlighted item in Group Contents. In other words, you cannot "run" a group; you can only display its menu.

Using a Mouse

One of DOS 4.0's new features is the ability to use a mouse to navigate around the screen. A mouse would have been meaningless for previous versions of DOS because everything had to be entered at the keyboard, but it makes perfect sense for DOS 4.0.

A mouse permits you to move the cursor anywhere on the screen without using the keyboard. It is particularly convenient that you don't need to use the F10 key to switch between the Group Contents area and the Menu Bar. You can simply move the mouse pointer to the item you want, wherever it is, and click the mouse button. You also do not need to scroll through menus to get to your choice; again, simply move the mouse pointer and click.

It takes little time to become proficient at using a mouse, and once you do, you will find it faster and much more convenient than using the keyboard.

THE SHELL HELP PROGRAM

The DOS 4.0 Shell includes a context-sensitive on-line Help system. When you press F1 (the Help key), a Help screen will appear that refers to whatever action, program, or group is currently highlighted. You can try this now. If the Command Prompt line of the Group Contents area is highlighted and you press F1, you will see the following window appear in the lower part of your screen:

```
┌────────────────────────────────────────────────────────┐
│                  Command Prompt                         │
│                                        More:   ↓        │
│  Choose this item or press the Shift+F9 keys            │
│  to display the Shell command prompt. This              │
│  prompt is useful because the Shell does not            │
│  refresh its screens while this prompt is               │
│  being used.  To return to the Start                    │
│                                                         │
├────────────────────────────────────────────────────────┤
│   Esc=Cancel     F1=Help     F11=Index     F9=Keys      │
└────────────────────────────────────────────────────────┘
```

The down arrow next to the message "More:" indicates that there is more information than will fit in this window, so you must scroll the screen downward to see the rest of the information. There are three ways to scroll downward: pressing the Down Arrow key scrolls one line at a time; pressing the PgDn (Page Down) key scrolls one window at a time; and using the mouse to click on the down arrow next to the "More:" message scrolls down one line at a time.

As soon as you have scrolled down one line, you will notice that an up arrow appears next to the down arrow, which indicates that there is information above that line displayed on the screen, and you can scroll up to it. When you get to the bottom of the Help text, the down arrow will disappear, and only the up arrow will remain.

The "More:" message always appears on Help screens, even if the entire Help message fits on one screen. The arrow symbols, however, only appear when there is additional information that does not fit on the screen.

Help on Help and the On-Line Help Index

There are Help screens for all the programs, groups, and actions included in the Shell. There are also Help screens for entry fields — places in which you enter information to direct the action that will be performed. There is even help on how to use the Help System. At the bottom of each Help screen is the message "F1 = Help." Pressing F1 while a Help screen is displayed brings up the following window:

```
        Help on Help
                                More:    ↓
Help is available for all selectable items
and entry fields within the Shell.  To get
help, move the selection cursor to the item
you want help for, then press the F1 key.
Use the PgDn and PgUp keys to scroll the
────────────────────────────────────────────
Esc=Cancel    F1=Help    F11=Index    F9=Keys
```

Note again that there is more information than will fit on the screen, so a down arrow appears next to the "More:" message.

Another way to use the Help System (and a good way to familiarize yourself with the DOS 4.0 Shell) is to press F11 when any Help window is displayed. Some keyboards do not include F11 keys — F11 and F12 keys were introduced with the enhanced keyboard, so PCs with standard keyboards include only 10 function keys. If your keyboard doesn't include an F11 key, holding down the Alt key and pressing F1 will accomplish the same purpose. If you are using a mouse, you can simply point to the "F11 = Index" message and click the mouse button. Pressing F11 from a Help screen brings up the Help System index:

```
        Indexed Help Selections
                                More:    ↓
    Introduction
    Selecting Instructions
    Start Programs Instructions
    File System Instructions
    Keyboard Instructions
────────────────────────────────────────────
Esc=Cancel    F1=Help    F11=Index    F9=Keys
```

When this screen appears, the first item — Introduction — is highlighted. Pressing the Return key will bring up a screen that displays the Help System introductory text. You can scroll the index to select other items. Using this Index function allows you to browse through the Help text and familiarize yourself with features of the Shell you may not otherwise discover.

Special Key Assignments

Many keys perform special tasks within the Shell. These special keys only perform special tasks at certain places in the Shell, and at those places a message is displayed that explains their purpose. For example, at the bottom of all Help screens are messages that describe the functions of four special keys — Esc, F1, F11, and F9.

To review the special key assignments available throughout the Shell, press F9 from any Help screen. The following window appears:

```
                    Key Assignments Help
                                        More:
        Enter       Places in system memory
                    the information you select
                    or type.

        Esc         Cancels the current function

    Esc=Cancel    F1=Help    F11=Index    F9=Keys
```

You can use the arrow keys to scroll through the descriptions of the special key assignments.

Because you are likely to add your own groups and programs to the Shell, DOS 4.0 includes the ability to attach Help screens to those items, which is very easy and is discussed in detail in Chapter 3.

By pressing the Esc key from any of these screens, you can return at any time to the section of the Shell from which you called the Help System.

THE GROUP CONTENTS AREA IN DETAIL

As discussed previously, there are four items in the Group Contents area for the Main Group: Command Prompt, File System, Change Colors, and DOS Utilities. You choose an item by highlighting it and pressing the Return key or by pointing the mouse cursor at it and clicking twice.

Moving Between the Command Prompt and the Shell

The first item on the menu is Command Prompt. When you choose Command Prompt, the traditional DOS prompt appears. On a floppy disk system, the prompt will look like the following:

```
A:>
```

If you have installed DOS 4.0 on a fixed disk, the prompt will look like the following:

```
C:\DOS>
```

This prompt includes a **path**, which indicates that the current directory is the DOS directory on drive C. Directories are explained in detail later in this chapter. The screen will look similar to that in Figure 2.2.

```
When ready to return to the DOS Shell, type EXIT then press enter.


DOS Version 4.00
        (C)Copyright International Business Machines Corp 1981, 1988
        (C)Copyright Microsoft Corp 1981-1986

C:\DOS>
```

Figure 2.2   *Command Prompt screen*

At the top of the screen is the message "When ready to return to the DOS Shell, type EXIT and press the Return key." You can execute any DOS commands at this point, just as you would in previous DOS versions. To return to the Shell, enter

exit

and press the Return key, which takes you back to the Start Programs screen.

Entering commands at the DOS prompt is discussed in Chapter 4.

DISPLAYING AND MANIPULATING FILES AND DIRECTORIES

The concept of files was discussed briefly in Chapter 1, but many aspects of file management must be understood for you to get the most out of your computer. DOS 4.0 provides the easiest and most powerful file management features of any DOS version yet released. These features are combined under the "File System" program.

When you select File System, a screen similar to Figure 2.3 appears.

```
┌─────────────────────────────────────────────────────────────────────────────┐
│  01-24-89                      File System                        4:02 pm     │
│    File  Options  Arrange  Exit                              |  F1=Help       │
├─────────────────────────────────────────────────────────────────────────────┤
│  A  B  C                                                                      │
├─────────────────────────────────────────────────────────────────────────────┤
│  C:\                                                                          │
├─────────────────────────────────────────────────────────────────────────────┤
│         Directory Tree    More:  ↓     │        *.*          More:   ↓        │
│  ► C:\                                  │   012345   .678      109    06-17-88 │
│    ├─DOS                                │   ANSI     .SYS    1,651    12-30-85 │
│    ├─C                                  │   AUTOEXEC.400      122    08-05-88  │
│    ├─MOUSE1                             │   AUTOEXEC.BAK      324    08-18-88  │
│    ├─SPREADS                            │   AUTOEXEC.BAT      334    08-19-88  │
│    │ └─ACCOUNTS                         │   AUTOUSER.BAT      106    10-03-86  │
│    ├─WORDPROC                           │   COMMAND  .COM  37,637    06-17-88  │
│    │ ├─LETTERS                          │   CONFIG   .A3       13    12-31-86  │
│    │ └─FONTS                            │   CONFIG   .LDS      67    12-19-86  │
│    ├─PASCAL                             │   CONFIG   .NIA      47    10-03-86  │
│    ├─LEARN                              │   CONFIG   .SYS     146    08-08-88  │
│    ├─DB                                 │   DJ       .BAT      29    04-13-87  │
│    ├─DBDATA                             │   GRNPC    .NOT   2,435    08-08-88  │
│    │ └─RECORDS                          │   DRIVER   .SYS   1,115    12-30-85  │
│    ├─MYDIR                              │   MYFILE   .COM  32,810    06-17-88  │
├─────────────────────────────────────────────────────────────────────────────┤
│  F10=Actions   Shift+F9=Command Prompt                                        │
└─────────────────────────────────────────────────────────────────────────────┘
```

Figure 2.3   *File System screen*

There are several distinct areas of this screen with which you can interact. The currently active area is indicated by the highlight bar. The F10 key moves between the currently active area, the Menu Bar, and back again. When you first enter the File System, the highlight bar is on the first file in the File List area, so the F10 key moves back and forth between the first item on the Menu Bar and the first file in the File List area.

The Tab key, on the other hand, cycles the highlight bar through all areas with which you can interact. When you use the Tab or F10 key to change to a new active area, you always return to the last item highlighted in that area. The only exception is the Menu Bar, in which you always return to the File choice.

In the second line down from the top of the screen, the Menu Bar contains the choices File, Options, Arrange, and Exit. Beneath the choices is a box known as the **Drive Identifier area** that displays information about your disk storage system. Recall that disk drives are referred to by letters of the alphabet; the first floppy drive is drive A, the second floppy drive is drive B, and the fixed disk drive is drive C. If your computer contains a fixed disk and only one floppy drive, the floppy drive is referred to as both drive A and drive B.

The Drive Identifier area displays the drive letters for the disk drives installed on your computer. In Figure 2.3, there are three drives: A, B, and C. The drive whose directories and files are being displayed is highlighted.

Directories, Subdirectories, and Paths

Beneath the Drive Identifier area is the **Path area**. The concept of paths is extremely important for keeping your files organized and easy to locate. To understand paths, you must first understand the concepts of directories and subdirectories.

With fixed drives and high-capacity floppy drives, it is possible to store many files on a single disk. Files on a fixed disk can easily number in the thousands. Keeping track of all these files could be difficult. Imagine one large file folder containing all the documents for a business. It would be almost impossible to find anything in the file; you would be required to sift through all of your correspondence, sales receipts, accounting information, and everything else in the folder. This situation is similar to what it would be like to keep all such information on a single disk if it were not for directories and subdirectories.

In a directory structure, you can think of the disk as a file drawer rather than a single folder. You can create directories to hold related files. These directories are analogous to file folders. The directory structure is actually much more powerful than the file drawer concept implies because within a directory you can create subdirectories, and within those subdirectories you can create more subdirectories, and so on. This structure permits you to organize files into logical and intuitive groupings, so it is always easy to find files of interest. A directory, then, is a place in which you can store groups of files. All directories except the root directory are also subdirectories.

A directory structure is also called a **directory tree** because of its branching nature. The first directory in the tree is known as the **root directory** because all other directories come out of it.

The term **path** refers to the route through the directory tree that takes you to a particular directory or file. When you specify a path, you separate the directory names by the backslash symbol (\). The root directory is always specified by a single backslash, so the root directory of drive C would be indicated by C:\ — the path shown in the Path area of Figure 2.1. The Path area is not an area in which you can enter information; it simply displays the path to whatever directory is currently selected in the Directory Tree.

On the left side of the screen in Figure 2.3 is the **Directory Tree area**, which shows the complete directory structure for the drive selected in the Drive Identifier area. In Figure 2.3, the drive is C. At the top of the Directory Tree — coming out of the root directory (C:\) — is a line leading down, and off of that line stem horizontal lines with attached subdirectory names. One of the subdirectory names is WORDPROC (for Word Processing). There are two subdirectories under WORDPROC: LETTERS and FONTS. At the bottom of the Directory Tree area is the name of another subdirectory, MYDIR. The MYDIR subdirectory is a subdirectory of the root directory, just as the WORDPROC: subdirectory is.

The vertical root directory line continues past MYDIR, and there is a down arrow next to the "More:" message, which indicates that there are subdirectories that do not fit on the screen. Using the arrow keys to scroll down (or highlighting the down arrow symbol with the mouse pointer) will scroll the Directory Tree down. You can move down one screen at a time with the PgDn key. Note that as soon as you start scrolling, the up arrow symbol also appears.

As you scroll, the highlight bar moves from directory to directory. The currently selected directory, however, does not change simply because of the scrolling. The arrowhead symbol indicates the currently selected directory.

To select a directory, you move the highlight bar to it and press the Return key. If you have a mouse, you can select a directory by moving the mouse pointer to the directory and clicking on it. Note that as you select a new directory, the Path area is automatically changed to indicate the path to the newly selected directory. Only one directory can be selected at a time. The ARRANGE option on the Menu Bar allows you to display and select two directories on the same screen; this is explained later in this chapter.

The File List Area

To the right of the Directory Tree area is the **File List area**, which lists files in the currently selected directory. As you change the selected directory, the filenames listed in the File List area change to reflect the contents of the new directory.

At the top of the File List area, in the center, the following characters appear:

    .

This is the **Filename area**, which indicates what files in the related directory will be displayed in the File List area. It can be used to limit the files from the currently selected directory that appear in the File List. This is useful if a directory has a large number of files and you only want to see a subset of them.

Filenames consist of two parts: the name and the extension. The name is required. It can be composed of one to eight characters. Legal characters include letters of the alphabet and numbers. No distinction is made between uppercase and lowercase. The extension is optional and can be from one to three characters long. The name and extension are separated by a period. The asterisk is known as a **wild card** symbol in filenames. When a filename is entered with an asterisk, it means that DOS should select any files that have any set of characters where the asterisk appears. For example, if *.BAT appeared at the top of the list, all files with BAT extensions would appear in the File List area. Because there is an asterisk before and after the period in Figure 2.3, the File List area includes all files in the C:\ directory.

Asterisks can be embedded within a file designator as well, but they should not be at the beginning of it. For example, the designator FILE*.BAT would select all files that begin with the letters FILE and have BAT extensions, which would include, for example, files named FILE.BAT, FILE1.BAT, FILEXYZ.BAT, and so on. The designator *A.BAT, however, would select all files with an extension of BAT, even if they did not include the letter A. DOS interprets a file designator beginning with an asterisk as indicating all files with the specified extension.

A question mark can also be used as a wild card in filenames. While the asterisk indicates that any set of characters can replace it, a question mark indicates that only one character can replace it. Consequently, if FILE?.BAT appeared at the top of the File List area, all files with names starting with the letters FILE followed by one more characters and an extension of BAT would appear. For example, if you had files named FILE1.BAT, FILE2.BAT, and FILE34.BAT, the names FILE1.BAT and FILE2.BAT would appear. FILE34.BAT would not appear because there would be more than one character replacing the question mark.

Changing the file designator in the Filename area is accomplished with the Options choice on the File System Menu Bar, which is discussed later in this chapter.

The filenames are listed alphabetically in the File List. To their right is a column of numbers that indicate the size in bytes of each file. For example, the first file listed is named 012345.678 and contains 109 bytes.

The final, right-most column is the date on which the file was last saved. The term "last saved" means the last time the file was written to disk. Files are written to disk when they are created or modified. The file 012345.678 was last saved on June 17, 1988. This can be very useful information because you sometimes have two versions of a file and want to identify the most current version.

An additional item of information that DOS saves about each file is the time of day the file was last saved. This information is not available on the File System screen; it can only be seen by executing a DIR command from the command prompt or adding the DIR command to the DOS Utilities menu as explained in Chapter 3.

When the File System screen first appears, the first file in the File List area is highlighted. You can change the highlighted file by scrolling the highlight with the arrow keys.

Only one file will be highlighted at any given time. Highlighting a file, however, does not automatically cause it to be selected. Note that there is no marker to the left of the highlighted filename. To select a file, you must first highlight it and then press the Space bar. (If you are using a mouse, clicking on a file highlights that file *and* switches the marker on and off.) Selecting a file causes an arrowhead marker to appear to the left of the filename.

You can have from 0 filenames selected to all filenames selected. You can also deselect a file that has been selected by highlighting it and pressing the Space bar (the marker will disappear).

As mentioned above, if you change the selected directory in the Directory Tree, the filenames displayed in the File List area are changed to reflect the new directory. When this happens, all selected files are deselected; if you change back to the first directory, you will see that the markers have disappeared from the selected files.

Running a Program from the File List Area

There are three ways to run a program from within the DOS 4.0 Shell. One is to include the program on a menu; another is to use the File choice from the File System Menu Bar. Both of these methods are discussed later in this book.

A third method is to highlight the filename for the program and press the Return key. If you are using a mouse, simply place the mouse pointer on the filename and click twice. This will cause a **dialogue box** to appear. A dialogue box is an on-screen box in which you enter information the computer requires to carry out a task. Some programs require that you enter **parameters** when you run them. Parameters are items of information that tell the program specifically what you want it to do. These parameters are entered into the dialogue box that appears before a program is run.

In Figure 2.3, the root directory is selected. The filenames that appear in the File List are some of the programs included with DOS. If the Format program is contained in this directory, scroll down the File List to the name of the Format program, highlight the name FORMAT.COM, and press the Return key. The dialogue box in Figure 2.4 will appear in the middle of the screen:

```
┌─────────────────────────────────────────────────────────┐
│                        Open File                          │
│                                                           │
│   Starting program:   FORMAT.COM                          │
│                                                           │
│   Associated file :                                       │
│                                                           │
│   Options. .   [                                     >    │
│                                                           │
│                                                           │
├─────────────────────────────────────────────────────────┤
│   <─┘ =Enter    Esc=Cancel    F1=Help                     │
└─────────────────────────────────────────────────────────┘
```

Figure 2.4   Dialogue box for running a program

The meaning of the phrase "associated file" is discussed later in this chapter. For now, consider the Options line in Figure 2.4. The Format program can accept a drive letter to instruct it to format a disk on a drive other than the current drive. For example, from the DOS prompt, you could enter the following command:

FORMAT A:

This command would instruct the program to format a disk in drive A. Because you are executing the program from the Shell, you do not manually enter the FOR-MAT command, so the Options line is used to indicate whatever drive letter you want before running the Format program. Entering A: on the Options line and pressing the Return key instructs the computer to format a disk in the A: drive.

THE FILE SYSTEM MENU BAR—FILE MENU

You can move from the Group Contents area to the Menu Bar by pressing the F10 key or by highlighting a choice on the Menu Bar with the mouse cursor and clicking once. After you have moved to the Menu Bar, you can move the highlight from one choice to another with the mouse or the Left and Right Arrow keys. To make a selection, you highlight the choice and press the Return key or click twice on the choice with the mouse pointer.

The first choice on the Menu Bar is File. Selecting this choice causes the File menu to appear, as shown in Figure 2.5.

```
01-23-89                        File System                      4:11 pm
File  Options  Arrange  Exit                              |  F1=Help
┌─────────────────────────┐
│ Open (start)...          ├─────────────────────────────────────────────
│ Print...                 │
│ Associate...             │
│                          │
│ Move...                  │   More:  ↓           *.*              More:  ↓
│ Copy...                  │    ▸ 012345  .678        109      06-17-88
│ Delete...                │      ANSI    .SYS      1,651      12-30-85
│ Rename...                │      AUTOEXEC.400        122      08-05-88
│ Change attribute...      │      AUTOEXEC.BAK        324      08-18-88
│ View                     │      AUTOEXEC.BAT        334      08-19-88
│                          │      AUTOUSER.BAT        106      10-03-86
│ Create directory...      │      COMMAND .COM     37,637      06-17-88
│ Select all               │      CONFIG  .A3          13      12-31-86
│ Deselect all             │      CONFIG  .LDS         67      12-19-86
└─────────────────────────┘      CONFIG  .NIA         47      10-03-86
      ├─LEARN                     CONFIG  .SYS        146      08-08-88
      ├─DB                        DJ      .BAT         29      04-13-87
      ├─DBDATA                    GRNPC   .NOT      2,435      08-08-88
      │  └─RULES                  DRIVER  .SYS      1,115      12-30-85
      ├─WP                        MYFILE  .COM     32,810      06-17-88

F10=Actions   Shift+F9=Command Prompt
```

Figure 2.5   *File menu in the Shell file system*

There are three groups of actions in this menu. The first group—Open (start), Print, and Associate—consists of actions that interact in some way with marked files. The second group—Move, Copy, Delete, Rename, Change Attribute, and View—consists of actions that perform some operation on marked files. The third group—Create directory, Select All, and Deselect All—consists of actions that involve the currently selected directory.

Note that most of the actions have ellipses (. . .) following them, which indicate that selecting these actions will lead to another screen on which you will enter information or make choices. Choices not followed by ellipses are carried out immediately upon selection.

The Associate Option

Although it is not the first item in the list, it is appropriate to first discuss the Associate option on the File Menu. The discussion of this option will affect some of the other options.

The Associate feature allows you to associate a program with all files that have a particular extension. Recall that you can run a program from the Shell simply by highlighting the program name in the File List area and pressing the Return key. It makes sense to only run files that are actual programs; running a file that contains, for example, a letter you produced with your word processor would not make sense.

If you want to edit such a file with your word processor, you must first run the word processor program and then open the letter file in your word processor for editing. You can streamline this operation by using the Associate feature. If you name the files that contain your correspondence with the extension .LET, you can associate your word processing program with that extension. Then, you can "run" a correspondence file. When you do, the Shell will actually run the word processing program, but it will pass to it as the parameter the name of the .LET file that you ran, so the file will automatically be opened in your word processor.

If your word processing program is named WP and the file that contains the WP program is named WP.EXE, marking that file and selecting the Associate option would cause the dialogue box in Figure 2.6 to appear in the middle of your screen.

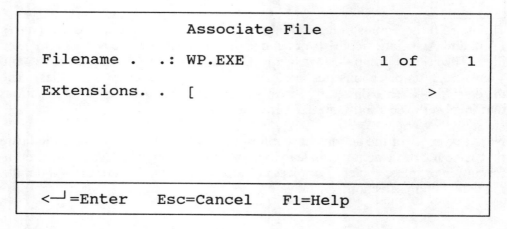

```
                        Associate File

   Filename .   .: WP.EXE                    1 of      1

   Extensions. .  [                            >



   <──┘ =Enter     Esc=Cancel      F1=Help
```

Figure 2.6   *Associate File dialogue box*

This box informs you that you will associate file extensions with the program file WP.EXE. The "1 of 1" indicates that only one file was marked when you chose the Associate option. If you had marked two files, the screen would show "1 of 2." After you were through with the WP.EXE file, the Associate File dialogue box would appear again with the second filename.

On the line that begins "Extensions. . " enter the extension(s) you want associated with the WP.EXE program. To enter an extension, simply type the extension *without* a period in front of it. To enter more than one extension, separate each one with blank spaces.

Note in Figure 2.6 that the Extensions line ends with a greater-than (>) sign, which indicates that you can enter more information than will appear on the screen. When you approach the maximum number of characters allowed, a right square bracket (]) will appear. You will not be able to type beyond the square bracket.

After typing the filename extensions you want associated with the program, press the Return key to bring up the dialogue box in Figure 2.7.

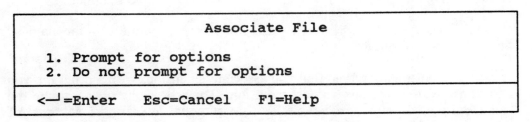

Figure 2.7   *Setting Parameters dialogue box for associated files*

Option 1 in Figure 2.7 will cause the Open File dialogue box, shown in Figure 2.8, to appear whenever you run files with the associated extension. The Open File dialogue box is used to enter any parameters the program can receive when it is run.

If files with the LET extension are associated with the WP.EXE program, marking a file named MERGER.LET and pressing the Return key will bring up the dialogue box in Figure 2.8.

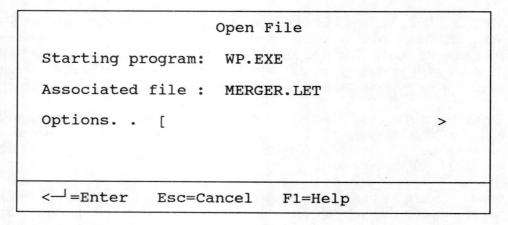

```
                      Open File

  Starting program:    WP.EXE

  Associated file :    MERGER.LET

  Options. .   [                                    >



  <──┘ =Enter    Esc=Cancel    F1=Help
```

Figure 2.8   Open File dialogue box for associated file

Compare Figure 2.8 with Figure 2.4. Note that the name of the program being started in Figure 2.8 is the name of the program associated with the marked file — not the name of the marked file itself. In Figure 2.4, there was no associated file. In Figure 2.8, the file that was run appears on the Associated file line.

If you choose Option 2 in Figure 2.7 — "Do not prompt for options" — the dialogue box in Figure 2.8 will not appear when you run your LET file.

It is important to understand that you associate extensions with a program; you do not associate programs with an extension. These procedures may sound the same, but marking a nonexecutable file (one without an .EXE, .COM, or .BAT extension) and selecting the Associate option causes the dialogue box in Figure 2.9 to appear.

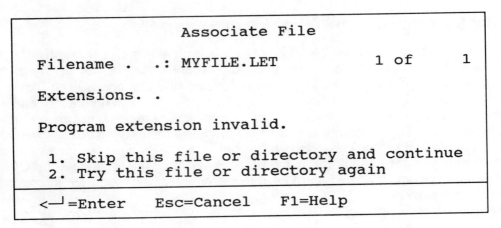

```
                   Associate File

Filename .   .: MYFILE.LET              1 of       1

Extensions. .

Program extension invalid.

   1. Skip this file or directory and continue
   2. Try this file or directory again

   <┘ =Enter    Esc=Cancel    F1=Help
```

Figure 2.9   *Attempting to associate extensions with a nonexecutable file*

The message "Program extension invalid" informs you that this is not an executable file and, therefore, cannot have file extensions associated with it. The reason for the "Try this file or directory again" option is because there is a possibility that an error occurred when the computer read the filename. If this dialogue box appeared when you were attempting to associate extensions with an executable file, then selecting this option would cause the computer to try again.

The Shell imposes a limit of 20 extensions associated with programs. You can have 20 extensions associated with one program, one extension associated with each of 20 programs, or any combination that does not exceed 20 extensions. Because this limit exists, it is a good idea to develop naming conventions for your file extensions. If each letter you wrote had a different file extension, you would be required to associate each extension separately, and you could only have twenty extensions associated with your word processor. If, on the other hand, you name all of your letter files with the same extension, you can associate them all with the word processor with only one extension.

The Open Option

Using the Open option on the File Menu Bar is an alternative to highlighting a filename and pressing the Return key. The difference is that the Open option operates only if exactly one file is marked in the File List area. If no files are marked or if more than one file is marked, the Open option on the File Menu Bar menu has an asterisk where the O should be, indicating that it is not an available choice. (If you are in graphics mode, the option will not have an asterisk but will appear blurred.) You can always run a file by highlighting it and pressing the Return key, regardless of how many files are marked. In either case, the Open File dialogue box shown in Figure 2.4 appears for entering parameters before running the program.

The Print Option

The Print option is used to send all marked files to the printer. This option can be selected when one or more files are marked. If no files are marked, the P in Print will be replaced by an asterisk, or "Print" will be blurred in graphics mode, each of which indicates that the option is not available.

The Print option makes use of the DOS **print queue**—an internal buffer that stores the names of files to be printed and automatically sends the files to the printer when it is ready for them. This feature is convenient because it means that you do not need to wait for your files to finish printing before you can use the computer again. DOS quickly lines up the files in the queue and allows you to go about your business.

If you continue working while DOS prints your files, you may notice that the computer pauses occassionally because the printer has finished printing the last information sent to it, and DOS needs to take over the computer momentarily in order to send the next chunk of information to the printer.

When you select the Print option, the first screen you will see is the one in Figure 2.10.

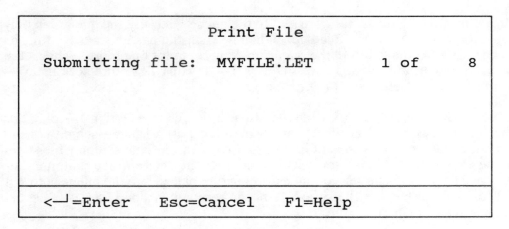

```
                    Print File
   Submitting file:  MYFILE.LET        1 of       8




   <─┘ =Enter    Esc=Cancel    F1=Help
```

Figure 2.10   *Choosing Print from the File menu*

This screen displays the action occurring between the computer and the print queue. When the screen only says "Submitting file:" followed by a filename, it is informing you that the computer is momentarily tied up sending a file to the print queue. Note that this is different from sending the information to the printer — that process takes much longer. At this point, DOS is simply placing the filename in the queue. The screen in Figure 2.10 may disappear before you even read it because filenames can be sent to the queue very rapidly.

The print queue can only hold ten filenames at a time (increasing and decreasing this number is discussed in Chapter 4). Consequently, if you send many files to the print queue, it may fill up. If this happens, you will see the box in Figure 2.11.

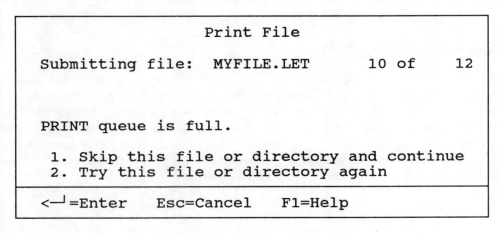

```
                    Print File
   Submitting file:  MYFILE.LET       10 of      12


   PRINT queue is full.

     1. Skip this file or directory and continue
     2. Try this file or directory again
   <─┘ =Enter    Esc=Cancel    F1=Help
```

Figure 2.11   *Print File dialogue box when queue is full*

In Figure 2.11, 12 filenames were sent to the queue. Because the queue can only hold ten filenames, it has filled up. When the first file has finished printing, its name will be removed from the queue, making room for one more. After a file has finished printing, you can press Option 2 — "Try this file or directory again" — to place the next filename into the queue.

If you do not want to wait for a file to finish printing, choose Option 1 — "Skip this file or directory and continue" — to display the next filename submitted and redisplay the Print File box in Figure 2.11. You can continue skipping files until none are left; at that point, you will be returned to the Shell and can continue your work. The print queue will continue printing files placed into the queue before it filled up, until they are all printed. You can resubmit skipped files as space becomes available in the queue.

If you submit a set of files and then submit a second set before the first set finishes printing, the Print File box will only indicate the number of files being submitted in the current set. However, the maximum of ten files in the queue applies to the total number of files waiting to print — not the number submitted in a particular set.

For example, if you submit four files, the Print File box will flash the messages "1 of 4," "2 of 4," and so on. After the fourth file is submitted, the box will disappear. If you then submit seven more files, the messages will be "1 of 7," "2 of 7," and so on. If the first file from the first set is still printing when the seventh file from the second set is submitted, the print queue will already be full (four files from the first set plus six files from the second set equals the maximum of ten files in the queue). For this reason, you may see the "Print queue is full" message when there are fewer than ten files being submitted in a particular set.

Customizing the Print Option

The Print option uses the traditional DOS PRINT command. Many aspects of the command modify how Print works: the number of files that can fit in the queue, the amount of memory used for buffering the files as they print, and other aspects. These modifications involve setting **switches** that instruct Print how to behave. The switches can only be set the first time a PRINT command is encountered; they are then set permanently until the machine is rebooted. These modifications are all explained in detail in Chapter 4.

If you examine the AUTOEXEC.400 file created during installation, you will see the command PRINT /D:LPT1. This is the DOS PRINT command with one modification specified by the /D parameter. If this command is not included in the AUTOEXEC.BAT file from which the Shell is started, the Print option will not be available. When the File menu is pulled down, the "P" in Print will be replaced by an asterisk, or the word Print will be blurred, both of which indicate that the option is not available.

After you have studied the PRINT command in Chapter 4 and learned how to modify it, you can do so by editing the PRINT /D:LPT1 line in your AUTOEXEC.BAT file. Alternatively, you can omit the line entirely and write a Shell program that prompts you for the options you want to include. Writing Shell programs is discussed in Chapter 3. If you use this method, you will add a Print choice to another menu (perhaps the DOS Utilities menu) and control the queue from there.

The Move Option

The Move option is used to change the directory in which a file resides. In previous DOS versions, the only way to accomplish this task was to copy the file from the directory it was initially in to the directory you wanted to move it to and then delete it from the first directory. This was tedious and, with large files, time-consuming. The DOS 4.0 Move option makes it possible to change the directory that contains a file without actually copying or deleting the file. If you want, you can also rename the file during the Move process.

To activate the Move option, you must have at least one file marked in the File List area. If you have more than one file marked, they will all be moved. If more than one file is marked, however, you cannot rename them during the Move process.

In Figure 2.3, the root directory (C:\) is selected, so the files in the File List area are all in that directory. To move the AUTOEXEC.400 and ANSI.SYS files to the DOS directory, you should mark them and then select Move from the File menu. The following dialogue box will appear on your screen:

```
┌──────────────────────────────────────────────────────────┐
│                      Move File                           │
│                                                          │
│   From:      [AUTOEXEC.400 DOS4.NOT              >       │
│                                                          │
│   To:        [C:\                                >       │
│                                                          │
│                                                          │
│                                                          │
│                                                          │
├──────────────────────────────────────────────────────────┤
│   <┘=Enter      Esc=Cancel      F1=Help                  │
└──────────────────────────────────────────────────────────┘
```

The names of the files being moved appear on the "From:" line, which is not an editable line (i.e., you cannot enter new filenames or change existing ones). If, however, the list of filenames extends past the right angle bracket (>), you can use the Tab key to place the cursor on this line and then press the Right Arrow key to review the filenames.

The "To:" line is where you enter the destination directory. At first, this line displays the current directory (i.e., the one in which the files now reside). It does not make sense to move files to a directory they are already in, so unless you are just renaming them, this line should be changed. The line can be changed either by editing it (e.g., moving to the end of the line by pressing the End key and adding a subdirectory) or by replacing it entirely. Pressing the Return key will cause the files to be moved to the destination directory.

Note that the destination directory must not end with a backslash (\) character. In this example, the correct destination directory would entered as

C:\DOS

The error message "Destination path incorrect" would appear if the destination directory were entered as

C:\DOS

If there is only one file on the "From:" line, you can include a new name on the "To:" line. If you do not specify a new directory but only a new name, the command is equivalent to a Rename command (discussed later in this chapter). If you attempt to specify a new name when moving more than one file, the error message "You have more than one file selected" will appear.

If the "You have more than one file selected" message appears, and you were not attempting to enter a new filename, check the name of the directory you have entered to make sure it exists. If the last subdirectory in the path is not a directory, it will be interpreted as a filename that should be used for renaming the files being moved. For example, if you entered the target directory as C:\DS by mistake, the DS would be interpreted as a name that the AUTOEXEC.400 and ANSI.SYS files should be renamed with. Because you cannot rename two files to the same name, the error message will appear.

If you attempt to move a file to a directory that already contains a file with the same name, the following confirmation box will appear:

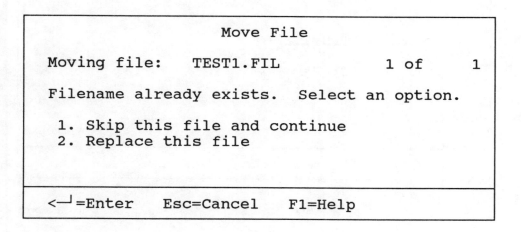

```
                      Move File

 Moving file:    TEST1.FIL              1 of        1

 Filename already exists.   Select an option.

   1. Skip this file and continue
   2. Replace this file



 <─┘=Enter      Esc=Cancel      F1=Help
```

You can choose either to not move the file or to replace the old file with the one being moved. If you want to move the file but not overwrite the file in the destination directory, you can rename the file being moved.

You can move a file to another disk as well as to another directory on the same disk. If you try this with a large file, note that it takes much longer than moving the file between directories on the same disk because the file must be copied to the target disk and then deleted from the source disk. When you move the file within a disk, the file itself is not changed; only the information that identifies its directory is affected. This technique is much faster than copying and deleting the file.

The Copy Option

The Copy option is used to make a duplicate copy of a file. The copy can reside in the same directory as the original if you rename it during the copy, or it can reside in a different directory with either the same or a different name. Choosing Copy brings up the dialogue box in Figure 2.12.

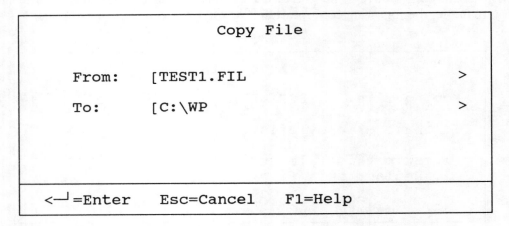

Figure 2.12   Choosing Copy from the File menu

As in the Move File box, you cannot edit or change the From: line, but you can use the Tab key to position the cursor on this line and scan it with the Arrow keys.

The "To:" line displays the current directory. If you press the Return key at this point, you will receive the following error message:

```
File cannot be copied to itself.

1. Skip this file or directory and continue
2. Try this file or directory again
```

It does not make sense to copy a file to itself, so you must either specify a new name for the file in the current directory or a new directory to copy the file to. As with the Move option, you can specify a new name only if you are copying a single file (otherwise, DOS will not know which file should get the new name). If you are copying multiple files and attempt to rename them, the error message "You have more than one file selected" will appear.

If you specify a directory that does not exist, the message "Path not found" will appear. If you include a backslash (\) at the end of the path, the message "Destination path incorrect" will appear.

If there is already a file with the same name in the directory you are copying to, a file confirmation box such as the one in Figure 2.13 will appear to confirm whether or not you want to overwrite the old file.

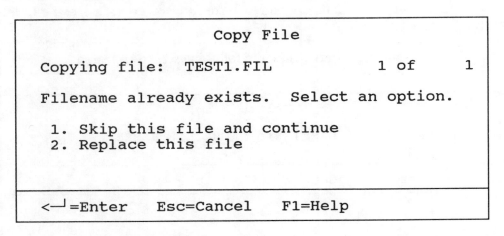

Figure 2.13   *Copy File dialogue box: trying to copy to an existing file*

As with the Move command, you can use the Copy command to copy files from one disk to another. To do this, enter the drive name of the new disk as part of the destination path.

It is important to understand how DOS interprets the path you include in a filename. If you specify a path whose final directory does not exist, that directory name will be interpreted as a filename. For example, if you enter the path C:\WP\TEST in Figure 2.12 and there is no TEST subdirectory in your WP directory, DOS will interpret TEST as a new filename and rename the TEST1.FIL in the WP directory because DOS has no way of differentiating between a filename and a nonexistent directory name that comes at the end of a path.

On the other hand, if one of the path's inner directories does not exist, DOS knows that it is an invalid directory because filenames cannot occur in the inner part of a path. For example, if you enter C:\DOS\TEST1\TEST2 as the pathname to copy to, DOS cannot tell whether TEST2 is a file or directory but knows that TEST1 must be a directory. If TEST1 does not exist, the error message "Path not found" will appear.

The Delete Option

The Delete option is used to remove files or a directory from your disk. If there are files marked in the File List area, they are deleted; if no files are marked, the selected directory is deleted. However, you are always presented with a confirmation panel before a deletion occurs to make sure you do not select the Delete option by accident.

If you are deleting one or more files, the following screen appears:

```
                     Delete File

   Delete . .      [NAME1.FIL NAME2.FIL NAME3.FIL N>

  <─┘=Enter    Esc=Cancel    F1=Help
```

This screen displays the names of all marked files. You can use the Arrow keys and the Home and End keys to scan the names if they do not all fit in the space provided on the screen, but you cannot edit them. Pressing the Return key will cause a confirmation box, as shown in Figure 2.14, to appear for each file in the list.

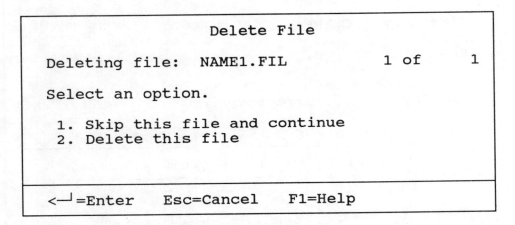

```
                         Delete File

Deleting file:   NAME1.FIL               1 of       1

Select an option.

   1. Skip this file and continue
   2. Delete this file



   <─┘ =Enter    Esc=Cancel    F1=Help
```

Figure 2.14   Delete File confirmation box

Selecting Option 1 — "Skip this file and continue" — will leave this file unchanged and display the next filename in the list. Selecting Option 2 — "Delete this file" — will erase the file from the disk and display the next filename. Pressing the Esc key will cancel the entire command for any files not already deleted.

The confirmation panel that comes up for each filename can be eliminated using the Options menu on the File System Menu Bar. This technique is discussed in the following section, but, in general, it is not advisable to turn the confirmation panel off. Even though it takes a little longer to confirm each file, it protects you against loss of valuable data and programs that may have been marked for deletion by accident.

Deleting a directory is a similar process; you mark the directory to be deleted and select Delete from the File menu. You cannot, however, delete a directory that contains files. If DOS allowed you to do this, it would open the door for disastrous mistakes because all files in the deleted directory would be lost. If you accidentally deleted your root directory, everything on your disk would be erased. If you want to remove a directory, therefore, you must first delete all of the files in it. You can then delete the directory itself.

When you select the Delete option for a directory, the following confirmation panel appears:

```
                    Delete Directory

    Directory:   C:\WP

    Select an option.

      1.  Do not delete this directory
      2.  Delete this directory


    <─┘ =Enter     Esc=Cancel     F1=Help
```

Note that there is no list of directories to be deleted because only one directory can be selected at a time. If the directory is not empty (i.e., it contains files), the error message "Access denied" will appear when you choose Option 2 — "Delete this directory." If the directory is empty, it will be deleted without an additional confirmation panel. There is no need for a confirmation because only one directory is being deleted. The additional panel for files is to ensure that each file listed should be deleted.

The Rename Option

The Rename option is used to rename files or a directory. If there is one or more files marked, the File Rename box will appear:

```
┌─────────────────────────────────────────────────────────────┐
│                      Rename File                             │
│                                                             │
│   Current filename:   SPELL.EXE          1 of       2       │
│                                                             │
│   New filename. .  [                    ]                   │
│                                                             │
│                                                             │
│                                                             │
│                                                             │
├─────────────────────────────────────────────────────────────┤
│   <─┘ =Enter     Esc=Cancel     F1=Help                     │
└─────────────────────────────────────────────────────────────┘
```

Entering the new name and pressing the Return key will cause the file to be renamed. If there are additional files, the box will appear for each one.

Renaming a directory involves the same process, except that the box title is "Rename Directory." Directory names follow the same rules as filenames: eight characters maximum for the name and an optional three-character extension, with a period separating the name from the extension. It is conventional, however, to not use extensions for directory names.

The Change Attribute Option

In addition to the filename, date last changed, and time last changed, one additional item of information is stored about each file — its **attribute settings**. Under most circumstances, you never need to consider the attribute settings, so they are not normally displayed. A file's attribute settings can be displayed and altered using the Change Attribute option on the File menu. You must select one or more files before you can choose the Change Attribute option. Selecting Change Attribute brings up the screen in Figure 2.15.

```
                       Change Attribute

     1. Change selected files one at a time
     2. Change all selected files at once

    <─┘=Enter     Esc=Cancel     F1=Help
```

Figure 2.15   *Setting confirmation for changing file attributes*

This screen gives you the option of reviewing each file before the attributes are changed. It is recommended that you choose Option 1 — "Change selected files one at a time" — unless you are very familiar with attribute settings and confident that you will not make a mistake.

Choosing Option 1 — "Change selected files one at a time" — will bring up the screen in Figure 2.16.

```
                      Change Attribute

     File:    012345.678                   1 of      1

     To change attribute highlight item and
     press Spacebar.  Press Enter when complete.

      Hidden
      Read only
    ▶ Archive

    <─┘=Enter     Esc=Cancel     F1=Help
```

Figure 2.16   *Changing file attributes*

This screen will appear for each file you have selected. The Up and Down Arrow keys are used to move the highlight bar from one choice to the next. Pressing the Space bar switches the attribute setting on and off. When an arrowhead appears to the left of a setting, it indicates that the setting is on. In Figure 2.16, the only attribute setting that is on is the Archive attribute setting.

Four types of attributes are defined for each file: the Read attribute, the Archive attribute, the Hidden attribute, and the System attribute. Each attribute is set to either on or off. The Change Attribute function only allows you to alter the first three attributes. The System attribute is used for special system files that you should never need to worry about.

The Read attribute determines whether a file can be read from and written to or only read from, which is useful to protect important files from being deleted or changed. If the Read attribute is on, the file can only be read. If the Read attribute is off, which is normal, the file can be read from, written to, and deleted.

The Archive attribute is used to indicate whether a file has been changed since it was last backed up. It is used by the DOS BACKUP, RESTORE, and XCOPY commands. When a file is backed up, the Archive attribute is set to off. As soon as the file has been modified in any way, the Archive attribute is set to on. This allows you to perform backups only on files that have been changed since the last backup.

The Hidden attribute is used to "hide" a file. When the Hidden attribute is on, the file does not show up when you perform a directory listing at the command prompt (with the DIR command) or if you list a directory from software within packages such as word processors. Hidden files appear in the File List of the Shell File System, however. Hidden files are most often used for certain types of copy-protection schemes and for certain system files required by DOS.

The System attribute is used to indicate that a file is a **system file** — one used by DOS for operating-system functions. Two system files are included with DOS. In the IBM version (PC-DOS), the system files are referred to as IBMBIO.COM and IBMDOS.COM. In the Microsoft version (MS-DOS), they are referred to as IO.SYS and MSDOS.SYS.

The View Option

The View option is used to view the contents of a file. It is intended to give you a quick way of checking a file's contents; it is not meant to be used for reading or reviewing files. You may want to make such a quick check before deleting a file or to locate a file you want to copy.

You will normally only want to view a text file (one that contains ASCII characters). **ASCII** stands for **American Standard Code for Information Interchange** and refers to a special set of codes used to represent text characters (such as letters, numbers, and punctuation) on computers. If a file contains only ASCII codes, it will appear as normal text when you view it.

An example of an ASCII file is the AUTOEXEC.400 file created by the installation program when you first install DOS 4.0. Selecting AUTOEXEC.400 and choosing the View option will present a screen such as the one shown in Figure 2.17.

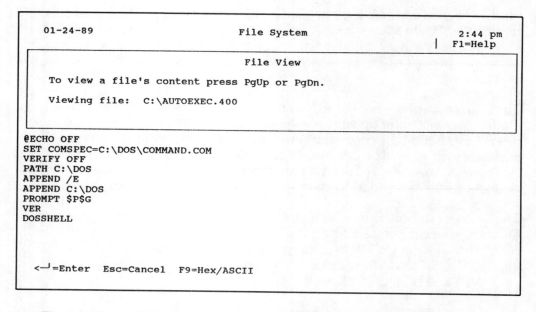

Figure 2.17   *Using the File menu View option to view contents of a file*

The contents of the file appear on the lower two-thirds of the screen, beneath the File View message box. If the file is long enough to extend beyond the bottom of the screen, you can use the PgDn and PgUp keys to scroll up and down through the text one screen at a time. Pressing the Return key also causes the screen to scroll down one screen. The arrow keys do not work for scrolling one line at a time.

Most word processors use additional codes to indicate special formatting commands for printers, such as centering and indenting. These commands will not display as text on the screen but rather as odd-looking symbols with no apparent meaning. For example, a small file created with a word processor to display centered and indented text is shown in Figure 2.18 as it appeared on the word processor screen.

```
This is a test file to see the different kinds of formatting codes used by
this word processor.

One code is for                              centering.

Another code is for      indenting.
```

Figure 2.18   Formatted text in a word processor

Figure 2.19 shows the contents of this file when displayed by the View function.

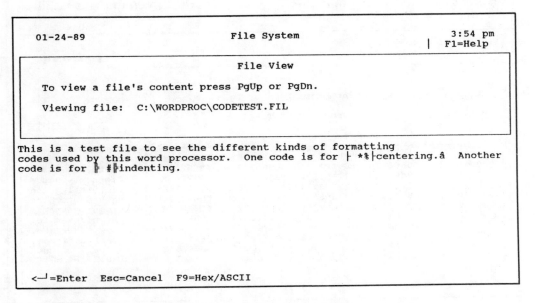

Figure 2.19   File in Figure 2.18 as seen with File menu View option

In the View function, text is not centered or indented; rather, the special symbols for centering and for indenting are displayed on the screen, though their meaning is not evident. In fact, they only have meaning to the particular type of word processor the file was created with because every word processor uses a different set of special formatting codes.

To the computer, all information is numbers — even the codes that appear on the screen as text characters. If a file contains many nontext characters (i.e., those that appear as garbage on the screen), it can be more meaningful to see the actual numbers than the characters if you know how to interpret the numbers.

The View function allows you to view the numbers by pressing the F9 key. If you press F9, most of the lower part of the screen displays the contents of your file as numbers rather than characters. The number system that is used is referred to as **hex** (for hexadecimal, which is base 16). At the bottom of Figure 2.19, you can see the message "F9 = Hex/ASCII," which tells you that F9 can be used to switch between displaying the text in hex format and ASCII format.

Even in Hex mode, the ASCII characters can still be seen; they appear in a small box to the right of the screen, with only meaningful text characters shown. All nontext characters, including spaces, are replaced with periods.

Pressing F9 for the screen in Figure 2.19 results in the screen in Figure 2.20.

```
 01-24-89                      File System                3:56 pm
                                                      |  F1=Help

                              File View
    To view a file's content press PgUp or PgDn.

    Viewing file:   C:\WORDPROC\CODETEST.FIL


 000000    54686973   20697320   61207465   73742066   This.is.a.test.f
 000010    696C6520   746F2073   65652074   68652064   ile.to.see.the.d
 000020    69666665   72656E74   206B696E   6473206F   ifferent.kinds.o
 000030    6620666F   726D6174   74696E67   0D636F64   f.formatting.cod
 000040    65732075   73656420   62792074   68697320   es.used.by.this.
 000050    776F7264   2070726F   63657373   6F722E0A   word.processor..
 000060    0A4F6E65   20636F64   65206973   20666F72   .One.code.is.for
 000070    20C3002A   25C36365   6E746572   696E672E   ......centering.
 000080    830A0A41   6E6F7468   65722063   6F646520   ...Another.code.
 000090    69732066   6F7220CC   0A23CC69   6E64656E   is.for.....inden
 0000A0    74696E67   2E                               ting.


 <─┘=Enter   Esc=Cancel   F9=Hex/ASCII
```

Figure 2.20   File in Figure 2.18 shown in hex format

A knowledgeable programmer will know that Hex code 54 corresponds to the ASCII character T. The upper left code in the Hex portion of Figure 2.20 is 54, and the upper left character in the ASCII portion is T. The left-most box indicates the position in the file.

The Create Directory Option

The Create Directory option allows you to create a new directory on your disk.

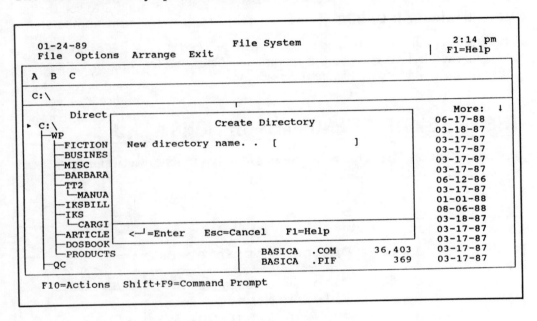

Figure 2.21   Creating a new directory in the File System

Note in Figure 2.21 that there is only room for the directory name; you cannot include a path when creating a directory. You can only create subdirectories of the currently selected directory, which is marked with an arrowhead to the left of the Create Directory dialogue box. After creating the directory, you can add files to it.

The Select All Option

The Select All option is used to instantly mark all files in the current directory, which can be a convenient shortcut if you want to perform an action on most or all of the files in a directory. It is quicker to mark all of the files and then deselect a few with the Space bar or mouse than to individually select a large number of files.

The Deselect All Option

The Deselect All option is used to unmark all marked files. All files do not need to be marked before you use this command. Choosing this option will unmark those that are marked and leave the rest alone.

THE FILE SYSTEM MENU BAR—OPTIONS MENU

Selecting "Options" from the File System Menu Bar pulls down the Options menu shown in Figure 2.22.

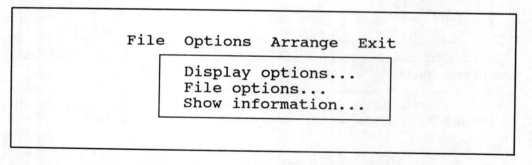

Figure 2.22   *Options menu on File System Menu Bar*

Customizing the File Selection Criteria and File List Sort Order

The first option — Display Options — is used to affect which filenames are displayed in the File List area and how those filenames are sorted. Selecting Display Options brings up the Display Options dialogue box shown in Figure 2.23.

```
                        Display Options
      Name: [*.*            ]

                                   Sort by:

                                ►  Name
                                   Extension
                                   Date
                                   Size
                                   Disk order
    _____

       <─┘ =Enter     Esc=Cancel     F1=Help
```

Figure 2.23   Defining the file selection and sort order of File List area

The default display options are to display all filenames, as specified in the *.* entry for names, and to sort them alphabetically by name.

When the Display Options dialogue box first appears, the cursor is positioned below the first asterisk in the "Name:" area. You can move it to the "Sort by:" area by pressing the Tab key. Pressing the Tab key again returns the cursor to the "Name:" area. Within the "Sort by:" area, the Up and Down Arrow keys are used to move from one Sort option to the next.

When referencing filenames, the asterisk is a **wild card**, which means that any set of characters can replace it. For example, if you enter "*.let" in the Name area, all files with "let" extensions will appear in the File List area, regardless of what the first part of their name is. Entering "invoice.*" will display all files whose name is "invoice," regardless of their extensions.

Another wild card you can use in filenames is the question mark (?). Whereas the asterisk substitutes for any characters, regardless of how many, the question mark substitutes for a single character. For example, if you had three files named "file1.let," "file2.let," and "file10.let," the designation "file?.let" would display the first two of these files but not the third. The designation "file*.let" would display all three files.

The "Sort by:" area is used to determine the order in which the selected files will be listed in the File List area. The default is by Name, which includes both name and extension. You can also sort by Extension, Date, Size, or Disk order. Date is the date of file creation or last modification, and Size is the number of bytes the file occupies on the disk.

The last option — "Disk order" — deserves special mention. Disk order is the order in which the filenames physically reside in the disk directory. It would not seem to be useful to sort the files this way, but if you don't care what order they are in, certain operations will be accomplished faster by the computer if this is the sort order. Operations that affect a large number of files can be performed faster. For example, if you have marked a large number of files and want to copy them or delete them, DOS will be able to perform this task faster if the files are sorted by disk order.

Eliminating Confirmation Boxes
for File Deletion and File Replacement

When you delete a file or overwrite a file with another file of the same name, the Shell displays a confirmation box such as those in Figures 2.13 and 2.14. These confirmation boxes are included to ensure you do not delete or overwrite files that should be left intact. If you are copying or deleting a large number of files, however, the confirmation boxes can be a nuisance because they force you to respond to every single file operation. Turning the boxes off allows the computer to operate on your entire list of files without pausing and frees you to do other things while it works.

Turning the confirmation boxes off is accomplished by selecting File Options from the Menu Bar Options menu, which brings up the menu in Figure 2.24.

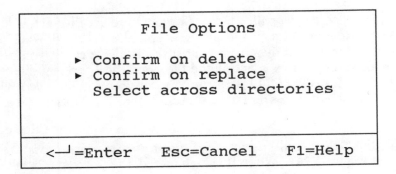

```
            File Options

   ► Confirm on delete
   ► Confirm on replace
     Select across directories


   <─┘ =Enter    Esc=Cancel    F1=Help
```

Figure 2.24   *Setting confirmation boxes for file deletion and replacement,
                    and setting multiple directory selection*

The File Options menu shows the default settings. "Confirm on delete" and "Confirm on replace" are selected, meaning that the confirmation boxes will appear before each file is deleted or replaced. You can use the Up and Down Arrow keys to move the highlight bar through the choices; pressing the Space bar switches them on and off.

The settings remain in effect until you change them again or exit the Shell. When you exit the Shell and start the Shell again, the default settings in Figure 2.24 are again in effect. Note that exiting the Shell does *not* mean moving to the command prompt by pressing [Shift/F9] or selecting Command Prompt from the Main Group menu; either of these two actions will not reset the File Options. Exiting the Shell means actually leaving the Shell by pressing F3 or selecting Exit from the Main Group Menu Bar.

Selecting Files in Multiple Directories

When you mark files in the File List area and then change the selected directory, the marked files in the previous directory are deselected. For example, if the root directory (C:\) were selected and you marked the file AUTOEXEC.BAT, changed the selected directory to C:\DOS, and then changed it back to C:\, the file AUTOEXEC.BAT would no longer be marked. This is a safety feature. When you switch directories, you can no longer see the files that have been marked in another directory, so it is easy to forget about them. This could lead to deleting files that you didn't want deleted, particularly if you have the "Confirm on delete" option turned off.

Despite this concern, you will sometimes want to select files across directories. You may want to move or copy files from several directories into one, or you may be eliminating unwanted files from your disk. In these cases, you may want to search multiple directories, mark all the files, and then perform the move, copy, or delete procedures for all of them in one step. This can be accomplished by turning on the "Select across directories" option in the File Options menu in Figure 2.24.

By default, the "Select across directories" option is set to off (there is no arrowhead next to it in Figure 2.24). When it is highlighted, the Space bar acts as a switch, turning the option on and off. When you exit the Shell (by pressing F3 or choosing Exit from the Main Group menu) and then return to the Shell, it is automatically reset to its default (off) status. It is *not* reset when you go to the command prompt by pressing F9 or when you choose Command Prompt from the Main Group menu.

Displaying Detailed Information about Disks, Directories, and Files

The Show Information option on the Menu Bar Options menu is used to display detailed information concerning the currently selected disk, directory, and file(s). The Show Information box also displays information about the last file highlighted, even if that file was not selected. Files are selected by highlighting them and pressing the Space bar. A selected file displays a marker immediately to the left of the filename. A sample Show Information box appears in Figure 2.25.

```
        Show Information
File
   Name  :  LETTER.FIL
   Attr  :  ...a
Selected                  C
   Number:              3
   Size  :      357,957
Directory
   Name  :  MYDIR
   Size  :    1,452,756
   Files :           20
Disk
   Name  :  MYDISK
   Size  :   32,598,016
   Avail :    5,928,960
   Files :        1,485
   Dirs  :           56

   Esc=Cancel    F1=Help
```

Figure 2.25   *Show Information box in File System*

The information under File in the Show Information box refers to the *most recently highlighted* file. It does not matter whether or not that file was selected. In Figure 2.25, the last file highlighted was LETTER.FIL, and its attribute settings were "a" (for archive) on and all others off.

The information under Selected in Figure 2.25 refers to the current disk drive and the currently selected files. In Figure 2.25, the current disk drive is C, the number of selected files is 3, and the sum of their sizes is 357,957 bytes. If the file referred to under File is not selected, it is not included in this information — i.e. if LETTER.FIL did not have a marker to the left of its name, then the sum of the files, and their cumulative size, would not include LETTER.FIL.

The Directory information refers to the currently selected directory. In Figure 2.25, this directory is named MYDIR. This directory contains 20 files, and the sum of all their sizes is 1,452,756 bytes.

The Disk information refers to the current disk, which is identified near the top of the box to the right of the word "Selected." In Figure 2.25, the disk is drive C. The disk has a volume label of MYDISK, which has a total capacity is 32,598,016 bytes. It has 5,928,960 bytes available for use (which means it has 26,669,056 bytes occupied by files and directories), and it contains a total of 1,485 files in 56 directories.

THE FILE SYSTEM MENU BAR—ARRANGE MENU

Choosing the Arrange option from the File System Menu Bar pulls down the menu in Figure 2.26.

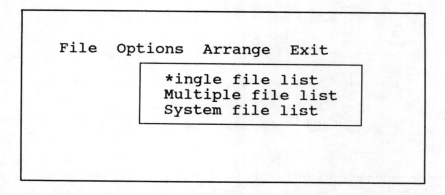

Figure 2.26   *Choosing the file list type from the File System Arrange menu*

The S in the Single file list option is replaced by an asterisk, indicating that this is the current selection and therefore is not available as a choice. In graphics mode, the selection will be blurred to indicate that it is not available. "Single file list" means that the screen contains one Directory Tree area and one File List area, which limits you to displaying only one directory at a time. You cannot have two different directories appear on the screen when Single file list is selected.

Displaying Two Directories at Once

The Multiple file list option allows you to display two Directory Trees and File Lists at the same time. Selecting this option splits the screen horizontally to appear as in Figure 2.27.

```
 01-24-89                      File System                      11:58 am
 File  Options  Arrange  Exit                            |     F1=Help
┌──────────────────────────────────────────────────────────────────────┐
│ A   B   C                                                              │
├──────────────────────────────────────────────────────────────────────┤
│ C:\WP\DOSBOOK                                                          │
├──────────────────────────────────────────────────────────────────────┤
│        Directory Tree      More: ↑↓    │         *.*       More:   ↓   │
│      ┌─IKS                             │  C1     .D4    23,453  09-06-88│
│      └─CLIENTS                         │  C2     .D4    95,053  09-11-88│
│      ─ARTICLES                         │  C2     .WP   106,928  09-06-88│
│    ► ─BOOKS                            │  C3     .D4    89,449  09-06-88│
│      └─PRODUCTS                        │  D4-2   .SCR    1,545  09-05-88│
├──────────────────────────────────────────────────────────────────────┤
│ A   B   C                                                              │
├──────────────────────────────────────────────────────────────────────┤
│        Directory Tree      More:  ↓    │         *.*       More:   ↓   │
│   ►C:\                                 │  012345 .678      109  06-17-88│
│    └─WP                                │  4201   .CPI   17,089  03-18-87│
│      ├─FICTION                         │  5202   .CPI      459  03-17-87│
│      ├─BUSINESS                        │  ANSI   .SYS    1,678  03-17-87│
│      ├─MISC                            │  APPEND .EXE    5,825  03-17-87│
│      └─LETTERS                         │  ASSIGN .COM    1,561  03-17-87│
└──────────────────────────────────────────────────────────────────────┘
```

Figure 2.27   Displaying two directories at once

The Tab key can be used to move the highlight bar from one area to another, or you can click the mouse pointer on the area you would like to activate.

In the two areas, you can display directories from different disk drives, different directories on the same drive, or the same directory. You can perform any of the File System operations in either directory. If you have the Select across directories option set off (under File options; see Figure 2.24), when you select files in one of the File Lists and then switch to the other File List, the files in the first list are deselected. Setting the Select across directories option on will allow you to have files marked in both File Lists at the same time.

Displaying Files Across Directories

You can display all of the files on your disk without regard to directory structure by selecting System file list from the Arrange menu, which changes the screen to appear as in Figure 2.28.

```
 01-24-88                        File System                     4:19 pm
 File   Options   Arrange   Exit                        |    F1=Help

 A   B   C

 C:\

 File                                         *.*                More:   ↓
   Name  : 012345.678           012345  .678        109   06-17-88   12:00pm
   Attr  : ...a                 100B3638         18,401   08-17-88    4:11pm
 Selected            C          4201    .CPI      6,404   06-17-88   12:00pm
   Number:           0          4208    .CPI        641   06-17-88   12:00pm
   Size  :           0          5202    .CPI        402   06-17-88   12:00pm
 Directory                      ADAPT   .BAT        133   03-07-88    5:10am
   Name  : ROOT                 ADDRESS .TUT        826   04-27-88    6:14pm
   Size  :      142,310         ADDRESS .WKB        642   04-27-88    6:14pm
   Files :           32         ADVANCED.TUT          3   04-27-88    6:14pm
 Disk                           AGENDA  .MEM      1,366   08-19-88    9:48am
   Name  :                      ALTA    .MAC          8   08-22-88    9:51am
   Size  :   21,309,440         ALTA    .MAC        107   09-02-88   10:37am
   Avail :    2,426,880         ALTI    .WPM        132   04-27-88    6:14pm
   Files :          688         ALTS    .MAC          3   09-02-88   10:40am
   Dirs  :           30         AMERHYPH.LEX     29,338   06-16-88    1:00am

 F10=Actions   Shift+F9=Command Prompt
```

Figure 2.28   *Displaying all filenames without reference to directories*

The left side of the screen is the same as the Show Information box in Figure 2.25. The contents of the Show Information box are explained in detail earlier in this chapter.

Locating a File on Your Disk

The various options discussed for the File System can be used to quickly locate a file, even if you don't remember its exact name. To do this, first choose System file list from the Arrange menu so that all files on the disk are available to the File List area. Then, choose Display options from the Options menu, and enter as much of the filename as you can remember, using wild cards for the rest. For example, if you remember that a file has a .LET extension, you would enter *.LET in the Name area of the Display Options dialogue box (Figure 2.23), which will cause only files that have extensions of .LET to appear in the File List area. Then, you can scroll through the list of files and highlight the one you are looking for. The directory name will appear on the left side of the screen.

Alternatively, if you remember the date on which you last saved the file, you can use the Display Options dialogue box to sort the files by date and then scroll down to the filename you are looking for.

Changing the Screen Colors Setup

The Change Colors option is used to change the colors that are used by the Shell. If your computer does not have a graphics adapter, you will not be able to use this function. Attempting to select it will result in the message "This Shell function is not available." If your computer does have a graphics adapter, the screen in Figure 2.29 is displayed.

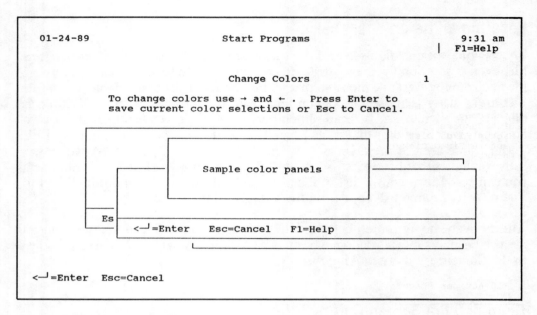

```
 01-24-89                    Start Programs                    9:31 am
                                                             |  F1=Help


                             Change Colors                     1

             To change colors use → and ← .  Press Enter to
             save current color selections or Esc to Cancel.



                        ┌──────────────────────────┐
                        │                          │
                        │     Sample color panels  │
                        │                          │
                        │                          │
                        │                          │
                  Es    │                          │
                        │  <─┘=Enter   Esc=Cancel    F1=Help │



  <─┘=Enter   Esc=Cancel
```

Figure 2.29   *Changing the color set*

There are four sets of colors to choose from. The first one displayed on the Change Colors screen is Set 1, as indicated by the 1 to the right of the Change Colors headline. Using the Right and Left Arrow keys will flip from one set to the next. Each set uses different colors for the foreground, background, File System screens, and so on. When you find the color set you like the most, press the Return key to select it. That color set remains in effect until you choose another one, using the Change Colors option, even if you exit the Shell or turn off the computer.

THE DOS UTILITIES SUBGROUP

Some of the most commonly used DOS commands are included in the DOS Utilities subgroup. These commands are used for setting the computer's internal clock and for managing disks. Selecting DOS Utilities brings up the screen shown in Figure 2.30.

```
01-24-89                    Start Programs                    4:55 pm
Program  Group  Exit                                      |  F1=Help
                          DOS Utilities...
              To select an item, use the up and down arrows.
            To start a program or display a new group, press Enter.

Set Date and Time
Disk Copy
Disk Compare
Backup Fixed Disk
Restore Fixed Disk
Format




   F10=Actions  Esc=Cancel  Shift+F9=Command Prompt
```

Figure 2.30   *DOS Utilities Group menu*

Each of these utilities is a Shell program. Shell programs are discussed in detail in Chapter 3. After reading that chapter, you might find it worthwhile to review the DOS Utilities programs to see how they are designed. Each utility executes a single DOS command (two commands in the case of DATE and TIME), but they use the Help screen and Parameter screen features of the Shell (discussed in Chapter 3) to make them easy to understand and use.

Setting the Computer's Date and Time

The first utility on the menu is Set Date and Time, which corresponds to the DOS DATE and TIME commands. Selecting this choice brings up the Set Date and Time Utility dialogue box, first for the date and then for the time. Figure 2.31 shows the box as it prompts for both date and time.

```
┌─────────────────────────────────────────────────┐
│                                                 │
│          Set Date and Time Utility              │
│                                                 │
│         Enter new date ??-??-??                 │
│                                                 │
│         Parameters . .  [         ]             │
│                                                 │
├─────────────────────────────────────────────────┤
│   <┘ =Enter    Esc=Cancel    F1=Help           │
│                                                 │
└─────────────────────────────────────────────────┘


┌─────────────────────────────────────────────────┐
│                                                 │
│          Set Date and Time Utility              │
│                                                 │
│          Enter new time hh:mm                   │
│                                                 │
│         Parameters . .  [      ]                │
│                                                 │
├─────────────────────────────────────────────────┤
│   <┘ =Enter    Esc=Cancel    F1=Help           │
│                                                 │
└─────────────────────────────────────────────────┘
```

Figure 2.31   *Setting computer's date and time*

You can use either the hyphen or the slash (/) as a separator when entering the date. The time can be entered in 24-hour format (i.e., 6:05 PM is 18:05) or 12-hour format, in which case you should specify a.m. or p.m. For example, 6:05 p.m. should be entered as 6:05P, and 6:05 a.m. should be entered as 6:05A. If no A or P is included, DOS assumes a.m. After entering the new date and time, the screen will clear momentarily and the message "press any key to continue" appears. Pressing any key will restore the DOS Utilities menu. The date and time at the top of the screen will reflect the new values entered.

Using the DISKCOPY Utility

The Diskcopy utility executes the DOS DISKCOPY command, which allows you to make an exact replica of a floppy disk. This procedure is different from simply copying all files from one disk to another in that DISKCOPY destroys any files already existing on the target disk and copies each piece of information from the source disk to exactly the same location on the target disk. The target disk is therefore identical to the source disk. A file copy, such as the File System Copy function, simply makes sure that files from the source disk are copied to the target; it does not consider whether they are in the same physical area of the target disk as on the source disk. If other files already exist on the target disk, they are left alone. The DISKCOPY command will also recreate the directory structure of a disk and copy files from all directories on the source disk to the same directories on the target disk. A file copy only copies files to and from one directory.

One disadvantage of using the Diskcopy utility is that it does not defragment files. File fragmentation occurs when you write a file to the disk, write another file to the disk, and then go back and add information to the first file. The first file is then located on two different parts of the disk; the second file is embedded between the two parts. This fragmentation is undesirable because it takes the disk drive longer to retrieve a fragmented file, and it also causes more wear and tear on the drive. When you use the File Copy function of the Shell File System, files are copied to contiguous sections of the target disk, eliminating file fragmentation.

Normally, it is preferable to use the File Copy feature of the File System to copy files. If, however, you want to be sure you have created an exact duplicate of a disk, use the Diskcopy utility.

Selecting Diskcopy from the Utilities menu brings up the Diskcopy Utility dialogue box shown in Figure 2.32. The first drive designated is the source drive (the one being copied from), and the second drive is the target drive (the one being copied to).

```
┌─────────────────────────────────────────────────────┐
│                  Diskcopy Utility                     │
│                                                       │
│      Enter source and destination drives.             │
│                                                       │
│         Drives . .  [a: b:              >             │
│                                                       │
├─────────────────────────────────────────────────────┤
│    <─┘=Enter     Esc=Cancel     F1=Help              │
└─────────────────────────────────────────────────────┘
```

Figure 2.32   *Using Diskcopy to duplicate a floppy disk*

The Shell assumes you want to copy from drive A to drive B, which is the most common situation. If you only have one floppy drive, that drive will be interpreted as both drive A and drive B. You can change the drive designators if you want.

Pressing the Return key will cause the screen to clear and the following message to appear:

Insert SOURCE diskette in drive A:

Insert TARGET diskette in drive B:

Press any key to continue . . .

After you have inserted the disks and pressed a key, the copying process will begin.

While the copying is being performed, a message similar to the following will appear on the screen:

Copying 40 tracks
9 Sectors/Track, 2 Side(s)

This message indicates the type and size of the disk being copied. When the DISK-COPY command is finished executing, it will ask whether you want to copy another disk, which allows you to copy multiple disks without having to return to the Shell each time.

Because the Diskcopy utility attempts to exactly duplicate the source disk, the two disk drives being used should be identical (i.e., you should not attempt a Diskcopy between different capacity drives or between 3-1/2" and 5-1/4" drives). The DISKCOPY command is for floppy disks only; if you specify either the source or target disk as a fixed disk, a network disk, a virtual disk, or a SUBSTed drive letter, you will receive an error message.

If your computer only has one floppy disk drive, you can still use the Diskcopy utility. In this case, specify the source and target drives as the same drive. You will be prompted when to switch disks, and the computer will pause and wait for you to press a key before it continues copying.

If the target disk is not formatted (formatting is discussed later in this chapter), the Diskcopy utility formats the disk as it performs the copy.

One additional parameter can be specified. Most floppy disks are double sided, which means they can hold information on both sides. There are, however, single-sided 5.25" disks. These disks are less expensive and are sometimes used for distributing software that will fit on one side of a disk. If you want to use Diskcopy to copy such a disk, you should specify the /1 parameter. This parameter should be entered after the target drive. Figure 2.32 would contain the following parameter line:

```
Drives . . [a: b: /1                    >
```

This parameter line will cause only the first side of the source disk to be copied. If you specify this parameter with anything other than a single-sided 5.25" disk for the source, you will most likely end up with an unusable target disk.

After performing a Diskcopy, it is a good idea to use the Diskcomp utility (discussed next) to compare the source and target disks to make sure they are identical.

Using the DISKCOMP Utility

The Diskcomp utility executes the DOS DISKCOMP command, which compares the contents of two diskettes. It compares the disks on a sector-by-sector basis, which means that the disks must have the same information in exactly the same location. This will only be true for disks that were written under identical circumstances, or if one disk was copied from the other with the Diskcopy utility. In fact, the most common use of Diskcomp is to compare two disks after a Disk-copy operation, to verify that the target disk is identical to the source disk.

Selecting Diskcomp from the Utilities menu brings up the Diskcomp Utility dialogue box shown in Figure 2.33.

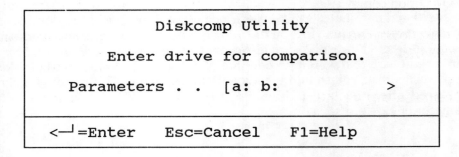

```
                    Diskcomp Utility

              Enter drive for comparison.

        Parameters . .  [a: b:                 >

      <─┘ =Enter     Esc=Cancel     F1=Help
```

Figure 2.33   *Comparing two floppy disks*

Because Diskcomp compares disks on a sector-by-sector basis, you must use the same type of drive for both disks. If you don't use the same type of drive, the results of Diskcomp are not reliable and may terminate with an error message. If you have only one floppy drive, or if your drives are for different disk sizes or densities, you should specify the same drive letter for the source and target disks. DOS will prompt you at the appropriate times to insert either the first or second disk in the drive.

The parameters shown in Figure 2.33 are the most common, but you can change them if you like. After pressing the Return key, the following message will appear on your screen:

    Insert FIRST diskette in drive A:

    Insert SECOND diskette in drive B:

    Press any to continue . . .

As the comparison is performed, Diskcomp will indicate how many tracks, sectors, and sides are being compared. If the disks are identical, it will report "Compare OK" upon completion and ask whether you want to compare another disk.

If the disks do not compare properly, Diskcomp will display error messages of the following type:

    Compare error on
    side 1 track 9

This message indicates that track 9 on side 1 of the second disk is different from track 9 on side 1 of the first disk, which informs you that the disks are not identical and gives you the physical location of the difference, but it does not tell you in which file the difference occurs. You must keep in mind, too, that if the second disk was not created with the Diskcopy utility, there may not be any difference in the files — the difference may only be in the way the files are arranged on the disk.

Two additional parameters can be specified for the Diskcomp utility; both are entered after the second drive letter. /1 tells Diskcomp to compare only the first side of the disks, even if they are double-sided disks. /8 tells Diskcomp to compare only 8 sectors per track, even if the first disk is a 9-sector-per-track or 15-sector-per-track disk. To tell Diskcomp to compare only side one, 8 sectors per track, and to use the same drive for both disks, you should include the following parameter line:

a: a: /1 /8

Diskcomp is for floppy disks only; if you specify either the first or second disk as a fixed disk, a network disk, a virtual disk, an ASSIGNed drive, or a SUBSTed drive letter, you will receive an error message.

Using the Backup Fixed Disk Utility

All disks, floppy and fixed, are subject to occasional failure. Because the data and programs stored on disks are often valuable, it is important to maintain backup copies. For floppy disks, you can simply use the Diskcopy utility or the File System Copy command to copy the files on one disk to another disk. It is not so simple, however, to back up fixed disks because they are not removable and often contain many files. Some files on a fixed disk may even be too large to fit on a single floppy disk.

The Backup Fixed Disk utility is provided to address these problems. This utility allows you to back up the files on one disk to one or more other disks and to restore them to the original disk or to another disk. Normally, you will back up a fixed disk onto multiple floppy disks, but it is possible to back up from any type of disk to any other type of disk.

Choosing Backup Fixed Disk from the DOS Utilities menu will bring up the Backup Utility dialogue box shown in Figure 2.34.

```
┌─────────────────────────────────────────────────┐
│              Backup Utility                     │
│                                                 │
│    Enter source and destination drives.         │
│                                                 │
│     Parameters . .   [c:\*.* a: /s      >       │
│                                                 │
├─────────────────────────────────────────────────┤
│                                                 │
│   <──┘=Enter     Esc=Cancel     F1=Help         │
│                                                 │
└─────────────────────────────────────────────────┘
```

Figure 2.34   Backing up a disk

The first parameter entered indicates the source drive, directory, and files to be backed up. In Figure 2.34, this parameter is c:*.*, which indicates drive C, the root directory, and all files. The second parameter is the drive to be used for the backup disks. This drive can be any type of floppy or fixed-disk drive. In Figure 2.34, it is drive A.

Six parameters can be entered following the backup drive. They are used to "fine-tune" your backups, making them as easy and fast as possible. The first of these, /S, is included as a default in the Backup Utility Dialogue Box because it is most often the one you'll want.

Backing Up Subdirectories

The /S parameter tells DOS to back up the files in all subdirectories of the specified source directory as well as the files in the source directory. For example, if you had a directory named WP containing two subdirectories named LETTERS and MEMOS, the following parameter line would back up all files in WP, LETTERS, and MEMOS as well as files in any subdirectories that may exist in LETTERS or MEMOS.

C:\WP A: /S

This parameter line will ignore all directories that do not include C:\WP in their path.

Backing Up Only Files Modified Since the Last Backup

The /M parameter is used to back up only those files that have been modified since the last backup was performed. This procedure can save a great deal of time, particularly if you perform frequent backups. For example, your program files will never change, so there is no need to back them up more than once, and there may be many data files that do not change between backups.

DOS is able to perform such incremental backups by setting the attribute byte of the file to off when it is backed up and setting it to on when the file is modified. File attributes are discussed in detail earlier in this chapter.

Saving Files on the Target Disk

The Backup utility normally erases any files that exist on the target disk, which makes it easy to reuse backup disks without first erasing the files on them. It is sometimes desirable to have backup files added to backup files already on the target disk rather than replace them. This task can be accomplished with the /A parameter.

When the Backup utility is used, the files are not copied in the usual manner to the target disk. If you look at the filenames on the target disk, you will see only two files: BACKUP.XXX and CONTROL.XXX. The XXX extension will be replaced by a number that indicates the backup disk sequence. For example, if a backup required two disks, the first disk would contain the file BACKUP.001 and the second would contain the file BACKUP.002. The BACKUP.XXX file contains all of the files that were backed up, and the CONTROL.XXX file contains all of the directory, path, and filename information. This procedure allows the Backup utility to fit as much information as possible on each backup disk.

Backing Up Only Files Modified Since a Specified Date and Time

You can also choose to back up only files that have been modified on or after a specified date. This task is accomplished with the /D parameter. For example, the following parameter line instructs the Backup utility to back up all files modified on or after December 1, 1988:

C: A: /D:12-1-88

You can also indicate the time as well as the last date on which backup files were modified by using the /T parameter. The following parameter line demonstrates this:

C: A: /D:12-1-88 /T:14:20

This parameter line will cause all files modified on or after 2:20 p.m. on December 1, 1988, to be backed up. If you specify the /T parameter without a /D parameter, the Backup utility will back up all files modified on or after the specified time on any date.

Creating a Log File During Backup

The /L parameter is used to create a log file for your backup. The log file contains the date and time of the backup and the diskette number and full pathname for each file backed up. This information is useful when you have a large number of backup disks and want to locate a particular file for restoration. A sample log file is shown in Figure 2.35.

```
9-16-1988   14:22:40
001   \SP.BAT
001   \WP.BAT
001   \DJ.BAT
001   \L.BAT
001   \PMTUTOR.BAT
001   \MM.BAT
001   \SETUP.BAT
001   \M.BAT
001   \QC.BAT
001   \TEST.BAT
001   \AUTOUSER.BAT
001   \SETPATH.BAT
001   \BT.BAT
001   \DOSSHELL.BAT
001   \AUTOEXEC.BAT
001   \BAN.BAT
```

Figure 2.35   *Log file created with /L backup parameter*

This file indicates that the backup occurred on September 16, 1988, at 2:22 in the afternoon. Following is the backup parameter line for this backup:

c:*.bat a: /L

All the files fit on disk 001. The log file indicates the path and name for each file. You can specify the destination of the log file as well. If the parameter line had been C:*.BAT A:/L:C:\DOS, the log file would be written in the DOS directory of drive C. If no destination is specified, the log file is written in the root directory of the source drive.

Using the Restore Fixed Disk Utility

Because files backed up with the Backup utility are stored in a special format, another program, Restore, is required to retrieve them. The Restore utility is used only with files written using the Backup utility.

Selecting the Fixed Disk Restore Utility from the DOS Utilities menu brings up the Restore Utility dialogue box shown in Figure 2.36.

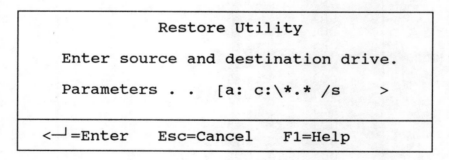

```
                      Restore Utility

        Enter source and destination drive.

        Parameters . .   [a: c:\*.* /s      >


     <─┘=Enter    Esc=Cancel    Fl=Help
```

Figure 2.36   *Restoring a file from a backup disk*

The most commonly used values are automatically entered on the parameter line. These values indicate that the source drive (i.e., the drive from which the files will be restored) is drive A, that the drive to restore files to is drive C, that all files in the root directory should be restored, and that subdirectories should also be restored (using the /S parameter).

The /S parameter for Restore, like the /S parameter for Backup, restores all files in the specified directory and all files in subdirectories that stem from the specified directory. Seven additional parameters can be entered on the parameter line.

Confirming File Replacement During the Restore Process

If you are restoring a file that already exists on your target disk, the file on the target disk will be replaced by the file on the source disk. You will not always want this to happen because the target disk file may be more recent than the source disk file. You can protect against this result by specifying the /P parameter. /P tells the Restore utility that if a file on the target disk has been modified since the last backup, the Restore process should pause and ask you whether or not you want to replace the target file with the source file. You can then choose which file you want to keep.

If /P is included on your parameter line, Restore will also pause and ask you whether you want to replace a file with the read-only attribute set to on. The read-only attribute is used to prevent the deletion, replacement, or modification of files.

Restoring Only Files Modified Since the Last Backup

The /M parameter is used to restore all files modified or deleted since they were last backed up. Without issuing a prompt, this parameter restores only those files. It can be used in conjunction with the /P parameter if you want DOS to pause and confirm each restoration.

Restoring Only Files That Do Not Exist on the Target Disk

With the /N parameter, you can choose to restore only files that no longer exist on the target disk. These files may have been deleted or they may be files that never existed on the target if the target is a different disk than the one you backed up.

Restoring Only Files Modified On or Before a Specified Date

The /B parameter is similar to the /D parameter for the Backup utility. /B, however, is used to specify all files modified on or before a particular date, whereas /D is used with Backup to specify all files that were modified on or after a particular date. For example, the following parameter line will specify all files modified on or before December 1, 1988:

a: c:*.* /B:12-1-88

Restoring Only Files Modified On or After a Specified Date

The /A parameter is the same as the /D parameter for backups — it specifies all files modified on or after a particular date. The following parameter line will restore all files modified on or after December 1, 1988:

a: c:*.* /A:12-1-88

Restoring Only Files Modified At or After a Specified Time

The /L parameter is identical to the /T parameter used for the Backup utility — it specifies that only files modified at or later than a specified time should be restored. The parameter can be used in conjunction with the /A parameter to specify that only files modified at or later than a given time on or after a particular date should be restored. The following parameter line specifies that all files modified at or after 2:20 p.m. on or after December 1, 1988, should be restored:

a: c:*.* /A:12-1-88 /L:14:20

Restoring Only Files Modified At or Before a Specified Time

The /E parameter is similar to the /L parameter, except that it is used in conjunction with the /B parameter; it specifies that all files modified at or earlier than a particular time should be restored. The following parameter line specifies that all files modified at or before 2:20 p.m. on December 1, 1988, should be restored:

a: c:*.* /B:12-1-88 /E:14:20

You can think of the /A /L combination as meaning After/Later and the /B /E combination as meaning Before/Earlier.

When you start the Restore utility, you are prompted for the backup disk that contains the file(s) you have specified. If you are restoring all files, or are uncertain which disk contains the file(s) to be restored, start with disk 001. If the file(s) being restored is not on that disk, DOS will prompt you for the next disk until all of the requested files have been restored.

Restoring to Create a Bootable Disk

The Restore utility cannot be used to create a bootable disk because it does not copy the three files that are necessary for booting. The first file is COMMAND.COM; the second and third files are IBMBIO.COM and IBMDOS.COM in PC-DOS and IO.SYS and MSDOS.SYS in MS-DOS. To create a bootable disk, first transfer the IBMBIO.COM/IO.SYS and IBMDOS.COM/MSDOS.SYS files to the target disk and then copy COMMAND.COM to the root directory of the target disk. Then, you can proceed with the Restore operation.

Using the FORMAT Utility

Before you can use a new disk, you must prepare it for use with the computer by using the Format utility. The Format utility prepares the disk for storing information in a format that DOS can read and write, for checking the disk for defective areas and marking them so they are avoided when DOS reads from and writes to the disk, and for creating a bootable disk.

You normally format only floppy disks. Fixed disks require formatting when they are new, but it is usually done by the manufacturer or dealer from whom you purchase your computer. The Format utility cannot be used with drives involved in a JOIN or SUBST (substitution) command or with network drives.

You can format a disk that has already been formatted and used, but the new format will destroy all information stored on the disk, so it is not usually advisable.

One of DOS 4.0's new features is the ability to format fixed disks with capacities greater than 32 megabytes. If you have a disk with a capacity greater than 32 megabytes that was set up under a previous version of DOS, it would have been partitioned into two or more logical drives, each of which is 32M or less. You can convert these drives to one logical drive if you like; however, you will be required to reformat the disk, which will destroy all information stored on it. You can perform these operations with the FDISK command.

The labeling of 3.5" disk capacity is a little confusing. There are two capacities in which these disks are provided: 720K and 1.44M (1440K). The disks, however, are labeled as 1.0M and 2.0M. The labeled capacity represents the unformatted capacity, but, after formatting, their capacities are reduced to 720K and 1.44M. It is important to remember that the actual DOS capacities of the disk are different from the labeled capacities.

When you select the Format option from the DOS Utilities menu, the Format Utility dialogue box shown in Figure 2.37 appears.

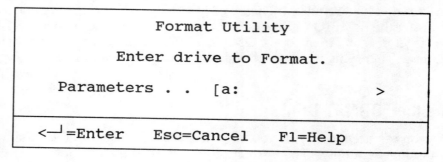

Figure 2.37   Formatting a disk

Because you normally only format floppy disks, the most common parameter is a:, which indicates that you want to format a disk on drive A. Eight additional parameters, however, can be used with the Format utility.

While your disk is being formatted, DOS will display the following message:

```
x percent of disk formatted
```

The x will change, reflecting how much of the formatting is complete, as formatting proceeds. When formatting is finished, you will be prompted for a volume label (unless you included one in the parameter list as discussed in the following section). After responding to the prompt, statistics reflecting disk space and allocation units are displayed, and you are asked whether you want to format another disk. At this point, the screen will appear as in Figure 2.38.

```
Insert new diskette for drive A:
and press ENTER when ready...

FORMAT complete

Volume label (11 characters, ENTER for none)?

     362496 bytes total disk space
     362496 bytes available on disk

       1024 bytes in each allocation unit
        354 allocation units available on disk

Volume Serial Number is 4328-15D5

FORMAT another (Y/N)?
```

Figure 2.38   *Typical screen after formatting a disk*

If you transferred the system files to the disk with the /S parameter or reserved space for them with the /B parameter, the "bytes available on disk" amount would be reduced by the amount of space needed for those files. The /S and /B parameters are discussed in the following section.

If there are defective sectors on the disk, the number of such sectors will also be indicated, and the "bytes available on disk" will be reduced by the number of bytes in bad sectors.

Creating a Bootable Disk with Format

The /S parameter tells the Format utility to transfer the system files (IO.SYS for MS-DOS or IBMBIO.COM for PC-DOS; MSDOS.SYS for MS-DOS or IBMDOS.COM for PC-DOS; and COMMAND.COM) to the disk being formatted, which means that you can start the computer with this disk in drive A. If the /S parameter is not included on the Format parameter line, you can transfer the IO.SYS/IBMBIO.COM and MSDOS.SYS/IBMDOS.COM system files later, using the SYS command, as long as the disk has no files or directories on it. These files must be placed in particular physical locations on the disk. The COMMAND.COM file can be copied at any time; it does not matter where this file physically resides as long as it is in the root directory. /S cannot be used if /B is used because it eliminates the need for /B (discussed next).

To reserve the physical locations required for the IO.SYS/IBMBIO.COM and MSDOS.SYS/IBMDOS.COM files without actually transferring them during the format, use the /B parameter. If a disk is formatted with /B, you can transfer the system files at any time — even after other files and directories have been placed on the disk — using the SYS command for IO.SYS/IBMBIO.COM and MSDOS.SYS/IBMDOS.COM and the Copy utility for COMMAND.COM. The only requirement is that there is enough room for COMMAND.COM because /B does not reserve space for that file. /B cannot be used if /S is used because there is no need to reserve space for the files after they are transferred.

Adding a Volume Label to Your Disk

A volume label is a title for a disk. It is displayed whenever you display a directory for the disk. Volume labels are useful for keeping track of your disks. A volume label is added using the /V: label parameter. Volume labels can be up to 11 characters long, and they do not use a period to create an extension as in filenames. The following parameter line will format a disk in drive A, reserve space to later add the system files, and assign the disk a volume label of MAY89MEMOS:

a: /B /V:MAY89MEMOS

If you do not include the /V parameter or include it without specifying a label, you will be prompted to enter a label after the Format is complete. If you do not want to give your disk a volume label, press the Return key at this point without entering a volume label.

The Format command automatically creates a volume serial number for each disk. This serial number is displayed whenever you list a directory for the disk. You can use the serial numbers rather than volume labels to keep track of your disk, but the serial numbers have no meaning other than being unique numbers.

A directory listing of a disk in drive A with no volume label will display the following three lines before listing the files on the disk:

```
Volume in drive A has no label
Volume Serial Number is 341E-14FD
Directory of A:\
```

You cannot use the /V parameter if you use the /8 parameter (discussed in the following section). You can add or change the volume label of a disk, using the LABEL command, which is discussed in Chapter 7.

Specifying Disk Density and Number
of Sides, Sectors, and Tracks for Formatting

DOS automatically formats disks for the maximum capacity of the drive in which they are being formatted. If you want to format a disk of lower capacity than the drive, you must include one or more parameters to inform DOS of the capacity of the disk.

The /8 parameter is used to specify eight sectors per track on 5.25" drives. This parameter is used if you want to be able to use the disk with the earliest versions of DOS (1.x). All later versions use nine sectors per track, which allows more information to be stored on the disk. All versions can read and write the eight-sector-per-track disks, while only versions 2.0 and later can read and write nine sectors per track. It is becoming increasingly unlikely that you will encounter DOS 1.x, but this parameter is still available if you want to be sure your disks can be used with it. It is useful only if you are distributing your disks to people who may have early versions of DOS. If you do not specify the /8 parameter, DOS will always create nine or 15 sectors for floppy disks, depending on the media size. You cannot use the /8 parameter if you use the /V parameter.

The /4 parameter is used to format a low-density (360K double-sided or 180K single-sided) disk in a high-density (1.2-megabyte) drive. Be aware, however, that the disks may not be reliably read or written in a low-density drive. Therefore, you should only use this parameter if you do not have a high-density disk available and must use a high-density drive.

You can format a single-sided 5.25" disk in a double-sided drive by using the /1 parameter. You can also use this parameter to format a double-sided 5.25" disk as a single-sided disk. The original version of DOS (1.0) was designed to use only single-sided disks. If you have a single-sided disk or want to use a disk with version 1.0 of DOS, you should format the disk with this parameter.

The /N parameter is used to format a disk with a different number of sectors per track than the default value for the specified drive. The /T parameter is used in conjunction with the /N parameter; if either is used, both must be specified or the format will abort with an error message. The /T parameter is used to format a disk with a different number of tracks per disk than the default value for the specified drive. For example, a 320K 5.25" disk formats to 40 tracks with eight sectors per track, while a 360K 5.25" drive defaults to 40 tracks with nine sectors per track. You would therefore specify the following parameter line to format a 320K 5.25-inch disk in the A drive:

a: /N:8 /T:40

To format a 740K disk in a 1.44-megabyte drive, use the following parameter line:

a: /N:9 /T:80

You cannot use the /N /T parameters if you specify the /F parameter (discussed next). You cannot use the /N /T parameters when formatting a fixed disk. If you do, the format will not be executed, and DOS will generate an error message.

The /F parameter is used to format disks to particular size media. For example, a 360K disk could be formatted to 160K. Table 2.1 indicates the various legal combinations of drives and /F parameter values. The "Default Size" column indicates the standard — the size used if no /F parameter is included. The "Other Sizes" column indicates the sizes that can be specified using the /F parameter. The "Parameter" column indicates the syntax of the /F parameter for the given "Other Size."

Disk Type	Default Size	Other Sizes	Parameter
160K 5.25" Single-sided	160K	none	none
180K 5.25" Single-sided	180K	160K	/F:160
320K 5.25" Double-sided	320K	180K	/F:180
720K 3.5" Double-sided	720K	none	none
1.2M 5.25" Double-sided	1.2M (1200K)	360K, 320K 180K, 160K	/F:360, /F:320, /F:180, /F:160
1.44M 3.5" Double-sided	1.44M (1440K)	720K	/F:720

Table 2.1   *Floppy disk types and /F parameter in the FORMAT command*

When using the /F parameter, you can enter the number with or without a K or KB ending. For example, all of the following are valid /F: parameters for specifying a size of 180K:

/F:180
/F:180K
/F:180KB

You cannot use the /F parameter if you use the /N /T parameters.

Table 2.2 indicates the Format parameters that can be used with the different disk types.

Type of Disk	Legal Parameters
160K/180K	/S, /V:label, /1, /8, /4, /F:size
320K/360K	/S, /V:label, /1, /8, /4, /F:size
720K/1.44M	/S, /V:label, /N, /T, /B, /F:size
1.2M	/S, /V:label, /N, /T, /B, /F:size
Fixed Disk	/S, /V:label, /B

Table 2.2   *Disk types and format parameters*

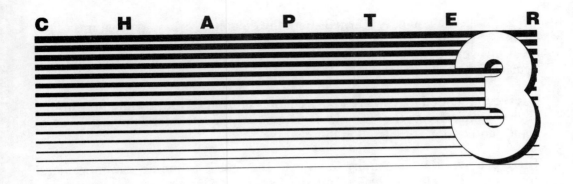

ADVANCED FEATURES OF THE DOS 4.0 SHELL

Up to this point, you have learned about the default screens and programs of the DOS 4.0 Shell as they result from a standard installation. The Shell, however, can be extensively modified and configured to suit your needs. Modifying and configuring the Shell is the subject of this chapter.

It is recommended that you read this chapter in front of your computer, with the Shell running. Trying the examples is the best way to understand the various commands and options discussed in this chapter.

There are two ways to modify the Shell: the first is to modify the menus and programs the Shell can execute, and the second is to modify the startup options. **Startup options** are aspects of the Shell that are generally "behind the scenes." They are instructions given to the Shell on startup that affect the way it behaves.

MODIFYING THE MENU SYSTEM

The startup options discussed later in this chapter modify the menu system as a whole. The options permit you to perform such operations as replacing the entire Main Group menu and eliminating the File System. This section will discuss modifications and extensions to parts of the menu system. These actions consist of adding, changing, or deleting groups and adding, changing, or deleting programs.

Adding Programs to the Main Group

Within the Shell, the term **program** refers to a sequence of commands executed when a menu choice is made. Each program has a title that appears on the menu. After the initial installation, the Main Group menu consists of three programs and one subgroup, as shown in Figure 3.1.

```
  01-24-89                    Start Programs                10:45 am
  Program  Group  Exit                                      F1=Help
                              Main Group
                To select an item, use the up and down arrows.
                To start a program or display a new group, press Enter.

  Command Prompt
  File System
  Change Colors
  DOS Utilities...










  F10=Actions   Esc=Cancel   Shift+F9=Command Prompt
```

Figure 3.1   *Start Programs Main Group screen*

The ellipses following "DOS Utilities" indicate that it is a subgroup.

Additional programs can be added to the Main Group by selecting the Program function on the Menu Bar. You can select the Program function by pressing the F10 key to highlight it and then pressing the Return key, or by clicking the mouse pointer on the word "Program." When Program is selected, the following pull-down menu appears beneath the Menu Bar:

```
Program   Group   Exit
┌─────────────────────┐
│ Start               │
│                     │
│ Add...              │
│ Cha*ge...           │
│ *elete...           │
│ *opy...             │
└─────────────────────┘
```

This menu indicates the choices available for modifying the programs on the Main Group menu. The Add option is used to add a new program to the menu. The other options — Change, Delete, and Copy — operate on the currently highlighted item in the Main Group menu. When the Shell is started, the highlighted item is Command Prompt. It is not possible to change, copy, or delete this option. Consequently, these options all have an asterisk appearing over the letter that would trigger their selection. If you are in graphics mode, there will be no asterisk, but the unavailable choices will appear blurred. The only option available at this time is Add, which can be selected by pressing the letter A, pressing the Return key while the word "Add" is highlighted, or clicking on the word "Add" with the mouse pointer.

Selecting Add will bring up the Add Program dialogue box. The screen will now appear as in Figure 3.2.

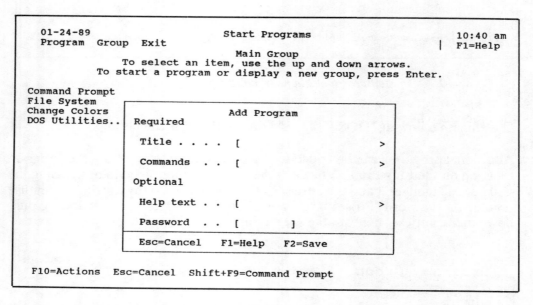

```
01-24-89                        Start Programs              10:40 am
Program  Group  Exit                                     |  F1=Help
                              Main Group
               To select an item, use the up and down arrows.
           To start a program or display a new group, press Enter.

Command Prompt
File System       ┌──────────────────────────────────────────┐
Change Colors     │              Add Program                  │
DOS Utilities..   │  Required                                 │
                  │                                           │
                  │    Title . . . .  [                    >  │
                  │                                           │
                  │    Commands  . .  [                    >  │
                  │                                           │
                  │  Optional                                 │
                  │                                           │
                  │    Help text . .  [                    >  │
                  │                                           │
                  │    Password  . .  [           ]           │
                  │                                           │
                  │  Esc=Cancel    F1=Help     F2=Save        │
                  └──────────────────────────────────────────┘

  F10=Actions   Esc=Cancel   Shift+F9=Command Prompt
```

Figure 3.2   *Add Program dialogue box*

There are two sets of entry lines in the Add Program Dialogue Box: required lines and optional lines. The required lines are the program Title and the program Commands. The Help and Password lines are optional.

Insert Mode vs. Overwrite Mode

When entering values into the various lines in the Shell dialogue boxes, you may be in either Insert Mode or Overwrite Mode. Pressing the Insert key toggles back and forth between these modes. **Insert mode** will cause anything you type to be inserted into the line at the point where the cursor is; anything to the right of the cursor is moved to the right. **Overwrite mode** causes anything you type to over-write what was already there.

On some screens, you can tell which mode you are in because the cursor will appear as an underscore in Overwrite mode and as a small box in Insert mode.

Entering the Program Title

The Title line is where you enter the text that will appear on the menu. For example, if you enter the text "My Editor," when you save this Add Program screen, a new item — My Editor — will appear at the bottom of the menu.

Note that the area in which you enter the title is marked at the left with a left square bracket ([) and at the right with a right angle bracket (>). The square bracket indicates the edge of the text; you cannot move the cursor to the left of the bracket. The angle bracket indicates that you can enter more text than there is room for. If you start typing your program title and it goes beyond the right edge, the text will scroll to the left and a left angle bracket (<) will replace the square bracket on the left, indicating that there is text off the screen in that direction as well. When you have entered the maximum amount of text (40 characters, including blanks, for a title), a right square bracket (]) will replace the right angle bracket, and you will not be allowed to type any further.

To move through the text for editing or reviewing, use the Left and Right Arrow keys. The Insert key can be used to toggle between Insert and Overwrite modes, and the Backspace key will delete characters. If you want to go to either end of the text you entered, you can use the Home and End keys. The Home key takes you to the left-most edge of the text you have entered (at the left square bracket); the End key takes you to the right-most edge of the text you have entered.

When you have finished entering the title, press the Return key to move to the Commands line. The Commands line has a large number of options, allowing you to develop fairly complex programs. These options will be discussed after the HELP and PASSWORD lines are reviewed.

Entering HELP Text for Your Program

You can create your own on-line Help screens for any item you add to the menu. This Help screen will appear when the F1 key is pressed while the item is high-lighted, in much the same way as the Help screens described in Chapter 2.

Entering Help text is similar to entering a title; you can enter more text than will fit in the area marked on the screen, and the square brackets and angle brackets indicate whether you are at the edge of the text.

Help text is not required, so you can leave this area blank if you do not need it. If, however, you need to remind yourself of something about the program when you run it, or if other users running it might not be familiar with its details, Help text is a useful feature.

Entering a Password for Your Program

The ability to include a password in your program allows you to provide security on your system. If your program permits access to confidential data, a password is a good idea. A password can be used to prevent anyone but yourself and other authorized individuals from viewing the data or using the program.

The Password line shows a left and a right square bracket. No angle bracket appears because you can only enter a maximum of eight characters for a password. These characters can include any characters that can be entered at the keyboard.

When you type the password into the Password line, it appears as you type it. When you enter the password to run the program, however, the password will not appear on the screen, which prevents other people from seeing the password.

Passwords are entirely optional and are not recommended if they are not needed. Passwords slow down a program because the program must pause and request that you enter the password each time you run the program. There is also a chance that you will forget the password.

If you include a password in your program, you will be forced to enter the password not only for running the program but also whenever you want to modify the program. If you forget the password, you will not be able to get at the Add Program screen to put in a new password. Therefore, you must be sure to use passwords you will remember or write them down so they can be referred to in hard copy form.

Retrieving a Lost Password

There is one technique for determining a password you have forgotten. It would be difficult to use this technique to determine a password you never knew, but if you will recognize the password when you see it, this technique should work.

Whenever you create a Shell program, the definition of the program is stored in a file with an MEU extension. There is one such file for each group. The name of the file for the Main Group is SHELL.MEU. The name of the file for the DOS Utilities group is DOSUTIL.MEU. The name of the file for groups that you add is specified by you in the Add Group dialogue box. The process of adding groups is discussed later in this chapter.

If you use the File System to view the contents of this file, you will see the program names, Help text, and other information. This information will be interspersed with nontext symbols, and there will be no indication as to what words correspond to programs, Help text, etc. The passwords for the programs in the group are also stored in this file. As you look at the contents of the file, you will see the passwords, although there is nothing to inform you that they are passwords. By carefully reviewing this file, you will find the password you have forgotten; all you must do is recognize it.

As an example, suppose you added a program named TEST to the Main Group. The word TEST will appear on the Main Group menu. If you had specified the password ALPHA for this program, the word ALPHA would appear in the SHELL.MEU file. When you view the contents of SHELL.MEU, you will see the word ALPHA.

ENTERING SHELL PROGRAM COMMANDS

Commands in the Commands line are known as **Program Startup Commands** (or PSCs for short). These commands are executed every time the menu item runs the program. It is possible to develop quite powerful programs, using the available commands. These commands are listed in Table 3.1 under "Summary of Program Startup Commands" later in this chapter.

The simplest command for a program is the command that executes the software you want to run. For example, if you used the title My Editor for your word processor, and the command to run the word processor was WORDPROC, you would enter the command WORDPROC on the command line. The Add Program screen for this setup, along with some Help text and a password, is shown in Figure 3.3.

```
                          Add Program
         Required

           Title . . . .  [My Editor                    >

           Commands  . .  [WORDPROC                      >

         Optional

           Help text . .  [If you want to use the>

           Password  . .  [ABCDEFGH]

         Esc=Cancel      F1=Help     F2=Save
```

Figure 3.3   Adding the WORDPROC program to the Main Group

The Start Programs screen will then appear as in Figure 3.4.

```
    01-24-89                    Start Programs                    10:52 am
    Program  Group  Exit                              |  F1=Help
                                   Main Group
                    To select an item, use the up and down arrows.
                 To start a program or display a new group, press Enter.

    Command Prompt
    File System
    Change Colors
    DOS Utilities...
    My Editor










    F10=Actions  Esc=Cancel  Shift+F9=Command Prompt
```

Figure 3.4   *Start Programs screen with "My Editor" choice added*

With this setup, whenever you select My Editor from the Main Group menu, the word processor program will start. When you exit the word processor, you will automatically return to the Main Group menu, with My Editor still highlighted.

For this procedure to work, the WORDPROC program must be in the default floppy disk drive or — if your computer contains a fixed disk — in the current directory or in a directory specified by the PATH command. If one of these conditions is not met, DOS will not know where to find the WORDPROC program. The PATH command is discussed in Chapter 4.

You can also include in the Command line any DOS commands that can be used in batch files (except IF, FOR, and GOTO). For example, rather than include the directory for your word processor in the PATH command of your AUTOEXEC.BAT file, you might want to make that directory the current directory before executing the WORDPROC command. You can do that by including a Change Directory (CD) command as one of your Program Startup Commands, which is done by typing the CD command, pressing the F4 key to separate it from other commands, and then typing in the WORDPROC command. Note that pressing F4 causes a double vertical bar to appear on the screen; this is the separator mark for Program Startup Commands. If your WORDPROC program was in a directory called WP, the command line would appear as follows:

CD \WP||WORDPROC

When the My Editor item is selected from the Main Group menu, the WP directory will be made the current directory. Then, the WORDPROC program will execute.

The Shell automatically restores the DOS directory as the current directory when you return to the Shell, so it is not necessary to include another CD (Change Directory) command after WORDPROC.

Passing Parameters to Your Programs

Some programs permit you to pass parameters to them; others require them. For example, your word processor may permit you to identify the file you will edit if you include the filename when you enter the WORDPROC command. If you enter the command WORDPROC MYFILE.LET, the word processor will appear with the file MYFILE.LET already loaded. The filename, however, should not be included in the command line because your word processor will always open with the same file. The filename should instead be passed to the program as a parameter that can be changed each time you run the program.

The Shell provides a number of special commands for entering, controlling, and manipulating such parameters. These commands can be entered in any order, except where noted otherwise. They are presented here in uppercase, but they can be entered in lowercase as well.

You needn't worry about making mistakes when you enter your commands. If there is an error in your command line, the Shell will detect it, display an explanatory Help message, and allow you to correct the error.

Using the Default Parameter Dialogue Box

If you include two square brackets as one of your Program Startup Commands, the Program Parameter Dialogue Box shown in Figure 3.5 will appear before the WORDPROC program is run. Your command should look like the following:

WORDPROC []

Note that the square brackets follow the WORDPROC command. The effect of the brackets is that whatever is entered into the Program Parameter box will be appended to the WORDPROC command, as if you had included it all on the command line.

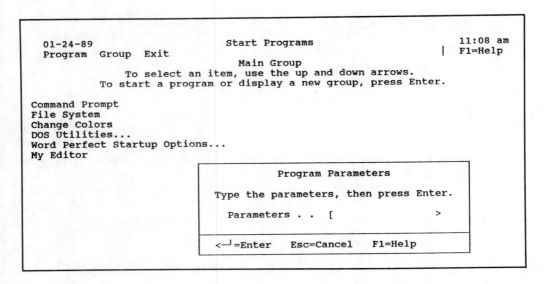

Figure 3.5   Start Programs screen with Program Parameters dialogue box

You can enter the name of the file to edit (MYFILE.LET in this example) on the Parameters line. The maximum length of the parameters line is 127 characters. You can reduce this limit by using the /L command.

Limiting the Number of Characters Allowed in the Parameters

The /L (for Length) command is used to limit the number of characters that can be entered as parameters. The command must be entered between the square brackets that bring up the Parameter Dialogue Box. The syntax for this command is

/L"n"

where n represents a number beween 1 and 127. If there is no /L command in your Program Startup Commands or if you use an illegal number (say 128), the default value of 127 will be used.

For the filename example, you may want to limit the number of characters to 12 (eight for the filename, one for the period that separates the filename from the file extension, and three for the extension). This can be accomplished with the following command line:

WORDPROC [/L"12"]

The Program Parameters box will now only allow twelve characters to be entered. The box appears as follows:

```
┌─────────────────────────────────────────────────┐
│              Program Parameters                   │
│                                                   │
│   Type the parameters, then press Enter.          │
│                                                   │
│     Parameters . .  [                    ]        │
│                                                   │
├─────────────────────────────────────────────────┤
│   <─┘=Enter    Esc=Cancel    F1=Help              │
└─────────────────────────────────────────────────┘
```

Note that the right angle bracket in Figure 3.5 has been replaced by a right square bracket, and there are 12 spaces between the square brackets.

Customizing the Title in the Program Parameters Dialogue Box

"Program Parameters" is a fairly generic title. To make your program more user-friendly, you may want to replace the title with a more informative one. For the word processing example, "Filename Entry Screen" is an appropriate title.

The /T command is used to specify a title. The syntax for this command is

/T".."

The two ellipses represent the title to be specified. You can enter a maximum of 40 characters, including blanks, for your title. The sample command line now looks like the following:

WORDPROC [/L"12"/T"File Name Entry Screen"]

The dialogue box for this command line appears as follows:

```
┌─────────────────────────────────────────────┐
│            File Name Entry Screen            │
│                                              │
│     Type the parameters, then press Enter.   │
│                                              │
│        Parameters . .  [              ]      │
├─────────────────────────────────────────────┤
│   <─┘=Enter    Esc=Cancel    F1=Help         │
└─────────────────────────────────────────────┘
```

Customizing the Instructions in the Program Parameters Dialogue Box

The instructions "Type the parameters, then press Enter" are, like the default title, generic and don't provide information specific to your program. To provide your own instructions, use the /I command. The syntax for this command is

/I".."

The two ellipses represent the instructional text. The maximum length of the text is 40 characters. To use the instruction "Enter the name of the file," use the following Program Startup Command:

WORDPROC [/L"12"/T"File Name Entry Screen"/I"Enter the name of the file."]

Remember that when you actually type this command line on your screen, it will not wrap around to a second line. Instead, it will scroll to the left as you type in more information than will fit in the area provided on the screen.

The Program Parameters dialogue box will now appear as follows:

```
┌─────────────────────────────────────────────┐
│            File Name Entry Screen            │
│                                              │
│      Enter the name of the file.             │
│                                              │
│        Parameters . . [              ]       │
│                                              │
├─────────────────────────────────────────────┤
│   <┘ =Enter    Esc=Cancel    F1=Help         │
└─────────────────────────────────────────────┘
```

Customizing the Prompt in the Program Parameters Dialogue Box

Another modification you can make in the Program Parameters dialogue box is to the prompt that appears to the left of the entry area. The default prompt is the word "Parameters .." and it is modified using the /P command. The syntax is as follows:

/P".."

The ellipses represent the text that will appear as a prompt. You can enter up to 20 characters as a prompt. To use the prompt "The name is:," the command line is written as follows:

[WORDPROC [/L"12"/T"File Name Screen"/I"Enter the name of the file."/P"The name is: "]

The Program Parameters dialogue box will now appear as follows:

```
           File Name Screen

      Enter the name of the file.

      The name is: [              ]

   <─┘=Enter    Esc=Cancel    F1=Help
```

In the command line, note that there is a blank space following the colon. If that space is not included, the prompt will "bump" against the left square bracket.

Displaying a Default Value in the Program Parameters Dialogue Box

There may be times when you will want to provide a default value in the prompt area. For example, you may have an assistant who only uses the word processor to print invoices. You could provide the name of an invoice template file as a default value. Such default values can be changed by typing over them, but they save you the trouble of typing them if the default value is wanted.

The command for displaying a default value is /D. The syntax is

/D".."

The two ellipses indicate the default value that will appear. You can use a maximum of 40 characters for your default value. To use the filename INVOICE.TMP (for invoice template), modify the command line to look like the following:

[WORDPROC [/L"12"/T"File Name Screen"/I"Enter the name of the file."/P"The name is: "/D"INVOICE.TMP"]

The screen will now appear as in Figure 3.6.

```
┌─────────────────────────────────────────────────┐
│              File Name Screen                    │
│                                                  │
│       Enter the name of the file.                │
│                                                  │
│       The name is: [INVOICE.TMP ]                │
│                                                  │
├─────────────────────────────────────────────────┤
│   <─┘=Enter     Esc=Cancel     F1=Help           │
└─────────────────────────────────────────────────┘
```

Figure 3.6   *Program Parameters dialogue box with customized Title, Instructions, Prompt, and Default Value*

When this screen appears, the cursor will be under the letter "I" adjacent to the left bracket. Pressing the Return key will accept the default value. If you want a filename other than INVOICE.TMP, you can simply type over it.

Providing Automatic Clearing of the Default Parameter

When a default parameter is specified with the /D command, you can edit it or accept it. If you do not want to use the default value, however, it is more likely that you will want to replace it completely rather than edit it. It can be replaced by overwriting the entire default value, but this can be tedious if you are replacing a long value with a short one. A better alternative is to have the default value disappear altogether as soon as you begin typing a new value, which is accomplished with the /R command. Adding the /R command to the example results in the following command line:

[WORDPROC [/L"12"/T"File Name Screen"/I"Enter the name of the file."/P"The name is: "/D"INVOICE.TMP"/R]

Now, when the screen comes up with the cursor under the first letter of the default filename INVOICE.TMP, as in Figure 3.6, pressing any alphanumeric key will cause the default name to disappear. The character you pressed will be the first character of the new name.

The alphanumeric keys are all letters, numbers, and punctuation keys. Pressing any other key, such as an arrow key, will not cause the default value to disappear. The Arrow keys can be used to scan the entire default value if it extends beyond the edge of the line.

Verifying the Existence of a Filename Entered as a Parameter

You may often want to only permit an existing filename to be entered as a parameter. In the example, you may want to prevent a user from starting the word processor with a file that does not exist. This can be accomplished with the /M"e" command. Including this command in the example results in the following command line:

[WORDPROC [/L"12"/T"File Name Screen"/I"Enter the name of the file."/P"The name is: "/D"INVOICE.TMP"/R/M"e"]

Now if you attempt to use a filename that does not exist, the following message will appear on your screen:

```
 File not found.



 <┘=Enter    Esc=Cancel    F1=Help
```

Verifying That the Correct Disk Is in the Drive

If the program to be executed is on a floppy disk, you want to be sure that the disk is in the drive. You can do this by checking for the program file on the disk, using the /F command. The /F command has the following syntax:

/F".."

The two ellipses represent the complete drive and path specification for the file. You can use up to 76 characters for this specification. If the word processor program is on the A drive, you should modify the command line so that it contains an A: prefix for the program name and the /F command to check for the program's existence. The command line would look like the following:

[A:WORDPROC [/L"12"/T"File Name Screen"/I"Enter the name of the file."/P"The name is: "/D"INVOICE.TMP"/R/M"e"/F"A:WORDPROC.EXE"]

Note that WORDPROC.EXE is the full name of the word processing file.

Regardless of where the /F parameter is placed in the command line, it is executed after the Return key is pressed in response to the parameter prompt. If the file specified with the /F command is not located, the computer beeps, and the Program Parameter dialogue box is redisplayed. If you have replaced the default parameter with another value, the new value will be cleared from the parameter line, and the default parameter will be restored.

Remember that the /F command executes *after* the Return key is pressed. Even if the file specified does not exist, you must still enter your parameter value and press the Return key before the computer beeps.

The Difference Between /M and /F

It is important to distinguish between the /M parameter and the /F parameter. /M checks for the existence of the file entered as a parameter; this file could be different every time the command line executes. /F checks for the existence of a file that is specified in the /F command; this file never changes unless you edit the command line itself.

Saving a Parameter Value for Multiple Uses

As your programs become more complex, you may find yourself typing the same parameter twice. For example, the following command line requests the name of a file to be edited and then requests it again for printing:

WORDPROC [/T"File Name Screen"/I"Enter the name of the file."/P"The name is: "]PRINT [/T"File Print Screen"/I"Enter the name of the file.."/P"The name is: "]

If you will always be printing the same file you just edited, you can set up the command line to save the parameter the first time you use it and automatically insert it when it is called for again. This procedure is set up with the %n command. The "n" in the command represents any number between 1 and 10.

When you include the %n command, you can have the value entered in the first parameter screen used for later parameters by replacing the parameter screen brackets with another %n symbol. Note that the second %n symbol is used to *replace* the brackets; it does not go inside the brackets. As an example, you could replace the previous command line with the following:

WORDPROC [%1/T"File Name Screen"/I"Enter the name of the file."/P"The name is: "]PRINT %1

When this command executes, you will only see one parameter screen — the one for the WORDPROC parameter. When the PRINT command executes, the Shell will replace the %1 with the parameter entered for WORDPROC. This command line will take you into your word processor to edit the file that you name in the parameter screen and then will print that file after you exit the word processor.

Most of the time, you will probably use the same parameters for both the WORDPROC and PRINT commands, but occasionally, you will want to use a different parameter for PRINT. This task can be accomplished with the /D"%n" command. This command uses the value entered in the first parameter screen for the default value in the second parameter screen, which can be edited. The command line for the previous example now looks like the following:

MYPROG [/T"File Name Screen"/I"Enter the name of the file."/P"The name is: "]PRINT [/T"File Print Screen"/I"Enter the name of the file."/P"The name is: "/D"%1"]

The first program parameter screen will look like the following:

```
┌─────────────────────────────────────────────────┐
│                File Name Screen                 │
│                                                 │
│     Enter the name of the file.                 │
│                                                 │
│     The name is: [                       >      │
│                                                 │
├─────────────────────────────────────────────────┤
│   <─┘=Enter    Esc=Cancel    F1=Help            │
└─────────────────────────────────────────────────┘
```

If you enter the filename LETTER.FIL, the second screen will look like the following:

```
┌──────────────────────────────────────────────────────┐
│                                                        │
│              File Print Screen                         │
│                                                        │
│        Enter the name of the file.                     │
│                                                        │
│        The name is: [LETTER.FIL          >             │
│                                                        │
├──────────────────────────────────────────────────────┤
│   <─┘=Enter    Esc=Cancel    F1=Help                   │
└──────────────────────────────────────────────────────┘
```

You can replace the name of the file by typing over it, or you can accept it by pressing the Return key.

There is one more technique for reusing a parameter. In the example just presented, both uses of %1 were in the same command line, and both occurred in response to one menu choice. You may find that you sometimes select two different menu items in a row and would like the option of using the same parameter value in both of the items, which can be done with the /C"%n" command. This command is placed in the command line of the second menu item. The command does not eliminate the parameter prompt screen, but if you press the Return key without entering a parameter value, the program will automatically substitute the %n value from the previously run menu item. An example will clarify this process.

Suppose you have two menu items named Choice 1 and Choice 2. Choice 1 has a command line that looks like the following:

WORDPROC [%1/T"File Name Screen"/I"Enter the name of the file."/P"The name is: "]

Choice 2 has a command line that looks like the following:

PRINT %1

If you run Choice 1 and enter a filename—for example LETTER.FIL—in the parameter screen, when you run Choice 2, you will see the following error message:

```
┌─────────────────────────────────────────────────────────┐
│                                                         │
│   Parameter uninitialized in Program Startup Commmand.  │
│                                                         │
│                                                         │
├─────────────────────────────────────────────────────────┤
│   <─┘=Enter    Esc=Cancel    F1=Help                    │
└─────────────────────────────────────────────────────────┘
```

This message appears because %1 has no meaning outside of the command line for which it is entered. However, if the command line for Choice 2 is modified to include the /C"%n" command, the value will be passed from the Choice 1 program to the Choice 2 program. The Choice 2 command line will look like the following:

PRINT %1 [/C"%1"/I"Leave blank for last parameter used."]

Now, when Choice 2 is run after Choice 1, a Program Parameters dialogue box will appear. Note the use of the /I command to notify users that the last parameter entered can be used here. The box looks like the following:

```
┌─────────────────────────────────────────────────────────┐
│              Program Parameters                         │
│                                                         │
│      Leave blank for last parameter used.               │
│                                                         │
│        Parameters . .  [                       >        │
│                                                         │
├─────────────────────────────────────────────────────────┤
│     <─┘=Enter     Esc=Cancel     F1=Help                │
└─────────────────────────────────────────────────────────┘
```

You can enter a value for the parameter or simply press the Return key to use the value entered in the previous screen.

Automatically Inserting Drive and Path Specifications into a Parameter Value

Under some circumstances, you may not know ahead of time which drive the Shell will be started from. This is especially true if you will be distributing your Shell programs to different machines. In this case, it can be convenient to refer in generic terms to the drive from which the Shell was started so that the correct drive letter will always be substituted into the command. This can be done with the /# command.

The /# command is entered *outside* the square brackets that define a parameter dialogue box. It affects the program filenames entered directly as Program Start-up Commands — not filenames entered as parameters.

As an example, suppose you started the Shell from drive C and that your word processing program — WORDPROC — is in the C:\WP directory. If the data file you will pass as a parameter will be on drive A, you will want to make drive A the current drive before running the WORDPROC program. Otherwise, you will be required to enter the A: prefix each time you enter the filename.

The following command line appears correct at first, but it will not work:

A:||\WP\WORDPROC

This command line will not work because once drive A becomes the current drive, DOS will look for the \WP directory on drive A; however, the \WP directory exists on drive C. The following command line will work:

A:||/#\WP\WORDPROC

This command line works because when the Shell executes this command, it replaces the /# symbol with the drive letter and colon from which the Shell was started. By the time DOS sees the command, it looks like the following:

A:||C:\WP\WORDPROC

The /@ command works the same way as the /# command, but it substitutes the path from the root from which the Shell was started, including the current directory rather than simply the drive letter followed by a colon.

Using the ECHO and PAUSE Commands to Display Messages

The ECHO command is one of the traditional DOS batch file commands; it is not a special Shell command. It can be included in a Shell Program Startup Command list just like any other DOS command.

The ECHO command serves two purposes: it acts as a toggle to turn ECHO mode on and off, and it displays a message on the screen. ECHO mode determines whether batch file commands appear on the screen as they are processed; it has no effect on Shell commands. ECHO mode use in batch files is discussed in detail in Chapter 5.

The ECHO command is used in Program Startup Command lists to display a message for the user. It is generally used in conjunction with the PAUSE command.

The PAUSE command is also one of the traditional DOS batch file commands. It causes the computer to stop processing a sequence of commands and display the "Press any key to continue ..." message. When any key is pressed, processing continues. Following is an example of using the ECHO and PAUSE commands in a Program Startup Command list:

ECHO Insert the word processor disk in drive A:||PAUSE||A:WORDPROC

When the menu item for this Program Startup Command list is selected, the message "Insert the word processor disk in drive A:" will appear on the screen. On the line beneath this, the message "Press any key to continue ..." will appear. After you press a key, the word processor program will be loaded and will run from drive A.

It is also often useful to place a PAUSE command at the end of each Program Startup Command list, which allows you to review any messages that DOS may display on your screen before returning to the Shell.

Using Batch Files in Program Startup Command Lists

If you are not familiar with DOS batch files, you should read Chapter 5 first. The following discussion relates to batch file use in Program Startup commands.

If you include the name of a batch file as a command in your Program Startup Command list, it will execute, but it will only return you to the DOS prompt; it will not return you to the Shell. To cause a batch file to execute and return properly, the CALL command is used. If you want to use a batch file named WP.BAT, the Program Startup Command is

CALL WP.BAT

If the batch file is set up to use parameters, you can use the Shell parameter-passing options just discussed to pass parameters to the batch file.

You may have already created many batch files and want to continue using them rather than creating all new Shell programs to replace them, but you may want to call them from the Shell. Batch files also allow certain kinds of programming commands not available in the Shell. These commands include the IF, FOR, and GOTO commands. These commands can provide needed functionality in some instances.

Another reason for using batch files is that there is a limit to the number of characters that can be included in a Program Startup Command list, whereas a batch file can contain as many commands as you want. For these reasons, you may sometimes want to use batch files in conjunction with the Shell.

Difference Between .MEU Files and Batch Files

Batch files are text files that can be created and edited with a word processor. There is no limit to how large batch files can be. Batch files can include conditional processing (IF commands), FOR loops, and GOTO commands. The ECHO command can be used to cause commands in batch files to appear on the screen as they execute or to cause a message to appear on the screen. Batch files do not provide the user-friendliness of the Shell; they do not include an automatic menu system; and they do not provide parameter entry screens or Help screens.

.MEU files are not text files, so they can only be created and edited within the Shell. The programs stored in .MEU files are limited in the number of characters that can appear in them, and they do not permit conditional processing, FOR loops, or GOTO commands. The ECHO command cannot be used to cause Program Startup Commands to appear on the screen as they execute; however, it can be used to cause a message to appear on the screen. Programs stored in .MEU files can make use of the Shell's Help screen and parameter entry screens.

Summary of Program Startup Commands

The commands you can use in developing Shell programs are summarized as follows:

Command	Description
[]	Causes a Program Parameter dialogue box to appear before executing the DOS command that precedes the brackets. If no other commands appear between the brackets, the default parameter box will be used.
/T".."	Defines a title for the Program Parameter dialogue box. It must be entered between the square brackets that cause the Parameter dialogue box to appear. If not used, the default title "Program Parameters" will be used. The maximum length of a title is 40 characters. The two ellipses represent the text of the title, and the quotation marks are required.
/I".."	Defines an instruction that will appear in the Program Parameter dialogue box. It must be entered between the square brackets that cause the parameter dialogue box to appear. If not used, the default instructions "Type the parameters, then press Enter" will be used. The maximum length of an instruction is 40 characters. The two ellipses represent the text of the instruction, and the quotation marks are required.

/P".." Defines a prompt that will appear in the Program Parameter dialogue box. It must be entered between the square brackets that cause the parameter dialogue box to appear. If not used, the default prompt "Parameters . . " will be used. The maximum length of a prompt is 20 characters. The two ellipses represent the text of the prompt, and the quotation marks are required.

/L"n" Specifies the maximum length of values entered in the Parameters area of the Program Parameters dialogue box. It must be entered between the square brackets that cause the box to appear. If not used, or if an illegal value is specified, the default value of 127 characters is used. The "n" represents the number of characters, and the quotation marks are required.

/D".." Defines a default value that will appear in the entry area of the Program Parameters dialogue box. It must be entered between the square brackets that cause the dialogue box to appear. The default value will be displayed in the dialogue box and can be edited before the program is run. The maximum length of a default parameter value is 40 characters. The two ellipses represent the default value, and the quotation marks are required.

/R Causes the default value in the entry area of the Program Parameters dialogue box to clear as soon as a character key is pressed. It must be entered between the square brackets that cause the dialogue box to appear. Only has effect if /D is used to specify a default parameter.

/M"e" Causes the Shell to verify the existence of a filename that has been entered in the entry area of the Program Parameters dialogue box. It must be entered between the square brackets that cause the dialogue box to appear. An error message will be displayed if the file does not exist. The "e" must be entered exactly as shown.

/F".." Used to check for the existence of a filename specified *on the command line*, as opposed to a filename specified as a parameter (see /M"e" command). It must be entered between the square brackets that cause the dialogue box to appear. The two ellipses represent the filename that should be checked, and the quotation marks are required. The name can include a drive and path specification, and it can be up to 76 characters long.

MANIPULATING SHELL PROGRAMS

How Shell Programs are Stored

For each menu in the Shell, a file exists with an MEU extension. The Main Group menu is stored in a file called SHELL.MEU. The DOS Utilities menu is stored in a menu called DOSUTIL.MEU.

Each Shell program you create is added to a menu — either the Main Group menu or one of the subgroup menus listed on the Main Group menu. All information about the program — the title, the Program Startup Commands, the Help text, and the password — are stored in the .MEU file for the menu on which the program appears. You can observe this by looking at the size and date of creation of the SHELL.MEU file before and after adding a program to the MAIN GROUP. After adding the program, the date last modified will be the date the program was added, and the size will be increased to reflect the information that has been added about the program.

How Shell Programs are Processed

DOS includes a batch file processor used for processing batch file commands. This processor is also used to process the Shell program commands. The Shell, however, prepares the commands before sending them to the batch processor.

There are basically three types of commands that the Shell passes to the batch processor: DOS commands appearing outside the brackets, Shell commands appearing outside the brackets, and Shell commands appearing inside the brackets. Commands that appear outside the brackets should be executed by DOS. Commands appearing inside the brackets are used for obtaining parameter values that will be passed to commands outside the brackets. The Shell commands that can appear outside the brackets are the %n, /#, and /@ commands.

When a Shell program executes, the Shell first looks at all sets of brackets and processes the commands in them, which is why programs that contain two or more parameter screens will display all of the parameter screens before executing any of the commands outside of the square brackets. After the commands inside the brackets are processed and the parameter values are determined, the Shell substitutes the parameter values for the commands used to obtain them. The Shell then replaces any %n, /#, and /@ commands with the appropriate values.

When all of these actions are finished, the Program Startup Command list has been converted to a set of traditional DOS batch commands that the Shell can pass to the batch processor. When the commands are finished executing, control is returned to the Shell.

Saving a Shell Program

When you are finished entering your title, commands, Help screen information, and password for a Shell program, you must save it before it is added to the menu. This procedure is performed by pressing the F2 key or clicking the mouse pointer on the "F2 = Save" message on the Add Program screen. This action will add the program to the menu and save the program definition in the appropriate .MEU file.

Modifying Shell Programs

After a program has been defined, you can modify it at any time with the Change option on the Menu Bar Program menu. Selecting Change will bring up the Change Program screen with the program definition for the currently highlighted program. This screen is the same as the Add Program screen except for the title. You can use the Left and Right Arrow keys, the Insert and Delete keys, and the Backspace key to edit the title, command line, etc. The Tab key can be used to move from one line to the next, and the Shift/Tab key combination moves you to the previous line.

Deleting a Program from a Menu

You can delete a program from a menu by selecting the Delete option from the Menu Bar Program menu. Note that built-in programs (Command Prompt, File System, and Change Colors) cannot be modified or deleted. They can, however, be activated or deactivated using the Shell Startup Commands discussed later in this chapter.

The Delete option works on whatever program is currently highlighted. If a subgroup or one of the built-in programs is highlighted rather than a program you have added, the D in Delete will be replaced by an asterisk or will appear blurred, both of which indicate that the option is not available for the currently highlighted item. The Delete option brings up the following Dialogue Box:

```
                        Delete Item

      1. Delete this item
      2. Do not delete this item

      <─┘ =Enter    Esc=Cancel    F1=Help
```

Choice 1—"Delete this item"—will be highlighted. You can delete the item by pressing the Return key. If you change your mind, you can choose not to delete it by pressing the Esc key or choosing Choice 2.

Copying a Program from One Menu to Another

You may find, after creating a program in a particular menu, that you would prefer it to be on another menu or that you would like it to appear in two menus. This task can be accomplished with the Copy choice in the Menu Bar Program menu.

To copy a program, first highlight the program title on the menu. Then, activate the Menu Bar by pressing F10, and select Program. This will pull down the Program menu. Selecting Copy will cause the following message to appear underneath the menu title near the top center of the screen:

To complete the copy, display the destination group,
then press F2. Press F3 to cancel copy.

The next step is to display the menu to which you want to copy the program. For example, if you wanted to copy the program My Program from the Main Group menu to the DOS Utilities menu, you would highlight the DOS Utilities option and press the Return key, which will bring up the DOS Utilities menu shown in Figure 3.7.

```
 01-24-89                      Start Programs              10:22 am
 Program  Group  Exit                              |      F1=Help
                           DOS Utilities...
              To complete the copy, display the destination group,
                     then press F2.  Press F3 to cancel copy.

 Set Date and Time
 Disk Copy
 Disk Compare
 Backup Fixed Disk
 Restore Fixed Disk
 Format




 F10=Actions   Esc=Cancel   Shift+F9=Command Prompt
```

Figure 3.7   *DOS Utilities menu*

Note that the instructions at the top of the screen continue to explain how to complete the copy. Pressing the F2 key will add the title My Program to the bottom of the program list, beneath Format. The program will continue to appear on the Main Group menu, so if you no longer want it there, you should use the Delete option to remove it.

If at any time during the process you change your mind, press the F3 key to cancel the copying process.

Adding Subgroups to the Main Group

Programs can be added to any group — the Main Group or a subgroup such as DOS Utilities. Subgroups can be added to the Main Group. Any group can contain up to 16 items, which means that subgroups can contain up to 16 programs, and the Main Group can contain up to a total of 16 programs and subgroups. The process of adding a group to the Main Group is similar to that of adding programs to a group.

To add a group, select the Group item on the Menu Bar, which will pull down the menu in Figure 3.8.

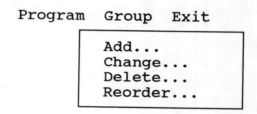

```
Program   Group   Exit
         ┌──────────────────┐
         │  Add...          │
         │  Change...       │
         │  Delete...       │
         │  Reorder...      │
         └──────────────────┘
```

Figure 3.8   *Group menu on Main Group menu bar*

The Add option displays the Add Group dialogue box shown in Figure 3.9.

```
                          Add Group
      Required

        Title . . . .  [                              >

        Filename  . .  [              ]

      Optional

        Help text . .  [                              >

        Password  . .  [              ]

      Esc=Cancel     F1=Help      F2=Save
```

Figure 3.9   *Add Group dialogue box*

This dialogue box is similar to the Add Program dialogue box in Figure 3.3. You provide a title that will appear on the menu, Help text that will be displayed on the Help screen, and a password. The Help text and password are optional.

Instead of the Command line appearing for entering Program Startup Commands, a Filename line appears that will contain the name of the MEU file that will store the programs for the menu items you will add to this group. You can use any legal filename you want. You must enter the name portion only; the extension MEU is automatically added. After adding the group (by pressing F2), the new filename will appear in the DOS directory. You can see the new filename by selecting that directory in the File System.

If you have more than one word processor, or if you want to provide different start-up options for your word processor, you might want to add a group called Word Processing Functions to contain the programs for running the different word processors. The completed Add Group screen would look something like the following:

```
                          Add Group
   Required

     Title . . . .    [Word Processing Functi>

     Filename  . .    [WP        ]

   Optional

     Help text . .    [If you want to use one>

     Password  . .    [           ]
   ────────────────────────────────────────────
     Esc=Cancel     F1=Help     F2=Save
```

By supplying a password at the Group level, you can restrict access to all programs within the group, which can eliminate the need for setting up a password for each program. It also allows a hierarchy of passwords. For example, you can restrict access to Word Processing Functions to a particular set of users and then selectively restrict access within that set by allowing only certain users access to certain functions within the group.

Selecting a Filename

Because the Shell automatically provides the extension .MEU, do not enter it as part of the filename; enter only the first part of the name, which can be up to eight characters long. The Shell also automatically places the file into the DOS directory, so there is no room to enter a path as part of the filename.

It is a good idea to choose a mnemonic filename (i.e., one that implies the purpose of the group). In the example, WP was chosen to indicate Word Processing. This strategy will make it easier to identify the file if you later want to erase it (after deleting the group from the Main Group menu) or if you want to copy it to another computer running DOS 4.0.

It is very important that each filename be unique. If you use the same filename twice, only one of the files will exist on the disk; you will lose the functionality of the other one. If this happens, you will need to redefine all programs in the lost file and give the group a new filename. The Shell does not provide a warning message when you are reusing a filename, so it is entirely up to you to be sure you don't make this mistake.

Modifying and Deleting Groups

The second and third items on the Group menu in Figure 3.8 are used for modifying and deleting groups from the Main Group.

Just as the Program Change option allows you to modify your programs, the Group Change option brings up a Change Group screen that allows you to edit any of the information entered on the Add Program screen. The Change Group screen is identical to the Add Group screen, except for the title.

To delete a group, select Delete from the Menu Bar Group menu, which will delete the group highlighted on the menu. Before the deletion is carried out, the Shell verifies that you really want to delete the group by displaying the Delete Item box:

```
                        Delete Item

     1. Delete this item
     2. Do not delete this item

    <─┘ =Enter    Esc=Cancel    F1=Help
```

Reordering Items in a Group Menu

When you add a new item to a group, the item automatically appears at the bottom of the Group Menu. You may want to order the items differently. It is particularly useful to put the most-used item at the top of the menu because this is the item that is highlighted when the menu comes up. You can then run the program by pressing the Return key without scrolling the highlight bar to your choice. Reordering can be accomplished with the Reorder option on the Group menu in Figure 3.8.

Reorder operates on the currently highlighted item in the group. Selecting Reorder changes the instructions under the group title to the following:

```
To complete the reorder, highlight the new
position, then press Enter. Press Esc to cancel.
```

To move the currently highlighted item, move the highlight bar to the position to which you want the item moved and press the Return key. The menu rearranges to reflect the new order.

Note that Reorder is the only item in the Group menu that operates on programs as well as subgroups. Reordering affects only the order of items in the group, not the items themselves. Because subgroups have only programs, and not subgroups, Reorder is the only option in the Group menu that can be used when a subgroup menu is displayed.

Restoring Deleted Groups and Copying Groups from One Installation to Another

When you save a new group, the definition for the group is saved in the DOS directory in the file specified on the Add Group screen. The file is automatically given the extension .MEU and contains the group definition as well as the definitions for the items that appear on the group's menu.

When a group is deleted from the Main Group menu, the .MEU file is not erased from the disk. The deletion simply removes the group reference from the SHELL.MEU file, which contains the menu items for the Main Group. This is a very useful feature because it allows you to restore a group with all of its menu items and programs simply by adding the reference back to the Main Group and identifying the .MEU file that contains it.

In the previous example, the Word Processing Functions group was saved in the file named WP.MEU. If this group was deleted from the Main Group, it could be restored by using the Add Group option. On the Filename line, you would enter WP. You should not enter the .MEU extension; the Shell knows the extension. Now, when the Word Processing Functions item is selected, the menu you created earlier for this group will be restored.

Because the complete definition for the group is stored in the .MEU file, you can also copy the file to other computers running DOS 4.0. The file must be copied into the DOS directory for the Shell to find it. After the file is copied, you can use the Add Group function to add the group to the Main Group menu. Again, name the file that stores the group on the Filename line; the entire group will be transferred to the new machine.

Where Group Information is Stored

When you think about how all of this works, keep in mind where the different items of information are stored. All information for a particular group is stored in the .MEU file for that group.

The SHELL.MEU file contains the definition for the Main Group menu. All program definitions for the programs on the Main Group are stored in this file. These definitions contain the Program Title, the Program Startup Command list, the Help Screen information, and the Program Password. In addition, the definitions of all of the subgroups are stored in SHELL.MEU. These definitions contain the Group Title, the name of the .MEU file that contains the program definitions for the group, the Help Screen information, and the Group Password.

Because the Main Group is the only group that can include subgroups, the other .MEU files contain only program definitions. These definitions contain the Program Title, the Program Startup Command list, the Help Screen information for each program, and the Program Password.

In the previous example, for Word Processing Functions, SHELL.MEU contains the Group Title (Word Processing Functions), the name of the .MEU file that contains the program definitions for the group (WP.MEU), the Help Screen information for the group, and the Group Password. The file WP.MEU contains the Program Title, the Program Startup Command list, the Help Screen information, and the Program Password for each program in the group.

Recovering a Lost Password

If you forget a password for a menu item (a program or group), you are not only prevented from using the item but also from being able to modify the item, which means you cannot change the password to provide access with a new one. With knowledge of where the password is stored, however, it is possible to find a lost password, as long as you will recognize it when you see it. In the above example, if there is a password of "xyz" on the WP group, the letters "xyz" will appear in the SHELL.MEU file because that file stores group names and passwords from groups that appear on the **Main Group** menu.

If you use the File System View feature (on the File pull-down menu) to view the contents of the SHELL.MEU file, you will see the Help text for Main Group items, the Main Group item names, and the passwords for the Main Group items, all interspersed with "garbage" characters—funny symbols that have no meaning to most users but that represent special codes to the computer. The screen will be similar to that in Figure 3.10.

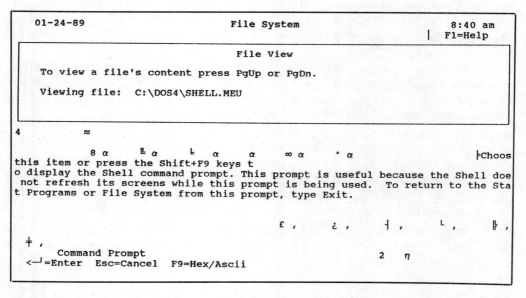

Figure 3.10   Viewing contents of a Shell menu file

The PgDn key can be used to scroll down one screen at a time. Eventually, you will see the Help text for the WP group, followed by the name WP. Following the name, and possibly separated from it with blank space, will be the password.

It might be easier to read these screens if you use the F9 key to shift to Hex mode; then, the text appears on the right side of the screen, without the garbage. There will be less information per screen this way, however, so you will need to press PgDn to scroll through more screens to locate your password.

MODIFYING THE SHELL WITH STARTUP OPTIONS

Startup options are settings that affect the Shell as a whole. The options offer tremendous power for customizing and tailoring the Shell to fit your particular needs. For example, you can tell the Shell to use your own custom-designed menu for the Main Group menu. You can remove the ability to leave the Shell for the command prompt. You can also remove the ability to modify the Shell menu system. You can tell the Shell what color setup to use, whether to include the File System in the current setup, etc.

There are three reasons for customizing the Shell with startup options. The first is to tailor the Shell to precisely fit your own needs and work habits.

The second reason to customize the Shell is to make it as user-friendly as possible. In today's work environments, many people use computers only for very specific tasks. The ability to customize the Shell allows you to create a menu system that addresses only those functions you need without burdening yourself with extra options and menus.

The third reason for customizing the Shell is to provide security on your system, which can be accomplished by excluding from the Shell those capabilities that would allow someone to access restricted parts of the computer system. For example, by removing the File System and the ability to leave the Shell for the command prompt, you prevent users from accessing your disk files, except through the programs you give them access to.

Once these options are selected, they remain in effect until you exit the Shell. This is unlike the menu modifications just discussed, which can be changed at any time.

Startup options are specified in a file named DOSSHELL.BAT, which resides in the DOS directory. Whenever the DOSSHELL command is entered, the DOS-SHELL.BAT file is read to determine startup options. If your computer automatically starts the Shell when you turn it on, the DOSSHELL command is in your AUTOEXEC.BAT file. The AUTOEXEC.BAT file is discussed in Chapter 4.

When you first installed DOS 4.0, the installation program automatically created a DOSSHELL.BAT file that contained the startup options specified by the menu options you selected. If you want to change those options, you must edit this file. A typical DOSSHELL.BAT file appears in Figure 3.11.

```
@C:
@CD C:\DOS
@SHELLB DOSSHELL
@IF ERRORLEVEL 255 GOTO END
:COMMON
@SHELLC /MOS:PCIBMDRV.MOS/TRAN/COLOR/DOS/MENU/MUL/SND/MEU:SHELL.MEU/CLR:SHELL.CLR/PROMPT/MAINT/EXIT/SWAP/DATE
:END
@BREAK=ON
```

Figure 3.11   *Typical DOSSHELL.BAT file*

Batch files are discussed in detail in Chapter 5. Of interest here is the line that begins with @SHELLC, which is the line that contains the Shell startup options. The options chosen in Figure 3.11 are those that are automatically installed if your system includes at least 360K of memory.

Each option begins with a forward slash (/). The first option listed is /MOS:PCIBMDRV.MOS; the second is /TRAN; and so on. The order in which the options appear is not important.

Activating the Main Group Menu

The /MENU option causes the Shell to open with the Start Programs screen, which contains the Main Group menu. If this option is not included on the @ShellC line, you will only have access to the File System part of the Shell.

There are several reasons why you may want to exclude the Start Programs screen. If you have only 256K of memory, you cannot include both the File System and Start Programs at the same time. You may prefer to have the File System available. Even if you have sufficient memory, you may prefer to work at the traditional DOS prompt for activities other than file management. In this case, it is faster to move right to the File System.

Activating the File System

The /DOS option makes the File System available in the Shell. If you exclude this option, the Shell will appear with the Start Programs screen, but attempting to access the File System will result in the screen shown in Figure 3.12.

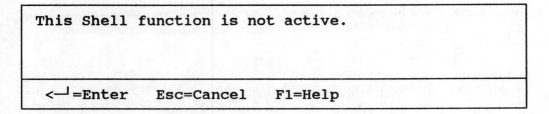

Figure 3.12　　*Message box for deactivated Shell functions*

Removing the File System from the Shell is necessary if you have only 256K of memory and want to use the Start Programs screen. It can also be useful to prevent access to the File System by untrained users. Making use of the power of the File System requires a degree of expertise, and misuse of that power can result in lost or damaged files and programs.

Activating Access to the Shell Command Prompt

The /PROMPT option activates access to the Shell command prompt. If this option is omitted from the DOSSHELL.BAT file, the Command Prompt item on the Main Group menu is rendered inactive, as is the use of [Shift/F9] to move to the command prompt from anywhere in the Shell. Attempting to use either of these items will result in the error message window in Figure 3.12 appearing on your screen. Omitting this option does *not* prevent you from exiting the Shell altogether by pressing the F3 key or choosing the Exit option from the Main Group Menu Bar.

Activating the Exit Option

The /EXIT option activates the EXIT item on the Start Programs screen Menu Bar. If this option is omitted, you cannot exit the Shell for the DOS prompt by pressing the F3 key or choosing Exit on the Main Group Menu Bar. Attempting to use either of these items will result in the error message window in Figure 3.12 appearing on your screen.

It is important to understand the difference between the /PROMPT and /EXIT options. /PROMPT prevents you from moving to the Shell command prompt; this prompt resembles the DOS prompt, but the Shell continues running in the background, and entering the EXIT command returns you to the Shell.

The /EXIT command does not prevent you from temporarily exiting the Shell. /EXIT does not restrict the ability to move to the command prompt (via the Command Prompt item on the Main Group menu or the use of [Shift/F9]), but it does prevent you from exiting the Shell altogether by selecting EXIT from the Start Programs screen menu bar or pressing F3. If you exit the Shell altogether, the only way back into the Shell is to restart the Shell with the DOSSHELL command.

Activating the Ability to Modify the Menu System

The /MAINT (for MAINTenance) option allows you to modify the menu system by adding, changing, and deleting groups and programs. Omitting this option does not prevent you from changing the Options in the File System (e.g., Confirm On Delete).

Choosing the Menu for the Main Group

The /MEU:SHELL.MEU option specifies that the Main Group menu will be in the file named SHELL.MEU. Whenever you create a new group, the menu setup for that group is saved in an .MEU file. You can specify any of these files to be the Main Group menu. Creating new groups is discussed earlier in this chapter.

This option provides tremendous power for tailoring a system to different user needs. You can design batch files that specify different DOSSHELL.BAT files for different users so that each user will have a unique startup menu. This technique is demonstrated in Chapter 6.

Specifying Buffers for Multiple File System Files and Directories

A program that sets aside part of the computer's memory for storage of a particular kind of information is called a **buffer**. When the /MUL option is specified, buffer space is set aside to store the names and directories from two disk drives at the same time when the File System is used.

If /MUL is specified, when you are in Single List mode in the File System, you can switch back and forth between two directories. The screen will change almost instantaneously because the computer will not perform a read operation on the drive you are switching to.

If /MUL is not specified, buffer space is set aside for the directory and filenames from only one drive. In this case, the computer will reread the directory and filenames from the disk you are switching to each time you specify a new drive, which takes much longer than when /MUL is specified.

If you are in Multiple List mode, you can display the directory trees for two different drives in the two Directory Tree areas when /MUL is specified. In fact, if you have read the directory trees for two different drives while in Single List mode and then switch to Multiple List mode, the Shell will automatically display the directory tree for one of the drives in the upper Directory Tree area and the directory tree for the other drive in the lower Directory Tree area without performing an additional read on either drive.

If /MUL is not specified, when you change the disk drive for one of the Directory Tree areas, both areas will change to show the directory and filenames for the new drive. You can display different directories for the same drive in the two areas, but you cannot display the directory trees for two different drives.

There is a disadvantage to storing the directory information in a buffer: because it eliminates the need for DOS to reread a drive when you return to it, any changes you have made to that drive will not be reflected on the screen. For example, if /MUL is specified and you have two drives, A and C, DOS has often already read the A drive. DOS does not read the drive again until you leave the File System. Consequently, if you change the disk in drive A and then select drive A again, the contents of the first disk will be displayed on the screen.

You can force DOS to reread drive A if you have a drive B by selecting the B drive and then going back to the A drive. Alternatively, you can exit the File System and perform some other function (e.g., running your word processor). This procedure will empty the File System buffers, so when you return to the File System, it will need to reread the drives.

Activating Sound Effects in the Shell

The /SND option causes the computer to beep when you try an action that is not allowed. For example, if you attempt to Open a file in the File System when more than one file is selected, the beep will sound. If the /SND option is omitted, no sound effects will occur.

Activating the Change Colors Option

/COLOR activates the Change Colors option in the Main Group menu. If /COLOR is not included in your DOSSHELL.BAT file, the option will not be available. If your hardware does not support the display of color, the message "This Shell function is not active" will appear (see Figure 3.12) when you select Change Colors, even if /COLOR is specified in the DOSSHELL.BAT file.

Causing the Date and Time to Be Displayed

The /DATE option causes the date and time to be displayed at the top of the Shell screen. Omitting it will turn off the date and time display.

Controlling the Shell's Use of Memory

The /TRAN and /B: options are used to control the Shell's use of memory. The /TRAN option causes the Shell to be installed in what is known as **transient mode**. The opposite of transient mode is **resident mode**, which is in effect if you omit the /TRAN option from the DOSSHELL.BAT file. The /B: option allows you to specify how much memory should be set aside for the File System buffer, which stores directory names and filenames.

When you select transient mode, the Shell provides more memory for running other programs from within the Shell by leaving only a small part of the Shell called the **base driver** in memory when you run your programs. This base driver is all that is needed to reload the rest of the Shell into memory from disk when you exit your program.

Another effect of transient mode is that the Shell is completely removed from memory when you choose the EXIT command from the Main Group. The Shell stops running, just as your word processor stops running when you exit from it. You must reload the Shell into memory when you want to run it again, but when you are not running it, the memory is available for other programs.

If you select transient mode, it will take more time to exit the Shell and return to it because the Shell program must be read from the disk. Furthermore, if you do not have a fixed disk, you must always have the Shell disk in your drive because part of the program is on disk rather than in memory. If you have a fixed disk, transient mode is recommended because of the high speed with which the program can be read from the disk. In this case, the memory saved is usually worth the extra time.

In resident mode, the Shell program remains in memory when you exit it. After it has been loaded, if you exit from the Shell, typing DOSSHELL will immediately bring the Shell menu up again without reading the program from the disk. If you had used the File System before exiting, all directory names and filenames were read in at that time, so if you go into the File System upon returning to the Shell, they will not need to be read again.

Resident mode is particularly advantageous if you have installed DOS 4.0 on a floppy-disk system because it allows you to remove the disk and use the drive for other purposes while running the Shell.

The disadvantage of resident mode is that the Shell occupies much memory. If you have access to programs that require more memory than is left after the Shell is loaded, you will get the message "Program too big to fit in memory" when you attempt to run them. Resident mode is recommended if your computer has enough memory and does not contain a fixed disk. If your computer has a fixed disk, the time saved by having the Shell remain resident does not usually justify the amount of required memory.

Fine-Tuning the Use of Memory with the /B: Option

The /B: option is not automatically included in your DOSSHELL.BAT file when you install DOS 4.0. You must edit the DOSSHELL.BAT file yourself to add the option.

If you install the Shell in resident mode without using the /B: option, you will probably find that many of your programs cannot be run because the Shell occupies too much memory. The /B: option can be used to reduce the amount of memory occupied by the Shell.

One of the largest demands on memory within the Shell is for the File System buffer, which is used to store all the directory and file information from your disk drives. By default, the Shell assumes you will want to store information from two large disks. This is a large amount of information, so the buffer is quite large. The /B: option can be used to limit the size of the buffer. The format for the option is

/B:n

where n represents the number of kilobytes you want to reserve for the buffer space. For example, you could add the following to the @SHELLC line in Figure 3.11:

/B:3

This command instructs the Shell to only use 3 kilobytes for the File System buffer, which is much less than the Shell uses by default and may well be sufficiently small to permit your programs to run while the Shell is in resident mode.

The drawback to limiting the buffer size is that it may not permit you to view your entire directory tree. If you limit the buffer to too small a number, when you enter the File System, the following window will appear on your screen:

```
┌─────────────────────────────────────────────────────────────┐
│                                                              │
│   Number of files exceed maximum.                            │
│                                                              │
│                                                              │
│                                                              │
├─────────────────────────────────────────────────────────────┤
│   <─┘=Enter    Esc=Cancel    F1=Help                         │
└─────────────────────────────────────────────────────────────┘
```

This window informs you that the directory contains too much information for the specified buffer size. If this happens, you may get the following message,

```
No files in selected directory
```

in the File List area when you select a subdirectory.

There are three ways of dealing with this problem: you can remove the /B: option from your DOSSHELL.BAT file; you can increase the number of kilobytes specified after the /B: option; or you can delete unwanted files from your disk if any exist.

The /B: option can be used in the same way in the transient mode, but it is not as likely to be needed because transient mode automatically frees up memory when you run a program.

Options to Try if You Are Running Out of Memory

From the previous discussion, it is clear that there are several options for reducing the memory requirements of the Shell. These include /TRAN, /MUL, /BIN, /DOS, and /MENU.

Increasing Shell Performance with the /SWAP Option

When you enter the File System, the Shell reads all directory names and filenames from the disk directory and stores them in memory. If you then attempt to perform some other task within the Shell, that same memory will be used for the new task. When you return to the File System, the directory and filenames must be read again from the disk directory. Using the /SWAP option allows you to speed up this process.

When /SWAP is included in the @SHELLC line of your DOSSHELL.BAT file (see Figure 3.11), the names of the directories and files are written to a temporary file on your disk. You can then perform other tasks that use the same memory as the File System used, and when you return to the File System, the directory names and filenames are read in from the temporary file. The Shell can read the names in from this temporary file much faster than it can read them in from the disk directory.

The /SWAP option is not recommended if you do not have a fixed disk because space is at a premium on floppy disks, and you do not want to use up space for temporary files. Disk access is also much faster with a fixed disk, so the increase in speed is more significant in those cases.

Normally, these temporary files are erased when you exit the Shell; however, if you have the /SWAP option set and you turn the computer off without exiting the Shell, these temporary files are not deleted. It is a good idea to occasionally check your DOS directory for these files. The files will have names that appear meaningless to you — e.g., "100B3638" with no extension — and their creation date will be recent (unless you haven't checked in a long time). Once you have identified these files, they can be deleted.

Installing the Shell for Use with a Mouse

To use a mouse with the Shell, you must indicate what type of mouse is being used and where that mouse is connected to the computer. Four options are available to inform the Shell about the mouse you are using. Three of these options identify different types of mice; consequently, you will never use more than one of these three. The fourth option informs the Shell where the mouse is connected to the computer.

Identifying Your Mouse Type

The first three mouse options are as follows:

- /MOS:PCIBMDRV.MOS
- /MOS:PCMSPDRV.MOS
- /MOS:PCMSDRV.MOS

The first option informs the Shell that you are using an IBM PS/2 mouse; the second option specifies a Microsoft Parallel Mouse (Microsoft part number 037-099); and the third specifies a Microsoft Serial Mouse (Microsoft part number 039-099). If you have one of these three types of mice, simply include the appropriate option in your DOSSHELL.BAT file.

Informing the Shell Where Your Mouse is Connected to the Computer

External equipment that plugs into your computer, such as printers and mice, connects through special plugs in the back of the computer. These plugs are known as **ports** because it is through them that information moves in and out of your computer. Some of the ports available to your computer are known as **communications ports**, (or **COM ports**). There are typically one or two COM ports; one is referred to as COM1, and the other is referred to as COM2.

When you install the Shell, it assumes the mouse is connected to COM1. If you have included the correct option for identifying your mouse and it does not work, the mouse might be plugged into the COM2 port on your computer. You can instruct the Shell to look to COM2 rather than COM1 by including the /COM2 option in your DOSSHELL.BAT file. If /COM2 is not specified, the Shell assumes the mouse is plugged into COM1.

Installing Mice Not Included in the Shell Options

If you have a mouse that is not one of the three included in the Shell options list, you can still use it with the Shell if its interface specifications match the Microsoft specifications. Most mice are built to these specifications, so there is a good chance your mouse will work.

You can also use this technique with the specified mice instead of including the /MOS option. This technique, however, uses between 4K and 11K of additional memory, depending on the mouse type.

First, remove all /MOS options from the DOSSHELL.BAT file. Next, install the mouse driver that came with the mouse; you will need to refer to the instructions that came with the mouse for this step. You can include the commands for this in your AUTOEXEC.BAT file, ahead of the DOSSHELL command, if you like. Finally, start the Shell program. The mouse should now be functioning with the Shell.

Note that the mouse driver must be installed before you start the Shell. If your AUTOEXEC.BAT file takes you right into the Shell, you must either insert the mouse driver installation commands ahead of it or exit the Shell, install the driver, and then enter the DOSSHELL command to restart the Shell.

Setting Up the Mouse for Left-Hand Use

You can set up the mouse for left-handed use by specifying the /LF option in the DOSSHELL.BAT file.

Selecting Text or Graphics Mode

If your computer has graphics capabilities, you can specify how you want them used. Graphics capabilities range from displaying images in anywhere from two to 16 colors. Resolution varies from low resolution to high resolution. If you make no specifications, the Shell will automatically determine the highest quality mode available on your computer and use it. Consequently, you only need specify one of these options if you want to force use of something less than the maximum your computer is capable of.

To understand the use of graphics modes, you must understand a bit about how images are displayed on your screen. Text mode is designed for only displaying text characters; these include numbers, letters of the alphabet, and special characters such as arrows and lines for drawing boxes. While text mode is limited to displaying only this limited set of images, and only in one color, it is also extremely sharp. Furthermore, systems that display only in text mode are less expensive than systems with graphics capabilities.

Graphics modes, on the other hand, create images by identifying very small spots on the screen and setting these spots to different colors. These spots are known as **pixels** (for picture elements). This is the same idea used for printing pictures in the newspaper; they are made up of many tiny dots.

What distinguishes different graphics modes is the number of colors and pixels they can display on the screen (i.e., their resolution). These differences are determined by the hardware installed in your computer.

One text mode and three graphics modes are available with the Shell. The graphics modes all require high-resolution graphics hardware (EGA or VGA). If you have a CGA (Color Graphics Adapter) card, you should install the Shell in text mode; it will still provide you with the use of four colors in the Shell.

If you aren't sure what hardware your computer has, you can simply try the various options. If you have specified a configuration that requires hardware your computer doesn't have, an error message will appear when you try to run the Shell. You can then edit the DOSSHELL.BAT file to change the configuration.

Text Only Mode

You can force the Shell to display all information in text mode by including the /TEXT option in your DOSSHELL.BAT file. If your computer has a CGA adapter, you will be able to use four colors.

Graphics Mode One

This mode is set by including /CO1 in your DOSSHELL.BAT file. It will display the Shell in 16 colors and has a resolution of 640 dots (horizontally) by 350 (vertically).

Graphics Mode Two

This mode is set by including /CO2 in your DOSSHELL.BAT file. It will display the Shell in two colors and has a resolution of 640 dots (horizontally) by 480 dots (vertically).

Graphics Mode Three

This mode is set by including /CO3 in your DOSSHELL.BAT file. It will display the Shell in sixteen colors and has a resolution of 640 dots (horizontally) by 480 dots (vertically).

The modes accepted by your machine depend entirely on your hardware. It is possible to replace the video parts of your computer to provide higher resolution and more colors.

Selecting the Initial Color Setup

When you change the color configuration of the Shell screens with the Change Colors option on the Main Group menu, the new configuration is automatically saved in a file named SHELL.CLR in the DOS directory. When you installed the Shell, the /CLR:SHELL.CLR option was automatically included, which instructs the Shell to use the color configuration defined in the SHELL.CLR file.

It is possible to have different color setups available without going through the Change Colors process, which can be convenient, for example, if you want to provide different color setups for different users.

The process for providing different color setups is straightforward. Choose one of the color setups you want to save. When you leave the Change Colors system and return to the Main Group menu, the new color configuration is saved in the SHELL.CLR file. You can then use the File System to copy that file into one named SHELL1.CLR. Repeat this procedure for each setup you want to save, changing the number in the filename for each setup. The second setup will be copied into SHELL2.CLR, and so on.

You can now create different DOSSHELL.BAT files for your different users. To use the color setup in SHELL1.CLR, you should include the option /CLR:SHELL1.CLR in the DOSSHELL.BAT file. A technique for creating different DOSSHELL.BAT files for different users is explained in Chapter 6.

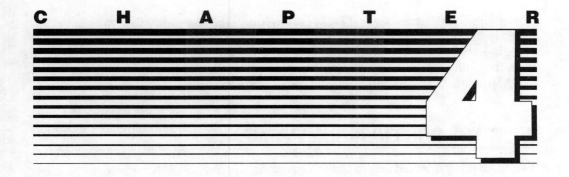

C H A P T E R

4

MANIPULATING THE DOS ENVIRONMENT

This chapter discusses several DOS commands used to modify the way your computer behaves. It is recommended that you experiment with these commands as you go — try out different commands with different parameters and see what effects they have. You won't damage anything if you make mistakes; the worst that can happen is that you will need to reboot your computer.

WHAT THE DOS ENVIRONMENT MEANS

The term **environment** refers to the context in which DOS interacts with the computer. You can think of the environment as the area that surrounds DOS and filters everything that passes to and from DOS. Figure 4.1 shows this graphically; the Shell talks to DOS through the environment and DOS talks to the hardware through the environment.

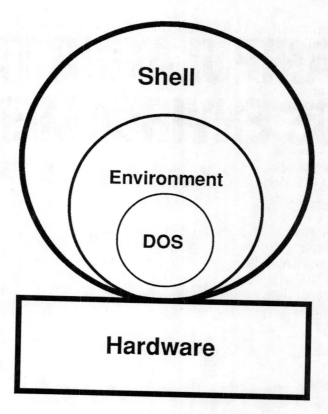

Figure 4.1   *Hardware/Shell/Environment/DOS relationships*

DOS environment commands can be used to modify the non-Shell DOS interface (i.e., the traditional DOS prompt screen). If you are setting up the computer for someone who will only occasionally exit the Shell to work at the command prompt, it is important to make that environment as user friendly as possible. Environment commands are also used to customize the way DOS functions, which can impact on the behavior of the Shell.

The environment can be modified by settings entered at the keyboard or included in the startup files (AUTOEXEC.BAT and CONFIG.SYS). Some of these settings can only be entered once. They remain in effect until the computer is rebooted. These settings are determined by configuration commands entered in the CONFIG.SYS file. Other settings can be entered and reentered at will, allowing you to change some aspects of the environment as you work. These settings are set by DOS prompt commands. They can be included in the AUTOEXEC.BAT file, or they can be entered at the command prompt.

Two of these commands, DATE and TIME, are included in the DOS Utilities menu. You can add any of the other commands to the DOS UTILITIES menu, using the techniques described in Chapter 3.

An example of an environmental setting is the DATE command. DATE is used to set the internal date of the computer, which is used for date stamping the creation or modification of files. The date is also displayed on the screen by some software programs, including the Shell.

The DATE command can be entered at the command prompt. It can also be included in the AUTOEXEC.BAT file. Once the date is set, it does not change until you reboot your computer or change it with another DATE command.

The DATE command is a DOS prompt command. It is becoming common for computers to have battery-operated internal clocks that automatically keep the date current, even when the computer is turned off or the power fails. If you have one of these clocks, you can still use the DATE command to change the computer's date setting. Depending on how the battery-operated clock works, you may need a separate command supplied with the clock to reset the clock itself.

THE STARTUP FILES—AUTOEXEC.BAT AND CONFIG.SYS

When you boot your computer, one of the first things DOS does is look in the root directory of the boot disk for a file named CONFIG.SYS. If the file is found, DOS executes the configuration commands contained within it.

CONFIG.SYS is a special file that contains various environmental settings. There are default values for each of these settings that are used if the file is not found, so it is not required that you have a CONFIG.SYS file. However, more and more programs are appearing on the market that require a modified DOS environment, so it is likely that you will need one. Some of these programs automatically create or modify the CONFIG.SYS file during installation, so you never need to worry about it. Other programs require you to modify it yourself, using a text editor such as EDLIN or SIDEKICK. As you become more proficient at using DOS, you may find that you want to customize your environment, using the CONFIG.SYS file to optimize your computer's performance.

After DOS has executed the commands in the CONFIG.SYS file, DOS looks in the root directory of the boot disk for a file named AUTOEXEC.BAT. AUTOEXEC.BAT is a batch file. (Batch files are discussed in Chapter 5.) If DOS finds this file, it executes the commands contained in the file. For example, if the DOS Shell appears when you boot your computer, it is because the command DOSSHELL, which starts the Shell running, appears in the AUTOEXEC.BAT file. If there is no AUTOEXEC.BAT file, when DOS starts it prompts you for the date and time, then presents you with the DOS prompt (e.g., C:) and waits for you to start entering commands.

Most environmental settings must be typed in at the command prompt. There is no facility included in the Shell for setting them, except for the Date and Time. However, you may want to change the environmental settings without having to exit the Shell, type the command, and reenter the Shell. This can be accomplished by adding a DOS Environment Command option to the DOS Utilities menu (or any other menu in which you would like to have this option appear).

The DOS Environment Command option can be added to a menu by selecting Add from the Program menu on the Menu Bar. Enter the name you would like to use for the choice (e.g., DOS Environment Command) on the Title line of the Add Program dialogue box, and enter an opening and closing square bracket on the Commands line. The box will appear as in Figure 4.2.

```
                     Change Program
        Required

          Title . . . .  [DOS Environment comman>

          Commands  . .  [[]                                    >

        Optional

          Help text . .  [                                      >

          Password  . .  [             ]

        ─────────────────────────────────────────────────────────
         Esc=Cancel     F1=Help     F2=Save
```

Figure 4.2   *Setting up a DOS Environment command*

This command line will add the item "DOS Environment command" to the menu. When this option is selected, the Program Parameters dialogue box in Figure 4.3 will appear.

```
                  Program Parameters

        Type the parameters, then press Enter.

          Parameters . .  [                    >

        ─────────────────────────────────────────────────────
         <─┘=Enter    Esc=Cancel    F1=Help
```

Figure 4.3   *Program Parameters dialogue box for DOS Environment command*

You can enter any DOS command on the Parameters line. For example, if you enter the command **PATH C:\DOS;C:\WP**, the screen will clear momentarily and then return to the Shell with the new path in effect. (The PATH command is discussed later in this chapter.)

You can also view the current path by entering just the command PATH with no directory following it. In this case, the screen will clear and momentarily display the current path before returning to the Shell. Depending on your hardware setup, DOS may not pause long enough to read the path. If that is the case, you can add a special PATH option to your menu that prompts you for parameters and then pauses (using the PAUSE command) after displaying the path.

DOS PROMPT ENVIRONMENTAL COMMANDS

Changing the Computer's Internal Date

The DATE command is used by the DOS Utilities' Set Date and Time function to display and/or change the date on the computer's internal clock. If you type the command DATE at the command prompt, the computer will display the following lines:

```
Current date is day mm-dd-yy
Enter new date (mm-dd-yy):
```

Pressing the Return key without entering a new date will leave the date unchanged. You can enter a new date in any of the following formats:

mm-dd-yy
mm/dd/yy
mm.dd.yy

yy can be either a two-digit or four-digit year. When you install DOS 4.0 with the SELECT program, if you select a country other than the U.S., the date format may be dd-mm-yy or yy-mm-dd. If you want to change the country after you have installed DOS 4.0, you can do so by including a COUNTRY command in your CONFIG.SYS file. The COUNTRY command is discussed later in this chapter.

If you enter an invalid date (e.g., 11/31/88), DOS will display the following error message and prompt:

```
Invalid date
Enter new date (mm-dd-yy):
```

This is the same error message you see when you enter an invalid date, using the Shell DOS Utilities' Date and Time function. The messages are the same because the Date and Time function is executing the DOS DATE command, except that it uses a parameter screen instead of the command line for entering the new date.

When DOS displays the date, it includes the day of the week (e.g., Tue). This is for information purposes only (e.g., it is often easier to remember that it is Tuesday rather than September 20). You should not include the day when you enter a date.

You can change the date without seeing the current date by appending the new date to the DATE command. The following command will set the date to January 2, 1989:

DATE 1/2/89

Changing the Computer's Time

The TIME command is also used by the DOS Utilities' Set Date and Time function to display and/or change the time of the computer's internal clock. If you type the command TIME at the command prompt, the computer will display the following lines:

```
Current time is hh:mm:ss.hsx
Enter new time:
```

The hs refers to hundredths of a second and the x refers to "a" for a.m. or "p" for p.m. If you press the Return key without entering a new time, the time is left unchanged. You can enter a new time in either of the following formats:

hh:mm:ss:hsx
hh.mm.ss,hsx

For example, to set the time to 9:35 p.m. you could enter either of the following two times:

9:35p
21:35

Note that you do not need to enter all of the parameters; just the hour and minute are sufficient. In fact, just the hour is sufficient. If you entered the time as "9p," DOS would set the clock to 9:00 p.m. Note also that even though people in the U.S. use a twelve-hour clock, you can set the clock, using either a twelve-hour or twenty-four-hour format. In either case, DOS will continue to display the time in a twelve-hour format.

If you do not include an "a" or a "p," DOS will assume it is morning. Simply entering "9:35" will set the clock for 9:35 a.m.

When you installed DOS 4.0 with the SELECT program, if you selected a country other than the U.S., the time format may be displayed as a 24-hour clock, in which case the a/p indicator will not be present. If you want to change the country after you have installed DOS 4.0, you can do so by including a COUNTRY command in your CONFIG.SYS file. The COUNTRY command is discussed later in this chapter.

If you enter an invalid time (e.g., 13:00P or 24:01), DOS will display the following error message and prompt:

```
Invalid time
Enter new time:
```

This is the same error message you see when you enter an invalid time, using the Shell DOS Utilities' Date and Time function. The messages are the same because the Date and Time function is executing the DOS TIME command, except it uses a parameter screen instead of the command line for entering the new time.

You can change the time without viewing the current time by appending the new time to the TIME command. The following command sets the time to 8:15 p.m.:

TIME 8:15p

Modifying the DOS Prompt

When you exit the Shell, you are presented with a screen that is blank except for a few characters that indicate the computer is waiting for you to type in a command. These characters are known as the **DOS prompt**. The DOS prompt is modified by the PROMPT command. If you do not have a PROMPT command in your AUTOEXEC.BAT file, the DOS prompt is set to its default value, which is the drive letter of the active drive followed by a greater than (>) sign. If the active drive is the A drive, the default prompt looks like this:

    A> _

If the prompt on your computer looks different from this, there is a PROMPT command in your AUTOEXEC.BAT file.

The PROMPT command is used to create a prompt that provides more useful information than just the drive letter. Different types of prompts will be appropriate for different users. If you are setting up the computer for people who will not normally use DOS commands, a text message that indicates what is expected of them may be helpful. For more advanced users, information about the current drive and directory is more appropriate. You may also want to display the current date and time as part of the prompt.

There are 13 parameters that can be used with the PROMPT command. Each parameter is preceded by a dollar sign ($). The dollar sign tells DOS that the character that follows it should be interpreted as a parameter rather than a text character. To include a dollar sign in your prompt, enter two dollar signs. For example, to change the prompt to "Enter your command$," use the following command:

PROMPT Enter your command$$

You can use parameters to construct a DOS prompt that looks almost any way you want.

Examples in this book always use uppercase letters for the Prompt parameters, but you can use lowercase letters just as well. You can intersperse text before, between, and after parameters. If you want to reset the DOS Prompt to its default value (the current drive letter followed by a greater than sign, e.g., C>), you can do so by entering the PROMPT command without any parameters.

Changing the DOS Prompt to a Text Message

You can change the prompt to a message, without any drive or directory designators, by entering the PROMPT command followed by the text you want to use. If you enter the following command:

PROMPT Type your DOS command here:

the DOS prompt will look like this:

```
Type your DOS command here:_
```

Including a Greater-Than Sign (>) in the DOS Prompt

It has been a standard convention since the first version of DOS to end the prompt with a greater than sign (>). However, you cannot simply use the greater than sign in your text message. The greater than sign has a special meaning to DOS. If you include it in the text of your prompt, you will receive an error message. You must therefore use the $G parameter to include a greater than sign in your prompt. To add a greater than sign to the prompt described above, you would use the following command:

PROMPT Type your DOS command here: $G

This will result in the following prompt:

```
Type your DOS command here:>_
```

Including a Less-Than Sign (<) in the DOS Prompt

The less than sign (<) also has a special meaning to DOS, so it too must be included by using a parameter. You can include a less than sign in your prompt with the $L parameter. To embed text between less than and greater than signs, you enter the text between the parameters. To make your prompt appear like the following,

```
Type your <DOS> command here:_
```

you would use the following command:

PROMPT Type your $LDOS$G command here:

Including the Current Drive Letter in the DOS Prompt

You can include the current drive letter in the prompt with the $N parameter, as in the following PROMPT command:

PROMPT The current drive is: $N

If your current drive is A, this command will result in the following prompt:

```
The current drive is: A_
```

Note that there is no colon or space after the drive letter. When you construct a prompt with the PROMPT command, only what you include in the command appears in the DOS prompt. A better way to write the above PROMPT command would be as follows:

PROMPT The current drive is $N:

Leaving a space at the end of the line will produce the following prompt:

```
The current drive is A: _
```

Including the Current Directory Path in the DOS Prompt

The $P parameter is used to insert the path from the root directory to the current directory into the DOS prompt, as in the following prompt:

PROMPT The current directory is $P:

If you are in the C:\DOS directory, this will produce the following prompt:

```
The current directory is C:\DOS: _
```

Again, be sure to include a space at the end of the PROMPT command. Otherwise, the cursor will be crowded up against the prompt.

Note that the path includes the drive letter so there is no need to combine the $N and $P parameters. In fact, if you used NP in a prompt, the drive letter would be duplicated at the beginning of the prompt.

One of the most common PROMPT commands is simply

PROMPT PG

This is the PROMPT command that DOS 4.0 automatically inserts into the AUTOEXEC.4XX file during installation. If you are in the DOS subdirectory, the prompt will look like this:

```
C:\DOS>_
```

This is a common prompt for fixed disk users because they will only be able to locate their files if they know where they are starting from. The current drive and directory is therefore considered essential information.

Using $P with a Floppy Disk Drive

If the current drive is a floppy disk drive, then the /P parameter will cause DOS to read the directory of the disk in that drive whenever the DOS prompt appears. To read the drive, DOS must have a formatted disk in it and the door must be closed. Consequently, if you are going to use a floppy disk drive as the current drive with the $P parameter, you must be sure the drive is ready. If it isn't, DOS will display the following message:

```
Not ready reading drive A
Abort, Retry, Fail?
```

There are two ways of handling this problem. The first is to put in a formatted floppy disk and select either A (Abort) or R (Retry). Either selection will result in the drive being read and the correct prompt appearing. The other option is to select F (Fail). This will result in the following prompt:

```
Current drive is no longer valid
```

Don't worry about this message. It does not disable the drive, and it allows you to take whatever appropriate action you want. Possible actions are as follows:

1. Insert a formatted disk in the floppy drive and press the Return key. This will cause DOS to read the drive again and set the prompt correctly.

2. Change the current drive to one that has a valid disk in it (either another floppy drive or a fixed disk drive). To change to your C (fixed) drive, enter C:. As a result, drive C will become the current drive, and the DOS prompt will display the current directory on drive C.

Including the Date in the DOS Prompt

The $D parameter is used to insert the system date into the DOS prompt. The following prompt demonstrates the use of the $D parameter:

PROMPT Today's date is $D. Enter your command$G

This will produce the following prompt:

```
Today's date is Wed 01-24-1989. Enter your command>
```

If you are concerned about your files having the correct date stamp on them, this parameter is useful. It tells you what the system date is so you will know to change it if it is incorrect.

Including the Time in the DOS Prompt

The system time can be inserted into the DOS prompt, using the $T parameter as part of the PROMPT command. The time will always be displayed in a 24-hour format regardless of whether the TIME command displays it in a 12-hour or 24-hour format. The COUNTRY command (discussed later in this chapter) determines the format used by the TIME commands. For example, if it is 2:06 in the afternoon, the TIME command may display the following:

```
Current time is 2:06:17.35p
```

The "p" at the end of the time indicates "p.m."; the time is displayed in 12-hour format. However, if you include the $T parameter in the PROMPT command, the time in the prompt will be displayed as "14:06:17.35." The following command demonstrates the use of the $T parameter:

PROMPT The time is $T. Enter your command$G

This command results in the following prompt (assuming it is 2:06:17.35 p.m.):

```
The time is 14:06:17.35. Enter your command>
```

Including the DOS Version Number in the DOS Prompt

If you are running different versions of DOS on your computer, or have more than one computer with different versions of DOS, it can be useful to know what version of DOS is running. You can display the version with the $V parameter. Both the version number and the manufacturer (IBM or Microsoft) appears. The following command demonstrates this feature:

PROMPT $V

If you are running IBM DOS 4.0, the following prompt will appear:

```
IBM DOS Version 4.0
_
```

The underscore indicates the cursor position. Note that there is a carriage return inserted after the prompt. This is to ensure that the version number is not obscured or confused by information following it. You can still include other parameters and text with the $V parameter. Anything that comes before the $V will appear in front of the version number on the same line with it, and anything that appears after the $V will appear on the following line. If you entered the following command,

PROMPT The version is $V The current directory is $P.

the prompt would appear as follows:

```
The current version is IBM DOS Version 4.0
The current directory is C:\DOS. _
```

Including a Vertical Bar Symbol in the DOS Prompt

The vertical bar symbol (|) can be included in the DOS prompt with the $B parameter. Like the greater-than and less-than signs, this symbol has a special meaning to DOS and therefore cannot be entered directly. The following command demonstrates the use of the $B parameter:

PROMPT Enter your command here$B

This command will produce the following prompt:

```
Enter your command here|_
```

Including an Equal Sign in the DOS Prompt

The equal sign is used by DOS as a delimiter (i.e., to separate commands and parameters on command lines). It is therefore necessary to use a special parameter to include an equal sign in the DOS prompt. The equal sign parameter is $Q, as in the following command:

PROMPT Today's date $Q DG

This command produces the following prompt:

```
Today's date = Wed 01-24-89>_
```

Using a Backspace in the DOS Prompt

You can include a backspace character in your PROMPT command with the $H parameter, which will erase the character immediately preceding the $H. For example, if you used the following command,

PROMPT This demonstrates the use of a b$Hackspace.

the prompt would look like this:

```
This demonstrates the use of a ackspace.
```

This seems at first to be a useless parameter; why not simply *not* type in the character you're going to erase? But remember, some of the other parameters display whole strings of characters as part of the prompt. For example, the $D (date) parameter displays the date as mm-dd-yyyy. You may prefer to have only the last two digits of the year displayed, rather than all four. If the date is 01-24-1989, the command **PROMPT The date is $D** will produce the following prompt:

```
The date is Wed 01-24-1989
```

You can use the $H parameter to display only the last two digits of the year as follows:

PROMPT The date is DHHH$H89

This will produce the following prompt:

```
The date is Wed 01-24-89
```

Of course, be sure you change the prompt when the next year comes around because you are actually writing in the digits for the year.

Another use of the $H parameter is to eliminate the hundredths of a second when including the time in the DOS prompt. This is done with the following command:

PROMPT The time is THHH

This command will produce the following time prompt:

```
The time is 15:16:56_
```

You can use additional $H parameters to eliminate the seconds if you want.

Displaying More Than One Line in the DOS Prompt

As the DOS prompt gets longer, it gets harder to separate the different pieces of information, and there is less room for you to type in your commands. DOS will allow you to wrap your commands to subsequent lines, but they are harder to read. The $_ parameter allows you to break your prompt into separate lines.

Take, for example, the following command:

PROMPT The current directory is $P. The date is $D. The time is$T.

This results in a prompt that is so long it actually wraps to the next line:

```
The current directory is C:\.  The date is Wed 01-24-1989.
The time is 14:24:38.48.
```

You can make this prompt more readable by using the $_ parameter as follows:

PROMPT The current directory is $P.$_The date is $D.$_The time is$T.

This command will produce the following prompt:

```
The current directory is C:\DOS.
The date is Wed 01-24-89.
The time is 14:24:38.48._
```

Use of the PROMPT Command to
Customize the Screen and Keyboard Characteristics

One way to modify the DOS environment is to install programs in memory that are called **device drivers**, which are used to communicate between the CPU and other devices, such as the keyboard and the monitor. DOS includes a device driver named ANSI.SYS, which can be loaded by including the command DEVICE =C:\ANSI.SYS in the CONFIG.SYS file. (If the ANSIS.SYS file is in a directory other than the root, you should include the complete pathname). This command is automatically included in the CONFIG.4xx file that the Shell creates during installation, so if you copied those commands into your CONFIG.SYS file, it is already there.

The ANSI.SYS driver allows you to modify the way the CPU responds to the keyboard and the way it displays characters on the screen. One way to send commands to this driver is through the PROMPT command, using the $E parameter. $E inserts into the command line a character known as the **escape** character. The escape character tells DOS that what follows is one or more commands that should be sent to the ANSI.SYS device driver. The combination of the escape character and ANSI.SYS commands is known as an **escape sequence.**

Keep in mind how these escape sequences work. Though they are not PROMPT commands per se, they use the PROMPT command to send another command to the ANSI.SYS driver. For this reason, entering another PROMPT command does not automatically cancel them the way it automatically cancels previous PROMPT commands. The only time a PROMPT command communicates with the ANSI.SYS device driver is when an escape sequence is included in the command. The only time a previous command to ANSI.SYS is cancelled is when a specific cancellation command is sent to ANSI.SYS.

The ANSI.SYS device driver can also receive commands from programs written in programming languages such as BASIC, PASCAL, and C; however, the discussion of these uses is beyond the scope of this book.

PROMPT Parameters Used for Positioning the Cursor

The escape sequence **$E[row;columnH** places the cursor at the point on the screen specified by "row" and "column." The H tells ANSI.SYS to interpret the preceding numbers as cursor positions. Be sure to use a capital H because a small h will send a command to ANSI.SYS that changes your screen display. (If this happens, refer to the next section in this chapter for information on how to restore your display.)

The following command demonstrates the use of PROMPT to position the cursor:

PROMPT $E[10;31HThis Is The DOS Screen$E[12;1H$P$G

This command displays the message "This Is The DOS Screen" on row 10, starting at column 31 (which centers the message horizontally, slightly above the middle of the screen). It then moves the cursor to the beginning of line 12 and displays a common DOS prompt: the current directory letter followed by a greater than sign.

This prompt appears at the specified location, regardless of whatever else is on the screen. It does not clear the screen first, so the prompt may appear in the middle of other information already being displayed. Whether this is a problem depends on your anticipated use of the DOS command line.

You can clear the screen before the message is displayed or only clear the lines on which the prompt will appear, using the escape sequences discussed in the next section. If you enter the CLS command (which clears the screen) after entering this PROMPT command, the screen will appear as in Figure 4.4.

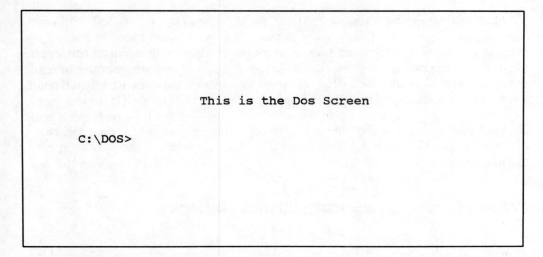

Figure 4.4   *DOS prompt using ANSI.SYS for cursor positioning*

If the screen is not cleared first, it could appear similar to that in Figure 4.5.

```
TEST2     FIL        20 10-09-88      3:01p
WP1       FIL        56 10-09-88      5:56p
WP2       FIL        56 10-09-88      5:57p
FILE1     BAT       110 10-09-88     11:10p
FILE2     BAT        81 10-09-88     11:11p
CALL1     BAT       134 10-09-88     10:53p
CALL2     BAT       131 10-09-88     11:11p
CALL3     BAT        35 10-09-88     10:53p
CALL2     BAK       136 10-09-88     10:54p
FILE1     BAK       122 10-09-8This is the Dos Screen
FILE2     BAK        87 10-09-88     11:01p
C:\DOS>   BAK         5 10-09-88     11:14p
MORE      TMP      2166 06-17-88     12:00p
MEM                   2 10-09-88     11:15p
FOREVER   BAT        16 10-09-88     11:17p
TEST      BAT       132 10-10-88      1:48a
D4        BAK       265 10-10-88      1:58a
HELP      BAT        80 10-10-88      2:09a
SHOW      BAT        41 10-10-88      2:10a
SHOW      BAK        29 10-10-88      2:09a
REPEAT    BAT        50 10-10-88      2:31a
D4        SCR       735 10-14-88     12:32a
        111 File(s)    9091072 bytes free
```

Figure 4.5   *DOS prompt in Figure 4.4 without clearing the screen*

You can also use escape sequences to move the cursor up, down, left, and right. The $E[numA sequence moves the cursor up *num* rows without changing the column it is in. The $E[numB sequence moves the cursor down *num* rows. The $E[numC sequence moves the cursor to the right *num* spaces without changing the row it is in. Finally, the $E[numD sequence moves the cursor to the left *num* spaces without changing the row it is in.

One use of the C and D sequences is to make detailed changes to the appearance of the date and time in the DOS prompt, as demonstrated in the following command:

PROMPT $E[1C$D$E[10D$HHHHHDate$E[11C$G

This command replaces the day of the week with the word "Date." The result is the following prompt:

```
Date 01-24-1989>_
```

The first escape sequence, $E[1C, moves the cursor one space to the right. This is necessary because the day of the week is abbreviated to three characters, while the word "Date" takes up four spaces. The next parameter, $D, inserts the date into the prompt. The next escape sequence, $E[10D, moves the cursor to the left 10 spaces, which puts it at the beginning of the date. The following four parameters are all $H, which erase four characters (the day of the week and the space that separates it from the date) and leave the cursor at the beginning of the line. Then the word "Date" is inserted, followed by the escape sequence $E[11C, which moves the cursor to the right 11 spaces, placing it at the end of the date. Finally, there is a $G parameter, which causes the prompt to terminate with a greater than sign.

PROMPT Parameters Used for Modifying the Screen Display

You can use escape sequences to modify the screen display itself, as well as to position the cursor. The extent to which you can modify the display is dependent on the type of monitor you have. If you have a color monitor, you can set the foreground and background colors of characters that appear in the prompt as well as anything that is displayed after the prompt. This includes information such as directory displays. The escape sequence settings do not, however, affect the display of the Shell or other programs you run; they only affect displays generated by DOS commands. On monochrome displays, you can define characters to be underlined.

The escape sequence $E[2J is used to erase the entire screen and position the cursor in the upper left corner. You can then use the cursor positioning sequences to place the cursor elsewhere if you want. This would be a useful sequence to add to the previous example that displays a message in the middle of the screen, using the $E[row,columnH sequence (see Figures 4.4 and 4.5).

The escape sequence $E[K erases the screen from the current cursor position to the end of the line. This sequence erases whatever is at the cursor position as well, so to avoid erasing the last character of the prompt, you may want to move the cursor to the right one space before using this sequence.

The format of the escape sequences for setting colors and other display attributes is as follows:

$E[setting1;setting2;...m

There can be any number of settings. The last setting is terminated with a small "m" rather than a semicolon, which indicates the end of the escape sequence. Each setting is a number between 0 and 47, though not all numbers are available. The available settings are as follows:

Setting	Description
0	Sets all other settings off. All new displays on the screen are set to the default of white letters on a black background. Information already on the screen is unaffected.
1	Turns on bold. Everything displayed after this setting will appear in bold (high intensity). This will affect everything displayed until an "all settings off" (setting 0) turns bold off. Anything displayed in bold will remain in bold on the screen; new characters will not be in bold.
4	Turns on underlining. This setting is effective for monochrome displays only; color displays cannot show a character as underlined. This setting will remain in effect until an "all settings off" (setting 0) turns off underlining.
5	Turns on blinking. Everything displayed entered after this setting will blink. Everything displayed until an "all settings off" (setting 0) turns blinking off will be affected. Anything displayed before the $E0m will continue to blink, but new displays will not blink.
7	Turns on reverse video. Everything displayed after this setting will appear in black letters on a white background. This setting will remain in effect until an "all settings off" (setting 0) turns off reverse video. Anything displayed in reverse video will remain in reverse video after this setting is turned off.
8	Turns off the display screen. Anything typed at the keyboard and anything that would normally appear on the screen will not appear. This setting is useful for entering passwords that you do not want to have appear on the screen when you enter them. This setting remains in effect until an "all settings off" (setting 0) resets the display mode.
30	Sets the foreground color to black.
31	Sets the foreground color to red.
32	Sets the foreground color to green.

33	Sets the foreground color to yellow.
34	Sets the foreground color to blue.
35	Sets the foreground color to magenta.
36	Sets the foreground color to cyan.
37	Sets the foreground color to white.
40	Sets the background color to black.
41	Sets the background color to red.
42	Sets the background color to green.
43	Sets the background color to yellow.
44	Sets the background color to blue.
45	Sets the background color to magenta.
46	Sets the background color to cyan.
47	Sets the background color to white.

You can also use escape sequences to set the screen mode. The term **mode** refers to how the screen as a whole displays information. There are two classes of modes: text and graphics. **Text modes** display only text and limited figures, but the resolution is very high. **Graphics modes** can display very complex graphic images, but when displaying text characters their resolution is sometimes not as high.

Text modes divide the screen into either 40 characters per line and 25 lines per screen, or 80 characters per line and 25 lines per screen. Graphics modes divide the screen into much smaller units called **pixels**. There can be up to 640 pixels across the screen by as many as 480 pixels down the screen. Pixels can either be in color or black and white.

In addition to setting either graphics or text mode, the Set Mode escape sequence can turn on or off the line-wrapping feature. By default, if you type past the end of the DOS prompt line, the cursor moves to the beginning of the next line and you can continue typing there. You can enter up to 128 characters on the DOS command line, so, depending on the length of the prompt, the line may wrap once or twice. If you do not want to allow line wrapping, you can use the Set Mode escape sequence to cause the cursor to stop at the end of the line. Whatever you type at that point overwrites the last character on the line.

Which modes are available on your computer is dependent on your hardware configuration. Some monitors can only display in a few modes, while others can display in all of them. All monitors will display in 40 × 25 and 80 × 25 text modes, and all monitors will allow the line-wrapping feature to be switched on and off. If you aren't sure which modes are available on your computer, the simplest way to find out is to try out the commands and see which ones affect your display.

The mode is set with the escape sequence $E[=numh, where *num* is a number that specifies the mode and the "h" marks the end of the command. The h must be a lowercase h. The allowable numbers and their effects are specified in Table 4.1.

Setting	Description
0	40 × 25 text mode - black and white
1	40 × 25 text mode - color
2	80 × 25 text mode - black and white
3	80 × 25 text mode - color
4	320 × 200 graphics mode - color
5	320 × 200 graphics mode - black and white
6	640 × 200 graphics mode - black and white
7	turns on line wrapping (the default)
14	640 × 200 graphics mode - color
15	640 × 350 graphics mode - black and white
16	640 × 350 graphics mode - color
17	640 × 480 graphics mode - color
18	640 × 480 graphics mode - color
19	320 × 200 graphics mode - color

Table 4.1   Screen mode settings using ANSI.SYS driver

You can use a lowercase L in place of the lowercase h to terminate these escape sequences. The effect is the same, except in the case of setting 7. The sequence $E[= 7l will turn off the line-wrap feature so that the cursor stays at the end of the line when you reach it.

PROMPT Parameters Used for Modifying the Keyboard

The $E escape sequences can be used to modify the way the CPU responds to the keyboard. Specifically, you can assign any key (including the Shift-key combinations and the function keys) to print a different letter than was originally assigned to it, or even to print a string of letters, numbers, and symbols. For example, you could assign the F1 key to automatically perform a DOS command, such as DIR, which lists the files in the current directory. You can also use this feature to cause a message to display whenever a particular keystroke is entered.

These keyboard commands work only for keystrokes entered at the DOS prompt; they will not affect the keystrokes entered within the Shell or within your software programs, such as your word processor. You can therefore use them to customize the DOS interface without worrying about interfering with other programs.

To understand how this process works, you must know a little about how the computer responds to the keyboard. Each key and each Shift, Alt, and Ctrl key combination produces a numeric code that is sent to the CPU. These codes are translated by the computer into ASCII codes. ASCII codes are codes that correspond to the common characters and symbols that we use for communicating (e.g., the uppercase and lowercase alphabetic characters as well as numbers and punctuation symbols). When the CPU sees one of these ASCII codes, it displays the appropriate character on the screen. For example, the ASCII code for capital A is 65, so when the CPU sees an ASCII code of 65, it displays a capital A on the screen.

Altogether, there are 256 ASCII codes. The first 128 of them (codes 0 through 127) are known as **standard ASCII** They share a common meaning with any computer system that uses ASCII codes, and they represent such common symbols as letters of the alphabet, numbers, etc.

The use of the last 128 codes (codes 128 through 255) is not shared among computer systems. IBM-compatible PCs use these codes for special symbols that can be displayed on the screen. They include letters of foreign alphabets, arrow symbols, and symbols that can be used for drawing lines and boxes on the screen. The entire 256-code ASCII table for IBM-compatible PCs appears in Table 4.2. Some of the ASCII codes produce two symbols: a caret (^) followed by a capital letter. Some of the ASCII codes do not produce printable characters at all; they are used for sending special messages to the display device (either a printer or the screen). An example of such a message is CR, which stands for Carriage Return. This tells the printer or screen to move to the beginning of the next line.

(see Table 4.2 on next four pages)

ASCII value	Character	Control character	ASCII value	Character
000	(null)	^@	032	(space)
001	☺	^A	033	!
002	☻	^B	034	''
003	♥	^C	035	#
004	♦	^D	036	$
005	♣	^E	037	%
006	♠	^F	038	&
007	(beep)	^G	039	'
008	◘	^H	040	(
009	(tab)	^I	041	)
010	(line feed)	^J	042	*
011	(home)	^K	043	+
012	(form feed)	^L	044	,
013	(carriage return)	^M	045	-
014	♫	^N	046	.
015	☼	^O	047	/
016	►	^P	048	0
017	◄	^Q	049	1
018	↕	^R	050	2
019	‼	^S	051	3
020	¶	^T	052	4
021	§	^U	053	5
022	▬	^V	054	6
023	↨	^W	055	7
024	↑	^X	056	8
025	↓	^Y	057	9
026	→	^Z	058	:
027	←	^[	059	;
028	(cursor right)	^\	060	<
029	(cursor left)	^]	061	=
030	(cursor up)	^^	062	>
031	(cursor down)	^_	063	?

Table 4.2   *ASCII table for IBM-compatible PCs*

ASCII value	Character	ASCII value	Character
064	@	096	`
065	A	097	a
066	B	098	b
067	C	099	c
068	D	100	d
069	E	101	e
070	F	102	f
071	G	103	g
072	H	104	h
073	I	105	i
074	J	106	j
075	K	107	k
076	L	108	l
077	M	109	m
078	N	110	n
079	O	111	o
080	P	112	p
081	Q	113	q
082	R	114	r
083	S	115	s
084	T	116	t
085	U	117	u
086	V	118	v
087	W	119	w
088	X	120	x
089	Y	121	y
090	Z	122	z
091	[	123	{
092	\	124	¦
093	]	125	}
094	∧	126	~
095	—	127	⌂

Table 4.2   *ASCII table for IBM-compatible PCs (cont.)*

ASCII value	Character	ASCII value	Character
128	Ç	160	á
129	ü	161	í
130	é	162	ó
131	â	163	ú
132	ä	164	ñ
133	à	165	Ñ
134	å	166	ª
135	ç	167	º
136	ê	168	¿
137	ë	169	⌐
138	è	170	¬
139	ï	171	½
140	î	172	¼
141	ì	173	¡
142	Ä	174	«
143	Å	175	»
144	É	176	░
145	æ	177	▒
146	Æ	178	▓
147	ô	179	│
148	ö	180	┤
149	ò	181	╡
150	û	182	╢
151	ù	183	╖
152	ÿ	184	╕
153	Ö	185	╣
154	Ü	186	║
155	¢	187	╗
156	£	188	╝
157	¥	189	╜
158	Pt	190	╛
159	ƒ	191	┐

Table 4.2   *ASCII table for IBM-compatible PCs (cont.)*

ASCII value	Character	ASCII value	Character
192	└	224	α
193	┴	225	β
194	┬	226	Γ
195	├	227	π
196	─	228	Σ
197	┼	229	σ
198	╞	230	μ
199	╟	231	τ
200	╚	232	Φ
201	╔	233	Θ
202	╩	234	Ω
203	╦	235	δ
204	╠	236	∞
205	═	237	$\emptyset$
206	╬	238	ϵ
207	╧	239	$\cap$
208	╨	240	$\equiv$
209	╤	241	$\pm$
210	╥	242	$\geq$
211	╙	243	$\leq$
212	╘	244	$\lceil$
213	╒	245	$\rfloor$
214	╓	246	$\div$
215	╫	247	$\approx$
216	╪	248	$\circ$
217	┘	249	•
218	┌	250	·
219	█	251	$\sqrt{}$
220	▄	252	n
221	▌	253	^{2}
222	▐	254	■
223	▀	255	(blank 'FF')

Table 4.2   *ASCII table for IBM-compatible PCs (cont.)*

Escape sequences can be used to change the ASCII code that is assigned to a key. The escape sequence used for this purpose is

$E[num;replacementp

In this escape sequence *num* stands for the ASCII code for the key, *replacement* stands for the new code or codes to be assigned to that key, and "p" indicates the end of the sequence. The reassignment codes can be either in the form of another numeric code or actual letters enclosed in double quotation marks. For example, the letter A (uppercase A) has an ASCII code of 65, and the letter B has an ASCII code of 66. Both of the following PROMPT commands will cause the letter B to appear when the letter A is entered:

PROMPT $E[65;66p
PROMPT $E[65;"B"p

Because these are PROMPT commands as well as commands sent to ANSI.SYS, they will change the DOS prompt. In fact, they will eliminate it because there are no PROMPT parameters other than $E in the command. To send this keyboard command to ANSI.SYS and leave a DOS prompt that shows the current directory followed by a greater than sign, you must enter one of the following commands:

PROMPT $E[65;66p$P$G
PROMPT $E[65;"B"p$P$G

After either of these PROMPT commands has been entered, typing a capital A at the DOS prompt will result in a capital B appearing on the screen. You can assign more than one ASCII code to a key, which allows you to have entire messages or commands appear at the touch of a key. These messages can be entered as either ASCII numeric codes or as character strings enclosed in quotation marks. Both of the following commands assign the word HELP to the A key:

PROMPT $E[65;72;69;76;80p$P$G
PROMPT $E[65;"HELP"p$P$G

Again, the PROMPT command is terminated with PG to leave a recognizable prompt appearing on the screen.

You can assign codes to the function keys rather than the regular keys by starting the numbers in the escape sequence with a 0. This tells ANSI.SYS that the next number refers to what is known as an **extended code**. The function keys are numbered with extended codes 59 through 68. The following PROMPT command reassigns the F1 key to type the message "HELP":

PROMPT PG$E[0;59;"HELP"p

In Table 4.2, the ASCII code 13 corresponds to a carriage return, and whenever the CPU sees the ASCII code 13, it sends a carriage return signal to the output device, which is the same as pressing the Return key. An ASCII code 13 can be included in the keyboard reassignment escape sequence to cause a keystroke to carry out a DOS command. For example, the following PROMPT command results in the letters DIR followed by a carriage return whenever F1 is pressed:

PROMPT PG$E[0;59;"DIR";13p

This command will cause the DOS DIR (directory) command to be entered when F1 is pressed, resulting in a directory listing of the current directory. You can extend this to have function keys execute batch files.

A particularly useful application of this technique is to use it with an appropriate DOS prompt to ensure that you or other users of your computer always know how to get back to the Shell. The following command will set up this prompt:

PROMPT Press F1 to return to the Shell$G$E[0;59;"EXIT";13p

This command will result in the following DOS prompt:

```
Press F1 to return to the Shell>
```

It will also assign to the F1 key the word EXIT followed by a carriage return, which is what is required for returning to the Shell when you choose Command Prompt from the Main Group menu or when you press [Shift/F9] to exit the Shell. Using the techniques described in Chapter 3, you can ensure that those are the only ways of exiting the Shell.

For the prompt to remain in effect when you exit and reenter the Shell, you must enter the PROMPT command at the DOS prompt (i.e., while the Shell is not running in the background), or use the DOS Environment Command option, which you can add to the DOS Utilities menu, as discussed at the beginning of this chapter in the section on Startup files.

DOS Delimiters and the DOS Prompt

Many DOS commands, such as the COPY command, can use more than one parameter. The following is an example of a COPY command that uses two parameters, one for the filename to copy from and one for the filename to copy to:

COPY file1 file2

The parameters must be separated by a delimiter. The delimiter can be a space, a comma, a semicolon, an equal sign, or a tab (from pressing the Tab key). The following versions of the COPY command all perform the same task, using different delimiters:

COPY,file1,file2
COPY = file1 = file2
COPY file1;file2
COPY   file1   file2

The last example uses a tab as a delimiter. Note that you can mix delimiters within one command, as in the **COPY file1;file2** command, which uses both a space and a semicolon as a delimiter.

You can use these delimiter symbols in the text part of PROMPT command text as long as they are not the first symbol. If they are the first symbol, DOS will interpret them as delimiters and ignore them, just as it ignores the space following the word PROMPT in all of the previous examples. Consequently, if you want to begin the prompt with one of these characters, you must trick DOS into thinking it is not the first character. This is accomplished by using a $ followed by a character that is *not* a legal PROMPT parameter. For example, there is no A parameter, so you could enter the following command:

PROMPT $A = Enter your command$G

This will result in the following prompt:

```
=Enter your command>
```

The $A is referred to as a **null parameter**, which means it has no meaning. However, in the command, it pushes the equal sign to the right so that the equal sign is no longer the first character. The $A is therefore made a part of the new prompt.

Summary of PROMPT Command Parameters

The PROMPT command parameters are summarized as follows. Each parameter must be preceded by a dollar sign ($).

Parameter	Description
$	Used to indicate that the following character is a parameter. It must precede all other parameters. To include a $ in the prompt, use two dollar signs.
G	Inserts a greater than (>) sign into the prompt.
L	Inserts a less than (<) sign into the prompt.

N	Inserts the current drive letter into the prompt. Only the letter is inserted; no semicolon or greater than sign follows it unless you include one of them in your PROMPT command.
P	Inserts the current directory into the prompt. The drive letter is considered part of the directory so you should not use the N parameter unless you want the drive letter displayed twice. Using the P parameter with a floppy disk drive requires that the drive always be ready because it will be read each time the computer displays the prompt.
D	Inserts the current date into the prompt. The format is country dependent. In the U.S., it is Day MM-DD-YYYY, where Day is a 3-character abbreviation of the day of the week.
T	Inserts the current time into the prompt. The format is country dependent. In the U.S., it is hh:mm:ss.hs, where hs refers to hundredths seconds.
V	Inserts the DOS version number into the prompt. Includes the copyright owner (Microsoft or IBM). The version number is always followed by a carriage return, so the cursor moves to the next line for the rest of the prompt.
B	Inserts a vertical bar into the prompt.
Q	Inserts an equal sign (=) into the prompt.
H	Inserts a backspace character into the prompt, erasing the immediately preceding character.
_	Inserts a carriage return into the prompt, allowing the use of more than one line for the prompt.
E	Inserts an escape character into the prompt, allowing the use of commands for the ANSI.SYS device driver in the prompt.

MANAGING THE PRINT QUEUE

When you use the Shell File System Print option, all of the files that are marked in the File List area are put into the print queue. The print queue is an area of memory that stores the names of files to be printed. When one file finishes printing, the next one in the queue is sent to the printer.

The Print option in the File System is enabled by including a PRINT command in the AUTOEXEC.BAT file. You can modify the PRINT command in the AUTOEXEC.BAT file, using the parameters discussed next. Many of the parameters can only be executed the first time the PRINT command is invoked. These parameters should be set in the AUTOEXEC.BAT file because that is where the PRINT command is first called. They can only be set once because the first time PRINT is executed, a portion of the program is loaded into memory, and the parameters are set in that portion of the program. They cannot be manipulated after being loaded.

The other parameters are used for manipulating the queue after it has been called. They allow you to remove files from the queue and add files to the queue, and they can be invoked as often as you want. These parameters are available by going to the command prompt and executing the PRINT command.

You can use as many or as few of the parameters as you want. If you do not include any parameters, the first time you invoke PRINT, DOS will prompt you for the device to print to (discussed in the next section). If you invoke PRINT without any parameters *after* the first time it has been invoked, it will simply list the files currently in the print queue.

If you want the flexibility of manipulating the print queue from within the Shell, you can add a PRINT QUEUE option to one of the menus (the DOS Utilities menu would be a logical choice). This option can then be used to set up and manipulate the print queue after you have placed files into it with the Print option of the File System.

To add this option to your DOS Utilities menu, bring up that menu and select PROGRAM from the Menu Bar. On the pull-down menu select Add. This will bring up the Change Program dialogue box. Use whatever title you want, and put the following commands into the command line:

PRINT [/T"Print Queue Manipulations"/I"Enter the print queue parameters"]

Press F2 to save this setup. The new option will appear on your DOS Utilities menu, and when you select it, the following screen will appear:

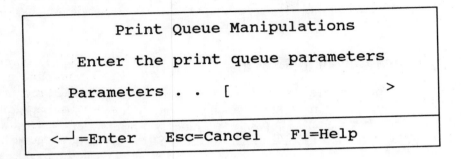

```
        Print Queue Manipulations

    Enter the print queue parameters

    Parameters . .  [                    >


    <─┘=Enter    Esc=Cancel    F1=Help
```

You may want to add a Help screen that will appear when you press F1. You can include notes in the Help screen about the various parameters and how they are used.

If you want control over the initial load parameters, remove the PRINT command from your AUTOEXEC.BAT file. You can then load the resident part of PRINT the first time you execute the PRINT command, either at the command prompt or with the additional menu option just discussed. You can specify the load parameters at this time.

After a file has been added to the print queue, you must not make any changes to it until after it has finished printing. If the file is on a floppy disk, you must leave the disk in the drive until the file has been printed.

If a disk error occurs when DOS attempts to read a file for printing, the following sequence of events occurs:

1. The file being printed is cancelled from the queue.
2. The disk error message is printed on the printer.
3. The printer paper is advanced to the next page.
4. The printer alarm is sounded.
5. The remaining files in the print queue are printed.

Do not attempt to use the printer for any other purpose while the PRINT command is operating. For example, you must not press the [Shift/PrtScr] combination to print a screen image. Doing so will cause the message "out-of-paper" to appear until all files have been printed or printing is terminated with a /C or /T parameter (discussed later).

Specifying the Device to Print to

Devices such as printers are attached to the computer through connections called **ports**. The Print program must know which port should receive information that is to be printed. For example, suppose you have two printers attached to your computer at ports named LPT1 and LPT2 (for Line Printer 1 and Line Printer 2). When you run PRINT the first time, you can specify where the information should be sent with a /D parameter.

The /D parameter can only be entered the first time you run the PRINT command. If you do use /D, it must be the first parameter specified. If you examine the AUTOEXEC.4XX file that is created upon installation of DOS 4.0, you will see the following line:

```
PRINT /D:LPT1
```

This installs the resident part of the print program and tells it to send all files in the print queue to the LPT1 port.

If you do not include a /D parameter, the first time you invoke PRINT, the computer will respond with the following message:

```
Name of list device [PRN]:
```

Pressing the Return key will accept the default value of PRN, which in most cases is the correct choice. If you have one printer attached to your computer on the LPT1 port, this default value will work. Otherwise, you can specify any other port you would like to send the print queue output to. Some possible choices are as follows:

LPT1	line printer 1
LPT2	line printer 2
LPT3	line printer 3
PRN	same as line printer 1
COM1	communications port 1
COM2	communications port 2
AUX	auxiliary port

Make sure the named port exists on your computer and that there is some device attached to it that can receive the output. If there is no such port, or if there is nothing attached to the port, using the PRINT command can cause problems in the functioning of your computer. For example, if you specify LPT2, your computer must have a port named LPT2, and there must be a printer attached to it.

Specifying the Size of the Print Buffer

When you run PRINT the first time, it sets up an area of memory known as a **print buffer**. Many printers can only receive a small number of characters at a time. After they have printed these characters, they request more from the computer. The computer must then suspend whatever it is doing, read the next characters to be printed from the disk, and send them to the printer. A great deal of the computer's time is then spent communicating with the printer.

The print buffer is used to alleviate this problem. It stores a large number of characters that are ready to go to the printer, so when the printer is ready for more characters, the computer does not need to suspend other operations in order to read them from disk. The only time the computer needs to suspend other operations for the printer is when the print buffer is empty.

The /B parameter is used to specify the number of bytes set aside for the print buffer. It can only be entered the first time you invoke the PRINT command. If you do not include it, the default value of 512 bytes is used. You can specify anywhere from 512 bytes up to 16K bytes. A larger value may noticeably increase the performance of the PRINT command, especially if you have a high-speed printer.

The following command demonstrates the /B parameter:

PRINT /B:1024

This command specifies a print buffer of 1024 bytes—twice the default value of 512. Because /B can only be used the first time you invoke PRINT, you will probably include a /D parameter, as follows:

PRINT /D:LPT1 /B:1024

Remember that the /D parameter must be the first parameter if it is to be included. The order in which the other parameters appear is not important.

Specifying the Maximum Number of Files in the Queue

The /Q parameter is used to specify the maximum number of files you can have in the queue at any one time. If you reach this maximum, DOS will not allow you to add any more files until the first one finishes printing. Then you can add one more, until the next one finishes, and so on.

The /Q parameter can only be added the first time PRINT is invoked. You can specify anywhere from four to 32 files. If /Q is not included, the default value is 10. The following command demonstrates the use of /Q:

PRINT /D:LPT1 /B:1024 /Q:15

This command specifies LPT1 as the printer port, 1024 bytes for the print buffer, and a maximum of 15 files in the queue at any given time.

Managing the Print Utility's Use of the Computer's Time

When the print queue is in use, it slows down any other operations you are performing with the computer. There is no way around this problem. The computer can only do one thing at a time, so when it tends to the print queue, it cannot tend to your other tasks. It is therefore important to have some control over how much of the computer's time is devoted to managing the print queue and how much of it is available for your other tasks.

There are three factors that determine how much of the computer's time is spent managing the print queue. To understand these factors you must understand a little about how the computer's clock controls what the computer does.

Like any clock, the computer's clock operates by "ticking" time away. It ticks very fast; there is a large number of clock ticks per second. Because a tick is such a tiny amount of time, the computer allocates much of its time in terms of "time slices" rather than "clock ticks." A **time slice** consists of 255 clock ticks, just as a minute consists of 60 seconds.

The computer operates in "time cycles." People also operate in time cycles called days. A person may get up at 6:30, have breakfast at 7:00, arrive at work at 7:45, leave work at 4:45, and so on. Each day repeats the cycle. Certain "time slices" of the day are allocated to particular tasks, such as having breakfast. In the same way, the computer breaks its cycle into different tasks. Each time the cycle comes around to a particular point, the same task gets some more time.

If you are working in your office on three projects, you can allocate the time from 1:00 to 3:00 for a particular one. Each day you work on that project from 1:00 to 3:00, and each day a little more of it gets done. In the computer's cycle, each time it gets around to the point where a particular task gets some time, a little more of that task gets done.

It is important to keep in mind that in the computer all of this is happening very fast — thousands of times per second — so you rarely notice the computer pausing in one task to give time to another.

In your computer's cycle, there are 255 slices available for all tasks, which means that the smallest amount of time the computer can allocate to any one task is 1/255th of its cycle. You can specify how many time slices per cycle get allocated to managing the print queue with the /S parameter. This parameter can only be entered the first time you run the PRINT command. You can specify anywhere from 1 to 255 time slices. If you do not specify the /S parameter, the default value of 8 is used. The following command demonstrates the use of the /S parameter:

PRINT /D:LPT1 /S:16

This command specifies the LPT1 port and 16 time slices per cycle, which is double the default value. The effect of this command is that more of the computer's time will go to making sure your files print as fast as possible, but less time will be available for whatever other task you are performing while the files are printing.

When you specify a number of time slices (e.g., 16), the computer does not bunch all of them together. It doesn't give the printer 16/255ths of its time all at once and then wait for a complete cycle to come around before the PRINT program gets any time again. Instead, it distributes the slices evenly throughout the cycle. This helps make the print operations more "transparent" to you because only very small amounts of time are being taken away from your other tasks. Those small amounts are just taken away more frequently.

When a time slice for the print queue comes around, DOS checks to see if the printer is still printing the last characters sent to it or if it is waiting for some more characters. If it is waiting for some more characters, DOS starts sending them.

However, DOS can send characters to the printer much faster than the printer can print them, so much of the time slice allocated to printing can be wasted. DOS may be able to send all of the characters the printer can print between now and the next printer time slice in the first few clock ticks of this slice, so the rest of the clock ticks for this slice are wasted. The /M parameter is used to recover those ticks for the next task in the computer's cycle.

/M is used to specify the number of clock ticks that DOS will use to send characters to the printer. If the printer is waiting for characters when a printer time slice starts, only the number of ticks specified with /M will be used to send characters to the printer. The rest of the time slice is released for the next task in the computer cycle.

You only specify /M the first time the PRINT command is invoked. You can specify anywhere from 1 through 255 ticks. The default value used if /M is not included is 2. The following command demonstrates the use of /M:

PRINT /D:LPT1 /M:10

This command specifies the LPT1 port and allocates 10 clock ticks per printer time slice for sending characters to the printer. Because no /S parameter is included in the command, the default of 8 time slices per cycle is used.

If the printer is still printing when a printer time slice comes around, DOS will continue checking the printer during the time slice. This can cause the entire time slice to be wasted if the printer does not complete its printing task during that time. The /U parameter is used to prevent this; it specifies how many clock ticks DOS will wait for the printer to complete its printing so it can receive new characters. If the printer does not finish in the number of ticks specified, the rest of the time slice is released for the next task in the computer's cycle.

/U can only be specified the first time PRINT is invoked. You can specify anywhere from 1 to 255. The default value if /U is not specified is 1. The following command demonstrates the use of the /U parameter:

PRINT /D:LPT1 /U:10

This command specifies the LPT1 port and 10 clock ticks to wait for the printer to be freed up. Because no /S or /M parameters were specified, the default values of 8 and 2 will be used for them.

The best use of the /S, /M, and /U parameters is highly dependent on both your hardware configuration and the use you will make of the Print utility. In most cases, the default values are satisfactory. However, if you find that the computer is taking too long to print your files, or that it is taking too much time away from your other tasks, you may want to try adjusting these parameters.

The parameter that is most likely to have an impact on how much the Print utility is slowing down your other tasks is the /S parameter because it determines how much total time out of each cycle gets devoted to PRINT. The /M and /U parameters are for fine-tuning; they determine how much of the time slices allocated to the printer can be wasted before releasing the rest of the slice for other tasks.

If your printer is pausing frequently and for long periods of time, try increasing /M first. This will provide a larger portion of the available time slice for sending characters to the printer without taking up more time slices for printing. If that does not work, increase /S. You may need to try several combinations of /M and /S before finding the one that provides the best printing speed with the least degradation of other computer performance.

The /U parameter should only be used if maximizing printer throughput is very important because it almost guarantees that time will be wasted waiting for the printer to become ready for more characters.

Managing Files in the Queue

There are three parameters used to manipulate the files in the queue. These parameters can be used at any time. They do not need to be included in the PRINT command the first time it is invoked.

/T is used to terminate printing the files in the queue. When you enter the PRINT command with a /T parameter, all files in the queue are removed from the queue. If a file is printing when the command is entered, the printing is terminated, a cancellation message is printed, the paper is advanced to the next page, and the printer's alarm sounds. The following command demonstrates the use of the /T parameter:

PRINT /T

If no files are in the queue when this command is entered, the message "PRINT queue is empty" will appear on the screen.

You can also specify one or more files to print after emptying the queue. These are included on the command line after the /T parameter. Often, the reason you cancel the print queue is because you want to print a file immediately, without waiting for all the other files in the queue to complete printing. The following command demonstrates this cancellation process:

PRINT /T letter1.fil letter2.fil

This command will cancel all files in the queue and put the files letter1.fil and letter2.fil into the queue. Letter1.fil will then print, followed by letter2.fil.

When /T is used while a file is currently being printed, the following sequence of events occurs:

1. The file being printed is cancelled from the queue.
2. A file cancellation message is printed on the printer.
3. The printer alarm sounds.
4. The printer paper is advanced to the next page.
5. Any files specified on the command line after the /T parameter are printed.

The /C parameter is used to cancel specified files from the queue. You can include one filename before the /C and as many as you want following it. Either of the following commands will remove the files letter4.fil and letter6.fil from the print queue:

PRINT letter4.fil /C letter6.fil
PRINT /C letter4.fil letter6.fil

You do not need to specify the filenames in the order that they occur in the queue. If /C is used to cancel a file that is currently being printed, the following sequence of events occurs:

1. The file being printed is cancelled from the queue.
2. A file cancellation message is printed on the printer.
3. The printer alarm sounds.
4. The printer paper is advanced to the next page.
5. The remaining files in the print queue are printed.

The /P parameter is used to add files to the print queue. The filename preceding the /P and all filenames following it will be added to the print queue. Files are added in the order in which they occur on the command line. Either of the following commands will add the files letter4.fil and letter6.fil to the queue:

PRINT letter4.fil /P letter6.fil
PRINT /P letter4.fil letter6.fil

/P is the default parameter. If no parameters are specified, but filenames are included on the command line, then the files are added to the print queue. The following two command lines are functionally identical:

PRINT letter4.fil /P letter6.fil
PRINT letter4.fil letter6.fil

The /C and /P parameters can be combined on one command line. The parameter specified first will be in effect up to the filename that precedes the parameter specified second. Either of the following command lines will remove the file letter4.fil from the queue and add the files letter5.fil and letter6.fil:

PRINT letter4.fil /C letter5.fil /P letter6.fil
PRINT letter4.fil /C /P letter5.fil letter6.fil

To experiment with the commands, you can turn off your printer and enter the PRINT command with various parameters. If you turn off your printer, the print queue will not empty out. Whenever any PRINT command executes, the entire queue is listed, so you can see what effect the command had.

Use of Wild Cards in PRINT Command Filenames

You can use the wild cards * and ? in filenames entered in the PRINT command. The * is used to replace groups of characters, and the ? is used to replace individual characters. For example, the filename *.fil refers to all files that have an extension of .fil, and the filename letter?.* refers to all files that begin with "letter" plus one more character and any extension. This would include letter1.fil, letter2.dat, etc. You can also embed the asterisk within a filename: let*.fil will include letter.fil, let.fil, lettuce.fil, etc. However, if you begin the filename with *, all filenames will be included. The designation *etter.fil will include all files with the extension .fil.

To print all files with an extension of .fil, enter the following command:

PRINT *.fil

To print all files that begin with "letter" followed by a number and the extension .fil, enter the following command:

PRINT letter?.fil

You can print all files that begin with "let" followed by any group of characters and the extension .fil with the following command:

PRINT let*.fil

The wild card symbols can be included with any of the PRINT parameters. The following command will remove all files that are named "letter" followed by an extension:

PRINT letter.*/C

Setting the DOS Path for Executable Files

On a fixed disk system there are many directories and subdirectories. When you execute a program from the command prompt, DOS normally only looks in the current directory for programs you want to execute. If you are executing a program from a menu choice you have added to the Shell, DOS will only look in the current directory unless you have specified the path on the command line of the Shell program. DOS does not check all of the directories on the disk because it would take a very long time to do so.

The PATH command is used to specify directories that DOS should search if it does not find the requested program file in the current directory. You can specify as many directories as you want, separated by semicolons, as long as you do not exceed the 128-character maximum for DOS commands. It is preferable to use the PATH command rather than include complete pathnames when you execute programs because it saves considerable typing, and it alleviates the burden of remembering all of the paths.

Always specify directory paths starting from the root directory. That way, DOS will always be able to find the directory, regardless of which directory you are currently in. The root directory is specified by the drive designator followed by a backslash. The root directory of drive C: therefore would be indicated by C:\.

The following PATH command tells DOS to look in the DOS, WP, root, and UTILITY directories when it cannot find a program file in the current directory:

PATH C:\DOS; C:\WP; C:\; C:\UTILITY

You can specify different drives to search as well as different directories. DOS will search directories and drives in the order in which they are entered in the PATH command, so you should place those used most often first.

You can see the current path by entering the PATH command with no parameters. This will result in a message similar to the following:

```
C:\DOS;C:\WP;C:\;C:\UTILITY
```

If you type PATH with just a semicolon after it (PATH;), the path will be reset to null (i.e., search only the current directory).

It is a good idea to include a PATH command in your AUTOEXEC.BAT file, so that the regularly used directories are automatically included in the search path. For example, if you use your word processor a lot and it is in the C:\WP directory, you should include the C:\WP path in the PATH command of your AUTOEXEC.BAT file. Then when you add a Word Processing menu option to one of your Shell menus, you will not need to specify the path as part of the file name to execute.

You can change the path at any time by using the PATH command at the command prompt or by using a DOS Environment Command menu option that you can add to your DOS Utilities menu (this is discussed in detail earlier in this chapter in the section on Startup files). When you enter a new PATH command, the previous path is eliminated. New paths replace old paths.

DOS only searches for executable files in the path (i.e., files with an extension of .COM, .EXE, and .BAT). It will not search the path for other files. If you want to use PRINT to print a file, that file must be in the current directory or you must include the full pathname to the file from either the current directory or the root directory. On the other hand, if you want to run your word processor, which will have an extension of either .COM or .EXE, that program file can be in any directory specified in the current path.

If two or more executable files in the same directory have the same name but different extensions, DOS will choose a file with the .COM extension first and then a file with the .EXE extension. Files with a .BAT extension only execute if their name is unique within their directory.

Setting the DOS Path for Nonexecutable Files

You may want to tell DOS to look in directories other than the current directory for nonexecutable files. These are typically overlay files for programs, as well as data files such as the files you create with your word processor. The APPEND command is used for this purpose.

If you keep your word processing data files in a subdirectory named C:\WP\DATA, the following command would allow DOS to find them regardless of which directory is current:

APPEND C:\WP\DATA

Now when DOS searches for a data file, it will look in the C:\WP\DATA directory if the file is not found in the current directory. Remember that even software programs such as your word processor use DOS to locate files, so your programs will locate data files in any APPENDed path.

There is one drawback to using the APPEND command for this purpose. If you retrieve a file that is not in the current directory but is in an APPENDed directory, then modify the file (e.g., by editing it with your word processor) and save it, it will be saved to the *current* directory. If the current directory is C:\DOS, then the edited copy of the file will be placed in the C:\DOS directory, and the original, unchanged copy of the file will be left in the C:\WP\DATA directory. This can result in several different versions of a file existing in different directories, which increases the risk of using or erasing the wrong file. For this reason, it is recommended that APPEND not be used for locating data files, but only for locating overlay files for your programs.

Overlay files are files that a program needs to perform some of its tasks. When one of these tasks is called for, the overlay file is loaded into memory and the task is carried out. Later, the overlay file can be released from memory to make room for another overlay. They are called "overlay files" because several files can be used to overlay each other in the same area of memory.

This need for the APPEND command is becoming rare in today's world. Most programs are designed to know where their overlay files reside and locate them without an APPEND command. You should therefore only need the APPEND command if you are running older copies of some programs.

If you would like to do away with the PATH command and only use the APPEND command, you can do so with the /X:ON parameter. /X:ON tells APPEND to search its path for executable files as well as nonexecutable files. Executable files are those that have an extension of .COM, .EXE, or .BAT. The default value for the /X parameter is /X:OFF, which turns off the search for executable files. Entering /X is equivalent to entering /X:ON. You can switch back and forth between /X:ON and /X:OFF by entering the APPEND command with the parameter you want.

If you enter a command to search for a file, and include a pathname in that file, APPEND will search its own paths if the file is not found in the path specified with the file. You may not want APPEND to do this. If you have specified a path and the file is not found, you may prefer not to have APPEND look for it in other directories. This can be accomplished with the /PATH:OFF parameter. You can enter /PATH:ON to enable the search for files that have a pathname included in their specification. If you specify no PATH parameter, PATH:ON is assumed. You can switch back and forth between /PATH:ON and /PATH:OFF by entering the APPEND command with the parameter you want.

The /E parameter can be used to keep the APPEND paths in the DOS environment space. This allows you to view and alter the APPEND paths with the SET command. However, if another command processor is loaded or the current one is exited, changes to the environment are lost. If you want to be sure that changes to APPEND are not lost with changes to the environment, such as entering and exiting the Shell, do not use the /E parameter.

You can view the list of APPEND paths by entering APPEND with no parameters.

Assigning One Drive Letter to Another Drive

You sometimes may want to have DOS respond to a call for one drive by searching a different drive instead. The most common reason for doing this is when you have a software program that always looks to a particular drive for certain files and you want to keep those files on a different drive. Suppose the software always looks to drive A for your data files, but you want to keep your data files on drive C. The following command will cause DOS to change all references for drive A into references for drive C:

ASSIGN A = C

Some programs will not recognize ASSIGNed drives, in which case the ASSIGN command is simply ignored and the drive that the program references is the one that is searched.

This need for the ASSIGN command is not encountered as often as it used to be. In early versions of some programs, drive letters were "hard-wired" into the program, but that is not a common practice anymore. There is one exception, however. Many software packages have installation programs that must be run in order to transfer them to your fixed disk. These programs often assume that you will use the A drive for this, and they therefore reference the A drive explicitly.

This reference to drive A is usually acceptable because a floppy drive is required for installing these programs, and the first floppy drive on a computer is always set up as the A drive. However, if your computer has two floppy drives and a fixed drive and the A drive breaks down, you cannot install your software. You can still boot your computer because you have your C drive. The ASSIGN command can come in handy here. By ASSIGNing the A drive to the B drive you can use the B drive to install your software. The following command accomplishes this task:

ASSIGN A = B

You can reverse any ASSIGNs in effect by entering ASSIGN by itself; this resets all drive letters to refer to themselves.

The Disk Copy and Disk Compare utilities on the DOS Utilities menu of the Shell File System will ignore any reassignment of drive letters.

THE DOS ENVIRONMENT AND COMMAND PROCESSORS

To understand how the environment commands will interact with the Shell, you must know a little about the DOS command processor, COMMAND.COM. When you boot your computer, DOS loads a program named COMMAND.COM into memory. COMMAND.COM is the program that reads everything you type in at the keyboard and determines how the computer will respond. When you type in a command, the first thing COMMAND.COM does is check to see if the command is for a program that is stored in the computer's memory. For example, when you type DIR, COMMAND.COM locates the DIR program in memory and executes it. The DIR program displays on the screen the names of files in the current directory.

If the command you enter is not for a program in memory, COMMAND.COM looks in the current directory, and any directory named in the current PATH, to see if it can locate an executable file with that name. If it can, it executes the file. If it can't, it displays the message "Bad command or file name," meaning that what you entered is neither an internal DOS command nor the name of an executable file in either the current directory or a directory in the current path.

Many parts of the DOS environment are stored with COMMAND.COM. Any modifications you make to the environment are held in memory and checked by COMMAND.COM any time it executes a command.

All of this is important in understanding the operation of the Shell because temporarily leaving the Shell by pressing the [Shift/F9] key combination or choosing the Command Prompt option from the Main Group menu causes a second copy of COMMAND.COM to be loaded on top of the one already operating. Control passes to this second command processor, along with all of the environmental settings of the first command processor. This is what is happening when the message "When ready to return to the DOS shell, type EXIT then press enter" appears at the top of the screen when you temporarily leave the Shell. You can then change the environmental settings that are controlled by DOS prompt commands. For example, you can change the date and time.

But many of the new environmental settings affect only the environment associated with the new copy of COMMAND.COM. They have no effect on the first copy. When you enter the EXIT command, the second COMMAND.COM is removed from memory, along with its environment. This restores the original environment associated with the first copy of COMMAND.COM and discards most of the changes made when the second command processor was in control.

You can see this effect if you go to the command prompt by pressing [Shift/F9] from within the Shell and then change the path, using the PATH command. Now type EXIT to return to the Shell, and return to the command prompt again with [Shift/F9]. Enter the PATH command, and you will see that the original path has been restored.

The path is changed permanently, however, if you change it after exiting the Shell altogether by choosing Exit from the Main Group Menu Bar or by pressing the F3 key from anywhere within the Shell except the File System (pressing the F3 key while in the File System returns you to the Main Group menu). If you return to the Shell with the DOSSHELL command, the new PATH settings will be in effect because the COMMAND.COM that is in effect at the DOS prompt after exiting the Shell is the same COMMAND.COM that is in effect when you run the Shell.

To change environmental settings without leaving the Shell, use the DOS Environment Command option, which you can add to a Shell menu. This process is described near the beginning of this chapter in the section on Startup files. Using this technique, the environment retains any changes because it does not invoke a secondary command processor.

CONFIGURATION ENVIRONMENT COMMANDS

Configuration commands are environmental commands that are entered in the CONFIG.SYS file, which is read and executed when you boot your computer. Many of these commands cannot be changed while the computer is running. They establish themselves as part of the computer's internal configuration when the computer is started and can only be changed by editing the CONFIG.SYS file and rebooting the computer. A complete discussion of all aspects of CONFIG.SYS commands would be very technical and is beyond the scope of this book. This chapter will focus on those commands that are commonly used to customize the DOS environment.

Setting Disk Buffers to Increase Disk Drive Performance

When DOS reads information from a disk, it usually reads more than just the information requested. For example, if you request that a database retrieve the name of a person (e.g., John Smith), DOS will not only read the name John Smith from the disk, but will also read the information that surrounds the name on the disk. This is done intentionally because a disk read, even with a fixed disk, is the slowest operation your computer must carry out. By reading in extra information, DOS minimizes the number of disk accesses it must carry out. To understand how all of this works, you should know a little about how information is stored on disks.

Disks are divided into **tracks**, which are concentric circles that go around the disk. These tracks are much like the grooves on a phonograph record, except that phonograph records have one continuous groove, whereas the tracks on a disk are not connected. Each track on a disk is divided into areas called **sectors**. Most disks are set up with sectors that store 512 bytes of information. The organization of a disk is shown in Figure 4.6. The number of tracks per sector varies with the type of disk; the minimum is eight.

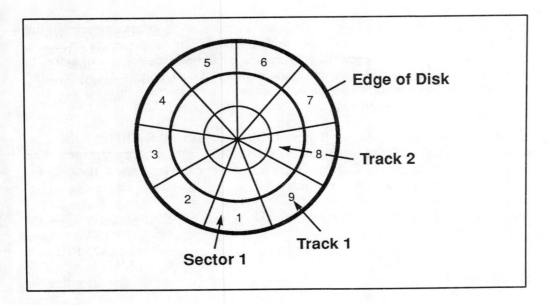

Figure 4.6   *Organization of a disk*

When DOS performs a disk read, the minimum amount of information it will read is one sector. If the name John Smith is in the middle of track 3 sector 2, when DOS reads John Smith's name it will also read the information on track 3 sector 2 that comes before and after his name. DOS stores this information (the entire sector) in a memory buffer.

The next time DOS receives a request to read information from the disk, it will first look in this memory buffer to see if the information is there. If it is, DOS reads it from memory and saves the time required to physically access the disk. There is a good chance the information will be in memory because it is common for two disk reads to be retrieving related information, and related pieces of information are often stored near each other on the disk. If you pay attention to your disk drive indicator light, you will notice that it does not always go on when you request information from the disk. When it does not go on, DOS is finding the requested information from the internal buffer. Also note that this information appears on the screen more quickly than information that requires a disk access. DOS also uses the memory buffers when writing to a disk, which further minimizes disk accesses.

DOS can have more than one memory buffer for storing information from the disk. Each buffer can hold one 512-byte disk sector. The more buffers DOS has, the more likely it is that the needed information will be in memory, thus avoiding additional disk accesses. However, as the number of buffers goes up, so does the amount of memory required for them. This memory is permanently set aside for these buffers, so it is taken away from other applications.

You can specify the number of buffers DOS contains with the BUFFERS command. This command is set in the CONFIG.SYS file and cannot be changed. The only way to change the number of buffers is to change the command in the CONFIG.SYS file and reboot your computer.

The following BUFFERS command tells DOS to set up 15 memory buffers for storing disk information:

BUFFERS = 15

The minimum number of buffers you can specify is 1. If no BUFFERS command is included in the CONFIG.SYS file, a default value is used. The default number of buffers is determined according to Table 4.3.

Default Number Of Buffers	Condition
2	none of the conditions for 3, 5, 10 or 15 buffers are met
3	a floppy disk drive greater than 360K is installed
5	computer has more than 128K memory
10	computer has more than 256K memory
15	computer has more than 512K memory

Table 4.3   Default number of disk buffers

The maximum number of buffers you can specify is 99 unless you have expanded memory in your system. If expanded memory is available, you can specify up to 10,000 buffers. If you specify more than 99 buffers, you must use the /X parameter to tell DOS to use expanded memory for the disk buffers. This causes the buffers to be placed in expanded memory so they do not decrease the amount of conventional memory available to your applications. If you do not have expanded memory, or if all expanded memory has already been allocated for another purpose, DOS will display an error message if you use the /X parameter. In this case, the BUFFERS command will be ignored, and the default value from Table 4.3 will be used.

There is one additional parameter that can be used with the BUFFERS command. This parameter specifies the number of look-ahead buffers. A **look-ahead buffer** is used to read more than one sector from the disk when a disk read is performed. When look-ahead buffers are specified, DOS reads the sector that contains the information requested into a buffer and reads the following sectors into buffers. The number of additional sectors read is specified by the look-ahead buffer parameter. The following command tells DOS to set up 25 regular buffers and 8 look-ahead buffers:

BUFFERS=25,8

You can specify anywhere from 1 to 8 look-ahead buffers. If you do not specify look-ahead buffers, none are used.

When to Modify the BUFFERS Command

For most purposes, the BUFFERS command that is defined when you install DOS 4.0 is suitable. However, there are circumstances when you will want to modify it.

If you purchase an application package, such as a database management system, its installation instructions may specify a higher number of buffers than is currently set in your CONFIG.SYS file. If the installation process does not automatically change the BUFFERS command, you will need to do it yourself. This can be done by editing the CONFIG.SYS file with a text editor.

Be aware that when an application package specifies a certain number of buffers, that specification is the minimum number of buffers. For example, if the instructions to your database system said there must be a BUFFERS=20 command in your CONFIG.SYS file, that means there must be a BUFFERS command that specifies at least 20. If you already have a command that specifies more than 20, you should not change it.

Even if none of your application packages require that you modify the BUFFERS command, you may want to do so to fine-tune your computer's performance. The following guidelines will help you determine when to change the BUFFERS command and what to change it to.

If you use a database system or another application that reads and writes large amounts of information to and from the disk, it may help to increase the number of buffers. Because these systems frequently access different sectors of the disk on each read or write, having more buffers available increases the likelihood that a requested sector will be in memory. For most database applications, setting from 10 to 20 buffers provides the best results.

If your computer has a fixed disk or a high-capacity floppy drive, you should have at least 3 buffers.

Because buffers take memory away from other applications, you may want to reduce the number of buffers to free up memory. In fact, the performance of some applications will actually decrease if the number of buffers is too large. Regular buffers take up 532 bytes of memory, and look-ahead buffers take up 512 bytes. The command BUFFERS=25,8 therefore takes up $(532 \times 25) + (512 \times 8) = 17,396$ bytes of memory.

If you have a performance problem that you believe may be alleviated by adjusting the BUFFERS command, try out different values and see how they affect the problem. For example, if your database seems to be performing poorly, it could be because you don't have enough buffers available, resulting in more disk accesses than necessary. It could also be because you have too many buffers specified, not leaving enough memory for the database application to efficiently perform its processing. Your database will then have to use the disk for tasks it would otherwise use memory for, resulting in poor performance. The only way to determine whether adjusting the BUFFERS command will help is to try different numbers of buffers and see what effect these settings have.

If your computer takes a very long time to carry out a task, changing the BUF-FERS command can only help if the computer is accessing the disk during the task. If the disk is never read from or written to, the problem is not one of disk access but rather a problem of processor speed. Adjusting the BUFFERS command will not help with this problem.

Changing the Country for Which Your Computer Is Set Up

During the SELECT program's installation of DOS 4.0, you were asked which country setup you wanted to install. The COUNTRY command determines the formats of the date and time, what currency symbol is used, what separator character is used for indicating decimal points, and other characteristics. Most of these characteristics are only available to programmers who write programs that interface with DOS. However, you can use the COUNTRY setting to set the display of the date and time to correspond to a particular country's conventions. Using the KEYB command, you can also set up a foreign keyboard.

To specify a country for the display formats (date, etc.), the COUNTRY = *code* command is included in the CONFIG.SYS file, where *code* refers to the country number. The following command sets the country code for Norway:

COUNTRY=047

Table 4.4 specifies the available countries and their associated codes.

Country	Code
Arabic-speaking	785
Australia	061
Belgium	032
Canada (French-speaking)	002
Denmark	045
Finland	358
France	033
Germany	049
Hebrew-speaking	972
Italy	039
Japan	081
Korea	082
Latin America	003
Netherlands	031
Norway	047
Portugal	351
Simplified Chinese	086
Spain	034
Sweden	046
Switzerland	041
Traditional Chinese	088
United Kingdom	044
United States	001

Table 4.4   Country codes for setting display formats

Setting the country code to 047 (Norway) displays the date in the following format:

```
Tue 01.24.1989
```

The time will be displayed as follows:

```
13.16.39,53
```

These formats are the same as the conventions used for displaying date and time in Norway.

Keyboards in different countries use keys differently. For example, a French keyboard has the "A" key where the U.S. has the "Q" key, and vice versa. Using the KEYB command, you can install a secondary keyboard layout. KEYB is a command that can be entered in the CONFIG.SYS file or at the command prompt as many times as you want in order to switch keyboard layouts. To include KEYB in the CONFIG.SYS file, you must preface the command with an INSTALL command, as follows:

INSTALL=KEYB.COM FR

This command specifies the French keyboard layout. If you put this command into your CONFIG.SYS file and reboot the computer, the A key on your keyboard will produce the letter Q. Some of the other keys will have different effects as well.

You can switch to the U.S. keyboard by simultaneously holding down the Ctrl and Alt keys and then pressing F1. To switch back to the French keyboard, hold down the Ctrl and Alt keys and press F2. You can toggle back and forth between the two keyboards in this manner as often as you want.

For example, to change the secondary keyboard to a Latin American keyboard, enter the KEYB command at the command prompt as follows:

KEYB LA

Now the [Ctrl/Alt/F1 or F2] key combination will switch the keyboard between the U.S. and Latin American keyboards. One of the differences between the U.S. and Latin American keyboards is that the Latin American keyboard will display an n with a tilde over it when you press the semicolon key.

You can see which secondary keyboard is installed at any time by entering the command **KEYB**. Even if you have pressed [Ctrl/Alt/F1] to switch to U.S. mode, KEYB will display the secondary keyboard that has been installed. If you enter the command **KEY BUS**, the secondary keyboard is replaced with the U.S. keyboard. The effect is that the U.S. keyboard is the only one available, and when you enter the KEYB command without a parameter, DOS tells you that the current keyboard is the U.S. one.

Table 4.5 shows the available countries and the codes that specify them in the KEYB command.

Country	Code
Belgium	BE
Canada (French-speaking)	CF
Denmark	DK
Finland	SU
France	FR
Germany	GR
Italy	IT
Latin America	LA
Netherlands	NL
Norway	NO
Portugal	PO
Spain	SP
Sweden	SV
Switzerland (French-speaking)	SF
Switzerland (German-speaking)	SG
United Kingdom	UK
United States	US

Table 4.5   *Country codes for keyboard layout*

Setting the Maximum Number of Files That Can Be Open at Once

All programs and all data are stored in files. For the computer to run a program or access the data in a file, it must first "open" that file. The DOS 4.0 Shell is itself a program, and therefore its file must be opened when you start the Shell. The various menu groups within the Shell are each stored in their own file. Each of these files must be opened when you display its menus. When you use the Print utility in the DOS Shell File System, that utility is a program that is stored in a file. The utilities on the DOS Utilities menu are also programs that are stored in files. Each time any one of these programs is run, DOS must open the file in which it is stored. In the case of the Print utility, DOS must also open the file that is being printed in order to retrieve the information in the file and send that information to the printer.

Opening a file involves identifying the filename, locating it, loading all or part of it into memory, and remembering where it is stored on the disk. A number, called a **file handle**, is associated with each open file. When an application opens a file, DOS assigns a file handle to the file and tells the application what that number is. The application then refers to the file handle, rather than the filename itself.

For example, when you want to edit a file called MYFILE.LET with a word processor, you first identify the filename. The word processor then passes that name to DOS, where the file handle is assigned and passed back to the word processor. If DOS assigns the file handle 8 to the file, the word processor then refers to "file 8" when it reads from or writes to that file.

All of this takes up memory, and when DOS is booted it must know how much memory to reserve for handling open files. The FILES command in the CONFIG.SYS file gives DOS this information. The following command specifies that DOS should reserve memory for having up to 16 files open at the same time:

FILES=16

The maximum number of files you can specify is 255. If you do not include a FILES command in your CONFIG.SYS file, the default value of eight is used. Eight is the minimum number you can specify. DOS requires 64 bytes of memory for each file that can be open, so if you specify 18 files, DOS will use 640 bytes more than the minimum value of eight files required.

For many applications, eight file handles are sufficient. However, if you ever see an error message that indicates there are not enough file handles available, you must increase the number of files specified in CONFIG.SYS.

Applications that require more than the minimum number of file handles usually point this out in their installation documentation. Some of them will automatically adjust the CONFIG.SYS file if the number of file handles is too low.

Including Remarks in the CONFIG.SYS File

CONFIG.SYS commands are not used very often. It is most common to set up the computer with the required configuration commands and then not think about them anymore because they automatically execute when the computer boots. The only time they are likely to be changed is when new software is installed on the computer that requires an additional configuration command or a modification to one that already exists. For this reason, you should include "remarks" in your CONFIG.SYS file that explain the purpose of the commands. If you come back to modify the file months after setting up the CONFIG.SYS file, the remarks will help you remember the purpose of the different commands and their settings.

A remark is entered by starting a line with the letters "REM." Everything that follows on that line will be ignored when DOS reads the CONFIG.SYS file. An example of a CONFIG.SYS file with remarks is shown in Figure 4.7.

```
REM The database system requires at least 16 buffers.  However,
REM expermintation has shown that performance is improved by
REM setting BUFFERS to 20.  The database system also requires a
REM minimum of 16 file handles.
REM
BUFFERS = 20
FILES = 16
REM
REM A secondary keyboard defined for Norway is included since we
REM are currently trading documents with Oslo Import-Export Ltd.
REM
INSTALL = KEYB.COM NO
REM
REM We want to use the ANSI.SYS device driver with the PROMPT
REM command, so we have installed that as well.
REM
DEVICE = ANSI.SYS
```

Figure 4.7   *Sample CONFIG.SYS file with remarks*

Figure 4.7 also uses REM to separate lines containing commands from the remark lines, making the file easier to read.

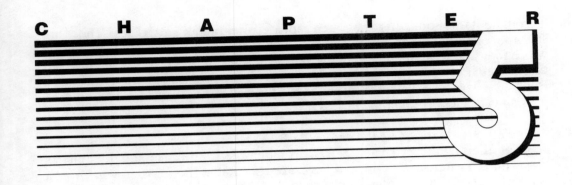

BATCH FILES

Throughout this book, there has been repeated mention of **batch files**. These are files that contain one or more DOS commands that are executed in the order in which they appear in the file. The term "batch" refers to the fact that the file contains a batch of commands, all of which are submitted to the computer at once. Batch files are also referred to as **batch programs** because they are, in fact, programs of DOS commands.

A batch file is identified by the extension BAT, just as the Shell group menu files are identified by the extension MEU. A batch file is an executable file, just as files with the extension COM and EXE are executable files. When you enter a command at the DOS prompt, DOS searches in the current directory and in any directories identified by the current path for a file that has the name you entered in, followed by an extension of COM, EXE, or BAT. DOS will only attempt to execute files with these extensions, and it does so in a different way for each extension. You could not name a batch file with a COM extension and have it execute. Batch files must only have BAT extensions.

Any DOS command, except configuration commands that can only be entered in the CONFIG.SYS file, can be included in a batch file. These include the commands that run software programs. For example, if a word processor is started by typing WORDPROC at the DOS prompt, then the command WORDPROC can be included in a batch file.

Batch files are used to simplify your work. They are not essential to performing any particular task because the commands contained in them could be typed in one at a time from the keyboard. However, by including sets of commands that you want to execute over and over again in a batch file, you save yourself considerable time and tedium.

When DOS executes a batch file, it stores the file in memory until all of the commands have executed. This means you can include commands that will execute both before and after a program that is run from within a batch file.

BATCH FILE PROGRAMS VS. SHELL PROGRAMS

With the ability to add menus to the Shell and write Shell programs, it may seem that batch programs are unnecessary. They have some of the same drawbacks as entering commands at the traditional DOS prompt: you must memorize their names; they must be typed in from the keyboard; and when they require parameters, there are no dialogue boxes or help screens to assist you. For these reasons, you should use Shell programs rather than batch files whenever possible. However, batch files have some advantages over Shell programs.

Shell programs are limited in the number of characters they can contain, and consequently in the number of commands that can be included in them. There is no such limit to the number of commands you can include in a batch file; you can make them as long as you want. You can also include remarks in batch files, just as you can include them in the CONFIG.SYS file. Remarks make the file much easier to read and understand, especially when you haven't looked at it for several months.

Shell programs are entered in one long line, and you can only look at a small part of the line at any time, which makes it difficult to follow a long sequence of commands. There are only very limited editing capabilities within the Shell for modifying program command lines, whereas a batch file can be edited with almost any word processor.

Finally, batch programs allow for certain powerful programming statements that are unavailable to Shell programs, such as the IF command, which allows conditional processing; the GOTO command, which allows branching within a batch file; and the FOR command, which allows repetitive execution of one or more commands within a batch program.

Both batch files and Shell programs have their place. There are advantages to each of them. The real power of DOS 4.0 lies not just in Shell programs or batch programs, but rather in the ability to combine both programs into one system. The best strategy is to use just a Shell program where that is sufficient. Batch files should be used where their additional power or size is required. When batch files are required, they can be called from within the Shell. This allows you to use the elegance of the Shell, with its menus and parameter dialogue boxes, as a front end to the batch files, thereby eliminating the clumsiness of the traditional DOS interface. This strategy is demonstrated in Chapter 6.

HOW TO CREATE BATCH FILES

There are several techniques for creating batch files. Each has its own place, depending on the size of the batch file and on your personal preference. The simplest way to create a batch file is with the DOS COPY command. You may be familiar with the COPY command being used to copy files. It can also be used to create files by entering the command in the following form:

COPY CON: FILENAME.BAT

The FILENAME can be any name up to eight characters. The above example uses an extension of BAT because it is intended to show the creation of a batch file. After this command is entered, the cursor will be at the beginning of the line immediately below the command. Anything you type will be saved in a file named FILENAME.BAT. Pressing the Return key will move the cursor to the next line, so you can create files with many commands in them. This COPY command is terminated by pressing the F6 key, followed by the Return key. When you press F6, you will see a Control Z appear, which will look like this:

^Z

You can also enter the Control Z by holding down the Ctrl key and pressing the Z key. Control Z is called the **end-of-file marker**; it is a special symbol that tells DOS the end of a file has been reached. When DOS sees this symbol following the COPY CON: command, it interprets it as meaning that all of the information has been entered into this file, and it should close the file. The message "1 File(s) copied" will appear on the screen, with the DOS prompt beneath it.

You must enter the Control Z in one of the two ways just specified. You cannot type a caret (^) followed by a Z. This represents two separate characters to DOS — a caret and a Z. Control Z, while it displays on your screen as two characters, is in fact just one character. If you look at the ASCII table in Table 4.2 (in Chapter 4), you will see that ASCII code 26 corresponds to ^Z.

To see how this COPY command works, enter the following lines at the DOS prompt:

```
COPY CON: TEST.BAT
ECHO OFF
DIR
^Z
```

If you press the Return key after the Control Z, your disk drive light will flash momentarily; this is caused by DOS writing the file to the disk. If you now enter the command TEST from the DOS prompt, you will see the directory scroll past on your screen. If you enter the command TYPE TEST.BAT, you will see the following two lines appear on your screen:

```
ECHO OFF
DIR
```

The ^Z, which is a symbol that DOS recognizes as marking the end of the file, is not displayed on the screen.

The COPY CON: command is useful for quickly creating short batch files. However, it provides no editing capabilities. If you want to change something, you must retype the entire file, and it becomes tedious if you are typing more than a few lines.

For larger batch files, a text editor is appropriate. You do not need to enter a ^Z character to terminate a file that is created with a text editor. ^Z is used only to terminate the operation carried out by a COPY CON: command.

A line editor, EDLIN, is provided with DOS. A **line editor** is a simple text editor. While it does not provide the power of a full-featured word processor, it is a substantial improvement over the COPY CON: technique. It also has the advantage of being very small. The EDLIN program is contained in a file called EDLIN.COM. This file can be found in the DOS directory of your fixed disk or on one of the DOS 4.0 program disks. It is only about 14K bytes, so it will conveniently fit on any floppy disk that has at least 14K bytes free. This makes it easy to carry it with you if you are working on computers other than your own. EDLIN is also fairly simple to use.

The disadvantage of EDLIN is that it is a line editor. It only works on one line of the file at a time, and it is not as easy to use as a screen editor. A **screen editor** is what we commonly call a word processor. It allows you to move the cursor around the entire screen and edit wherever you want. It also contains many convenient commands for copying, deleting, and moving blocks of text. The only requirement of a text editor for batch files is that it must produce ASCII text files. Most word processors today have this ability, though they often require a special form of their SAVE command to ensure that the file is saved in strict ASCII format.

Memory-resident word processors, such as Sidekick, are particularly useful for creating batch files. They permit you to "pop up" the word processor at the touch of a key, create or edit a batch file, and then — at another touch of a key — return to DOS and execute the file. This feature provides for a very fast development environment.

Simple Batch Files

The simplest batch files have only a few commands in them. A common application for a simple batch file is to change the current directory to one that contains a program you want to use, start the program, and then when the program is finished return to the root directory. For example, if the word processing program WORDPROC is in the directory WP, the batch file in Figure 5.1 will take you to that directory, run the word processor, and, when you exit the word processor, return to the root directory.

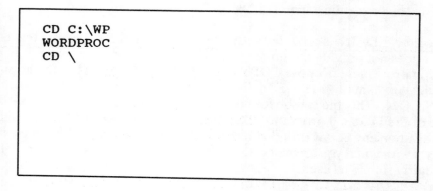

```
CD C:\WP
WORDPROC
CD \
```

Figure 5.1   *A simple batch file*

The CD command stands for "Change Directory." Each command in a batch file appears on its own line. As each line executes, it appears on the screen. This process is called **echoing**. The commands are echoed on the screen as they are processed.

Displaying Messages and Temporarily Suspending Execution of Batch Files

Just as the PAUSE and ECHO commands are used in Shell programs, they are also used in batch programs. The ECHO command is used to cause a message to appear on the screen. The PAUSE command is used to suspend the batch file from executing until a key is pressed. ECHO has an additional use in batch files. It acts as a switch that either prevents or causes the commands within a batch file to appear on the screen as they execute. The batch file in Figure 5.2 demonstrates these commands:

```
ECHO OFF
CLS
ECHO Make sure the word processor disk is in drive A:
PAUSE
A:WORDPROC
```

Figure 5.2   *Use of ECHO and PAUSE commands in batch files*

If this batch file were named WP.BAT, entering the command WP would cause the screen to clear and the following two messages to appear:

```
Make sure the word processor disk is in drive A:
Press any key to continue . . .
```

After a key is pressed, the WORDPROC program in drive A will execute.

The first ECHO command turns off echoing, which means that as the subsequent batch file commands execute, they will not appear on the screen. However, any output they may produce does appear on the screen. The next command in this batch file, CLS, causes the screen to clear. It is a good idea to start batch files with CLS in order to remove any distracting information that may still be there from the last command that was executed. This is not necessary for batch files that are called from a Shell program because the Shell automatically clears the screen when it executes a program.

The next ECHO command is used to display a message on the screen (in this case, a prompt to put a disk in drive A, where it will be needed by the command following the PAUSE command). The PAUSE command causes DOS to stop executing the commands in the DOS file and display the message "Press any key to continue . . ." on the line beneath the ECHO message. When you press a key, DOS will resume executing the batch file. The last command, A:WORDPROC, will execute a program named WORDPROC on the A drive.

When a batch file finishes executing, DOS restores the ECHO state to whatever it was when the batch file was called. Thus, if ECHO is ON when a batch file is called, after the batch file finishes executing, ECHO will be turned ON again, even if it was switched OFF by the batch file. If ECHO is OFF when the batch file is called, it will be switched OFF again when the batch file is finished executing, even if it was switched ON by the batch file.

Another use of the PAUSE command is to display more than one screen of information that the user may want to read. For example, suppose you have two screens of help information that you want available to users. The information could be in two files, called HELP1.FIL and HELP2.FIL. The batch file in Figure 5.3, named HELP.BAT, will display the help information one screen at a time when the HELP command is entered:

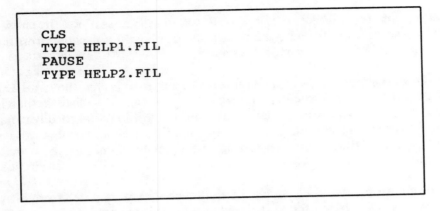

```
CLS
TYPE HELP1.FIL
PAUSE
TYPE HELP2.FIL
```

Figure 5.3   *Use of TYPE command in batch files*

The TYPE command is used to print the information in a text file on the screen. The command TYPE HELP1.FIL will write the information in the file HELP1.FIL on the screen. However, it does not stop if the screen fills up; it just keeps on going, letting the information at the top of the screen scroll away. You must therefore be sure that each file only has as much information as will fit on one screen, allowing room at the bottom for the "Press any key to continue . . ." message.

If the PAUSE command is not included in the HELP.BAT file, the first screen will scroll away when the second screen is displayed. The PAUSE command halts the execution of the batch file after the first file is displayed and waits for the user to press a key. DOS then displays the second screen of information.

Passing Parameters to Batch Files

The term **parameters** refers to variables in your batch files. These items are referenced within the file, but their specific value can change each time the file is run. A batch file that clears the screen and then lists the WP directory on drive C would contain the following two commands:

CLS
DIR C:\WP /P

The /P parameter at the end of the DIR command causes DOS to pause each time a new screen of information appears and display the message "Press any key to continue . . ." at the bottom of the screen.

If this file were named D.BAT, all you would need to do is type the letter D to list the files in the C:\WP directory. However, if you wanted to list the files in different directories, you would need a separate batch file for each directory, and you would need to remember the name of each file. It would probably be easier to just type the DIR command each time, specifying the directory you want to see each time.

A better solution is to use a batch file that accepts a parameter to tell it which directory to list. A batch file that demonstrates this process is shown in Figure 5.4.

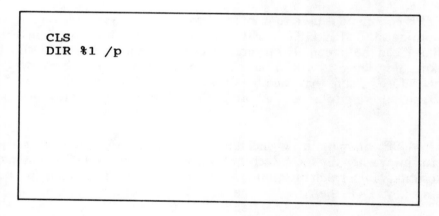

```
CLS
DIR %1 /p
```

Figure 5.4   Use of parameters in batch files

Batch file parameters are represented within the batch file by the % sign followed by a number from 1 to 9. When the file is executed, each parameter is replaced by the corresponding item from the DOS command that called the file. For example, if the above two commands were in a file named D.BAT, then entering the command D C:\WP would cause the %1 to be replaced by the letters C:\WP. This results in the command DIR C:\WP /P being executed. The next time the file is run, it can be entered as D A:, which will display the directory of drive A.

This is not a very useful example because typing D C:\WP is almost as much trouble as typing DIR C:\WP /P, but it serves to illustrate the use of parameters in batch files.

Figure 5.5 shows an example of a batch file using two parameters. It first creates a new directory and then copies files from an existing directory to the new one.

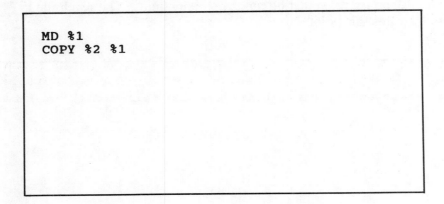

```
MD %1
COPY %2 %1
```

Figure 5.5   *Use of multiple parameters in batch files*

If the file in Figure 5.5 is named TEST.BAT, the following command will create a new directory named NEWDIR and copy all of the batch files from the C:\ directory into the NEWDIR directory:

TEST NEWDIR C:*.BAT

If you are in the Shell, the File System can be used to get a much better picture of how your files are organized than the DIR command provides. The Shell File System also provides more convenient ways to create directories and copy files into those directories. These are not, therefore, batch files you would want to execute from within the Shell. However, if you are already at the DOS prompt, it may be quicker to execute these batch files than to go into the Shell and call up the File System.

CREATING BATCH FILES THAT CALL THEMSELVES

The names by which batch files refer to parameters start with %1 and end with %9. However, you can also use %0 in your batch files. %0 is a special parameter symbol that refers to the name of the batch file in which the parameter occurs. This allows you to call a batch file from within itself. It might not seem useful at first to do this, but there are circumstances in which it can be a very efficient way to accomplish a task that must be repeated many times. The batch file in Figure 5.6 demonstrates this point.

```
@ECHO OFF
ECHO Place source disk in drive A and target disk in drive B
COPY A: B:
PAUSE
%0
```

Figure 5.6   A batch file that calls itself

If the file in Figure 5.6 is called CCOPY.BAT (for Continuous COPY; you must not give batch files the same name as DOS commands, in this case COPY), then entering the command CCOPY will result in the message "Place source disk in drive A and target disk in drive B" appearing on the screen. On the line beneath it will be the "Press any key to continue . . ." message. After you have placed the disks in drives A and B and pressed a key, all of the files will be copied from drive A to drive B.

The %0 command will cause this sequence to repeat. The message "Place source disk in drive A and target disk in drive B" will appear, followed by the "Press any key to continue ..." message. The batch file will continue executing like this until you hold down the Ctrl key and press the Break key (or [Ctrl/C]). This will always cause a batch file to stop execution, as explained in the following section. Pressing [Ctrl/Break] will cause the prompt "Terminate batch job (Y/N)?" to appear. Pressing Y will return you to the DOS prompt. The CCOPY program (in Figure 5.6) will result in a screen similar to the one in Figure 5.7.

```
Place source disk in drive A and target disk in drive B
Strike a key when ready . . .
A:JOHN.LET
A:MARY.LET
A:BILL.LET
A:GEORGE.LET
        5 File(s) copied
Place source disk in drive A and target disk in drive B
Strike a key when ready . . .
A:ACCNTS1.RBF
A:ACCNTS2.RBF
A:ACCNTS3.RBF
        3 File(s) copied
Place source disk in drive A and target disk in drive B
Strike a key when ready . . .
A:JULY.WK2
A:AUGUST.WK2
A:SEPT.WK2
        2 File(s) copied
Place source disk in drive A and target disk in drive B
Strike a key when ready . . . ^C

Terminate batch job (Y/N)? y

C:\>_
```

Figure 5.7   *Result of running the batch file in Figure 5.6*

Halting the Execution of a Batch File

You may encounter situations in which you want to stop a batch file before it is finished executing. You might realize after starting it that it is going to take too long to complete, or that it is going to do something you don't want it to do. You may even have created a batch file that never terminates on its own, such as the example above for copying large numbers of disks from drive A to drive B. Batch file execution can be stopped by holding down the Ctrl key and pressing the Break key (or [Ctrl/C]). This command, known as a **control break**, is a special signal that DOS recognizes as a command to stop whatever it is doing and return to the DOS prompt.

Conditional Execution of Batch File Commands—Use of IF Command

A powerful feature of DOS batch files is the ability to execute a command only if some condition is true, or alternately if some condition is not true. Conditions that can be tested for are listed in Table 5.1.

Conditions That Can Be Tested in a Batch File

1) the existence or nonexistence of a file that is named in the batch file
2) the existence or nonexistence of a file passed as a parameter
3) whether a parameter matches a value that is specified in a batch file
4) whether or not the previous command in the batch file terminated normally

---

Table 5.1   Conditions that can be tested in a batch file

The first condition listed in Table 5.1 can be demonstrated with a batch file that will display the directory information for a file named TEST.FIL only if the file exists in the current directory. The commands to enter in this file are as follows:

```
ECHO OFF
CLS
IF EXIST TEST.FIL DIR TEST.FIL
IF NOT EXIST TEST.FIL ECHO TEST.FIL DOES NOT EXIST
```

Note that echo is turned off with the ECHO OFF command, and the screen is cleared with the CLS command at the start of this batch file. You may occasionally want to have commands display on the screen when a batch file executes, but in general it is good style not to display them. They tend to be confusing, especially because they often flash by too quickly to read. Clearing the screen is almost always a good idea; it removes clutter that makes it difficult to locate important messages or other information.

This file demonstrates the use of the NOT operator. You can place NOT in front of the condition tests in batch files to test for the failure of the condition rather than for its success.

When this file is executed, if TEST.FIL exists in the current directory, the screen will appear as in Figure 5.8.

```
    Volume in drive C has no label
    Volume Serial Number is 1A5A-20AE
    Directory of   C:\SPRINT\DOSBOOK

TEST       FIL         7 10-09-88    3:29p
           1 File(s)     9228288 bytes free
C:\
```

Figure 5.8   *Result of batch file testing for a file's existence*

If the file TEST.FIL does not exist, running the batch file will result in the screen shown in Figure 5.9.

```
THE FILE TEST.FIL DOES NOT EXIST
C:\>
```

Figure 5.9   *Result of batch file testing for a file that does not exist*

The second test in Table 5.1 — checking for the existence of a file entered as a parameter — can be demonstrated with a batch file that starts a word processor named WORDPROC with the specified file loaded, if the specified file exists. If the file does not exist, the batch file displays an error message. The commands for this batch file are as follows:

ECHO OFF
CLS
CD C:\WP
IF EXIST %1 WORDPROC %1
IF NOT EXIST %1 ECHO %1 DOES NOT EXIST - CHECK THE NAME
CD C:

This batch file changes directories to the word processing directory C:\WP before checking for the existence of the file that is passed as a parameter. It is important to include a CD (Change Directory) command in batch files that serve the type of function demonstrated here because the batch files are almost always in the root directory, and the program and data files are generally in subdirectories. It is also a good idea to return the user to the root directory, as done here with the CD C:\command, because that is where other batch files they might want to execute will most likely be found.

If this batch file is named WP.BAT, and a file named MYFILE.LET exists in the
C:\WP directory, then the command WP MYFILE.LET would result in the word
processor WORDPROC starting up with the file MYFILE.LET loaded. If
MYFILE.LET does not exist in the C:\WP directory, the screen will appear as in
Figure 5.10.

```
MYFILE.LET DOES NOT EXIST - CHECK THE NAME
C:\>
```

Figure 5.10   *Result of batch file testing for a file that does not exist*

The third condition in Table 5.1, testing whether a parameter matches a value
that is included in the batch file, can be demonstrated with a batch file that carries out one command if the name Mary is entered as a parameter, and another
command if the name Bill is entered. The commands for this batch file are shown
in Figure 5.11.

```
IF %1 == Mary WP
IF %1 == Bill DB
ECHO A valid name was not entered.  Try again
```

Figure 5.11   *Batch file comparing a parameter to a specific value*

If the batch file in Figure 5.5 is called NAME.BAT, then the command NAME Mary will cause a batch file named WP.BAT to run. The command NAME Bill will cause a batch file named DB.BAT to run. If the name entered is neither Mary nor Bill, the ECHO command will execute, displaying the error message. Note that there are two equal signs in the condition tests. If you use only one equal sign, DOS will terminate execution of the batch file and display the message "Syntax error."

If WP and DB were program files that ended with a .COM or .EXE extension, rather than being batch files, the ECHO command would always execute because when the WP or DB programs ended, control would return to the NAME.BAT file. But when one batch file executes a second batch file in the manner demonstrated here, control does not return to the first batch file. If you want control to return to a batch file after it runs a second batch file, you must use the CALL command, which is discussed later in this chapter.

The names Mary and Bill must be spelled exactly the same on the parameter line and in the batch file. This includes case sensitivity. If you entered the command NAME MARY or NAME mary, the IF condition would fail and the ECHO command would execute.

The last condition in Table 5.1, testing for normal termination of the previous command, only works with certain DOS commands and certain programs. When these commands terminate, they leave a code known as the **exit code** in a location of the DOS environment memory. Batch files can access this code to determine the status of the last command's termination (i.e., whether it terminated normally or abnormally).

Usually, an exit code of 0 means the command terminated normally — it carried out its intended purpose with no interruption or error. A nonzero exit code will indicate an abnormal termination. This can occur when the user interrupts the operation or when an error occurs during the operation. The exit code will indicate what caused the interruption. Generally, the higher the exit code, the more serious the problem. A list of the DOS commands that produce exit codes and the meanings of those codes for each command can be found in the Appendix.

One of the DOS commands that sets an exit code is the BACKUP command. The BACKUP command is discussed in Chapter 2. It is used to back up a disk, usually a fixed disk, onto one or more floppy disks. A backup utility is built into the DOS Utilities menu of the Shell. This utility uses the DOS BACKUP command.

The batch file in Figure 5.12 will test for an exit code from the BACKUP command and takes an action based on that code.

```
BACKUP %1
IF ERRORLEVEL 0 ECHO Backup finished normally
IF ERRORLEVEL 1 ECHO No files were found for backing up.
IF ERRORLEVEL 1 ECHO Check the file specification and try again
IF ERRORLEVEL 2 TYPE BUERR.2
IF ERRORLEVEL 3 ECHO User terminated the backup
IF ERRORLEVEL 4 TYPE BUERR.4
```

Figure 5.12   *Batch file testing for an exit code from the BACKUP command*

This file relies on two text files, BUERR.2 and BUERR.4, that contain lengthy error messages and instructions if the BACKUP command returns an exit code of either 2 or 4.

Use of Remarks to Help Make Batch Files Easier to Understand

As batch files become larger and more complex, they also become harder to understand. The REM command is used to help make batch files easier to understand. REM stands for "remark." When a batch file line begins with the letters REM, everything on that line is ignored by DOS when the batch file executes. The line is used to contain a remark, which is a comment that explains something about the batch file. A REM line can also be used to separate commands from one another, making the batch file easier to read. It is a good habit to use remarks liberally in your batch files.

Remarks will be echoed to the screen if ECHO is set on, so it is a good idea to always start your batch files with the ECHO OFF command. If there are particular lines in your file you want echoed, you can turn ECHO back on for those lines.

Many of the examples in the rest of this chapter will make use of REM lines to help explain how the files work.

An On-Line Help System Example

If you anticipate users will work at the DOS prompt to start application packages, rather than start them from the Shell, an on-line Help system can be developed using the batch file techniques present so far. This system is not as easy to use or as elegant as the one provided in the Shell, but it will work at the DOS prompt.

Suppose there are three topics for which you want to provide help: starting the word processor, starting the database system, and starting the spreadsheet system. Using a text editor, create three files, each containing one screen or less of help information for one of the topics. Make sure that the file is saved in standard ASCII format. If you use EDLIN or SIDEKICK, ASCII is the only format the file can be saved in. If you use another word processor, refer to its documentation for instructions on saving files in ASCII format.

The file that contains the help information for word processing should be named WP1.FIL; the file that contains the help information for the database system should be called DB1.FIL; and the file that contains the help information for the spreadsheet system should be called SS1.FIL. If you want to provide more than one screen of information for any of these subjects, type the second screen into a 2.FIL file (e.g., a second screen of information for the spreadsheet goes in SS2.FIL and a third screen goes in SS3.FIL, and so on).

Now copy the commands in Figure 5.13 into a file named HELP.BAT.

```
@ECHO OFF
REM filename: HELP.BAT
REM This file is used to display help screens that are stored
REM in files named XX1.FIL, XX2.FIL, and so on.  The XX's stand
REM for the application for which the help is provided.  For
REM example, the word processor help screens are stored in files
REM named WP1.FIL and WP2.FIL.  This file is executed by entering
REM the command HELP XX - e.g. HELP WP
CLS
IF NOT EXIST %11.FIL ECHO No help files for that command.
IF EXIST %11.FIL TYPE %11.FIL
IF EXIST %12.FIL PAUSE
IF EXIST %12.FIL TYPE %12.FIL
IF EXIST %13.FIL PAUSE
IF EXIST %13.FIL TYPE %13.FIL
```

Figure 5.13   A batch file for building a simple on-line help system

To use this help system for assistance in starting the word processing program, a user would enter the command HELP WP. The HELP.BAT file would then check for the existence of a file named WP1.FIL. If the file does not exist, it will display the message "No help files for that command." If the file does exist, HELP.BAT will display the contents of the file on the screen and then check for the existence of a file named WP2.FIL. If WP2.FIL exists, the PAUSE command will execute, displaying the "Press any key to continue . . ." message on the screen. When a key is pressed, the contents of WP2.FIL will be displayed. The process will then repeat for the file named WP3.FIL.

This system can be expanded to provide as many HELP screens as you want for as many applications as you want.

Make sure that you allow for the maximum number of help files you have written for any one of the commands. If you have five help files for the database system (DB1.FIL, DB2.FIL, DB3.FIL, DB4.FIL, and DB5.FIL), and three for each of the others, then you must have IF EXIST commands for five files.

If you have been typing in and executing the examples up to now, you may have noticed that whenever there is an ECHO OFF command, that command echos on the screen. This makes sense because ECHO is set ON when the command is executed. But it can also be annoying. The goal is to make the batch file commands transparent to the end user; you can't do that if they echo on the screen. The ECHO OFF command in the example for the online help system didn't appear on the screen because it begins with an @ sign. The @ sign tells DOS not to echo the command on the screen, regardless of the ECHO status. You can use this in front of any batch command to selectively suppress it from echoing.

This Help system demonstrates the ability to insert a parameter into a text string. When DOS executes a batch file that contains parameters, it literally inserts the parameter values directly into the command.

Branching of Program Control with the GOTO Command

The GOTO command can be used in conjunction with the IF command to add greater flexibility and power to batch files. The GOTO command causes control to jump from one line in the file to another. It is used in conjunction with a label that indicates the point in the file to jump to. For example, the batch file in Figure 5.14 uses a GOTO to display one message if the file passed as a parameter exists, and it displays another message if the file does not exist.

```
 1   @ECHO OFF
 2   REM This file is named JUMP.BAT.  It tells the user whether
 3   REM or not the file passed as a parameter exists.
 4   REM
 5   IF NOT EXIST %1 GOTO NOFILE
 6   ECHO The file %1 exists.
 7   GOTO :END
 8   :NOFILE
 9   ECHO The file %1 does not exist.
10   :END

(Line numbers are for reference only; they should not be included
in the batch file.)
```

Figure 5.14   *Use of the GOTO command in batch files*

The batch file in Figure 5.14 first checks to see if the file passed as a parameter exists. If it does, the GOTO on line 5 does not execute, and control continues with line 6, which displays the message "The file (filename) exists." Then the GOTO on line 7 executes, causing control to jump past lines 8 and 9 to line 10, which is the end of the file.

On the other hand, if the file passed as a parameter does not exist, then the GOTO on line 5 executes, causing control to jump past lines 6 and 7 and continue on line 9 (line 8 is a **label line**, which does not execute; it simply marks the point to jump to). Line 9 displays the message "The file (filename) does not exist."

The line on which the label appears must begin with a colon (:), and the label must be the only thing that appears on the line after the colon. Lines containing a label in a batch file are not echoed on the screen, even if ECHO is set to ON. This provides an alternative to the REM command for including remarks in a batch file. Start the line with a colon, which identifies it as a label to DOS, then place your remark after the colon. The line will not be echoed on the screen, as REM lines are if ECHO is ON. The only thing you must guard against is having a comment that matches a label specified in a GOTO command; this may cause control to jump to the comment, rather than the true label.

The batch file in Figure 5.15 sets up the online help system described earlier, in Figure 5.13, except that in Figure 5.15 the GOTO command is used to reduce the number of IF commands.

```
@ECHO OFF
REM filename: HELP.BAT
REM This file is used to display help screens that are stored
REM in files named XX1.FIL, XX2.FIL, and so on.  The XX's stand
REM for the application for which the help is provided.  For
REM example, the word processor help screens are stored in files
REM named WP1.FIL and WP2.FIL.  This file is executed by entering
REM the command HELP XX - e.g. HELP WP
CLS
IF NOT EXIST %11.FIL GOTO NOFILE
TYPE %11.FIL
IF NOT EXIST %12.FIL GOTO END
PAUSE
TYPE %12.FIL
IF NOT EXIST %13.FIL GOTO END
PAUSE
TYPE %13.FIL
:NOFILE
ECHO No help files for that command.
:END
```

Figure 5.15   *Use of the GOTO command to improve on-line help*

Repetitive Execution of Batch File Commands with the FOR Command

The FOR command is used in batch files to cause a command to repeat a specified number of times. The FOR command specifies a variable that takes on each of the values in a set that is specified in the command. The variable is named with two percent signs followed by any one character, for example, %%A. The set of values that the variable will take on is specified by placing the values within parentheses in the FOR command. Figure 5.16 contains a simple batch file that uses the FOR command.

```
@ECHO OFF
REM This file is named SHOW.BAT.  It is used to display the
REM directory listing of the three files entered in the
REM parentheses.
REM
FOR %%F IN (FILE1 FILE2 FILE3) DO DIR %%F
```

Figure 5.16   Use of the FOR command in batch files

When the file SHOW.BAT in Figure 5.16 is called, the FOR command gets translated by DOS into three separate commands that look like the following:

DIR FILE1
DIR FILE2
DIR FILE3

The variable %%F takes on each value in the set (FILE1 FILE2 FILE3) and is passed to the DIR command for each of these values. This may not seem useful at first, but the values in parentheses (called the SET of the FOR command) can be replaced by parameters passed to the batch file on the command line. The file in Figure 5.16 could be rewritten as in Figure 5.17.

```
@ECHO OFF
REM This file is named SHOW.BAT.  It is used to display the
REM directory listing of the three files entered in the
REM parentheses.
REM
FOR %%F IN (%1 %2 %3) DO DIR %%F
```

Figure 5.17   *Use of parameters with the FOR command in batch files*

With the SHOW.BAT file in Figure 5.17, you could enter the command SHOW FILE1 FILE2 FILE3, and DOS would display the directory listing for each of the three files specified on the command line. You could take this a step further and, as shown in Figure 5.18, display messages about files that don't exist and also display the directory listing for files that do exist, all with only two commands.

```
@ECHO OFF
REM This file is named CHECK.BAT.  It is used to display the
REM directory listing for files that are entered on the command
REM line.  If a file does not exist, a message is displayed that
REM lets the user know a non-existent file name was entered.
REM
FOR %%F IN (%1 %2 %3 %4) DO IF EXIST %%F DIR %%F
FOR %%F IN (%1 %2 %3 %4) DO IF NOT EXIST %%F ECHO %%F does not
exist
```

Figure 5.18   *Combining FOR and IF commands in batch files*

If the file in Figure 5.18 were executed with the command CHECK FILE1 FILE2 FILE3, and only FILE2 existed, the result would appear similar to that in Figure 5.19.

```
C:\DOS>TEST FILE1 FILE2 FILE3

 Volume in drive C has no label
 Volume Serial Number is 1A5A-20AE
 Directory of  C:\DOS

FILE2                  7 01-24-89   5:23p
        1 File(s)     9166848 bytes free
FILE1 does not exist
FILE3 does not exist
C:\DOS
```

Figure 5.19   Sample output from Figure 5.18 batch file

Note in Figure 5.19 that only three file names were entered, even though the batch file allows for four parameters. The fourth parameter is ignored if nothing is entered for it, so make sure you allow for the maximum number of parameters in the FOR command set.

The online help system shown in Figures 5.13 and 5.15 can be greatly simplified by using a single FOR command and two batch files. The batch files are shown in Figures 5.20 and 5.21.

```
@ECHO OFF
REM This file is named HELP.BAT.  It is used to disply help
REM files that have been prepared for one of the applications
REM available to users of this computer.  There can be up to
REM four help files per application.  This number can be
REM increased simply by adding additional parameters to the
REM FOR command set.
REM
CLS
FOR %%F IN (%11.FIL %12.FIL %13.FIL %14.FIL) DO CALL SHOW %%F
```

Figure 5.20   *Use of FOR command to improve on-line help*

```
REM This file is named SHOW.BAT.  It is called from the file
REM HELP.BAT.  It displays the help screen file that is passed
REM to it as a parameter, then pauses so the user will have time
REM to read the screen.  It checks for the existence of the file
REM because HELP.BAT is going to pass four file names, even if
REM they don't all exist.  Checking for their existence prevents
REM the appearance of extraneous messages appearing on the
REM screen.
REM
IF EXIST %1 TYPE %1
IF EXIST %1 PAUSE
```

Figure 5.21   *SHOW.BAT file called from HELP.BAT (Figure 5.20)*

After you take out the remarks, there are only five commands in these two files taken together, as opposed to eight and 12 commands in Figures 5.13 and 5.15, respectively. The CALL command in HELP.BAT is discussed later in this chapter.

The most important improvement in the system shown in Figures 5.20 and 5.21 is that it is much easier to understand and modify. If you want to add additional help files, simply increase the number of parameters in the set of the FOR command.

As you can see, the FOR command can be very useful for concisely repeating the processing of a DOS command or program file. You can even use it to cause another batch file to execute a specified number of times, without passing any additional parameters to the batch file. A batch file that uses the FOR command in this way is shown in Figure 5.22.

```
@ECHO OFF
REM This file is named REPEAT.BAT.  It calls the batch file
REM NEXT.BAT 10 times.  This number may be adjusted simply by
REM changing the numbers in the set of the FOR command.
REM
FOR %%N IN (1 2 3 4 5 6 7 8 9 10) DO CALL NEXT
```

Figure 5.22   Using the FOR command to repetitively execute a DOS command

This batch file will call the batch file NEXT.BAT ten times.

The FOR command can be executed at the DOS prompt by using a % variable instead of %% variable. Everything else is the same as in batch files. For example, to execute the batch file NEXT.BAT ten times, you could enter the following command at the DOS prompt:

FOR %N IN (1 2 3 4 5 6 7 8 9 10) DO CALL NEXT

Note that only one percent sign is used for the variable when the FOR command is entered from the DOS prompt.

CREATING BATCH FILES THAT CALL OTHER BATCH FILES

As seen in some of the previous examples, a batch file can cause another batch file to execute simply by having the name of the second batch file occur as a command in the first. When this happens, the first batch file gives up control to the second one. In the first batch file, any commands after the command that calls the second batch file will not execute, unless there is a GOTO that can cause control to branch to them. The batch files in Figures 5.23 and 5.24 demonstrate this process:

```
@ECHO OFF
REM This file is named GREETING.BAT
REM
ECHO Hello.
RESPONSE
ECHO Goodbye
```

Figure 5.23   *GREETING.BAT file with nonreturnable call to RESPONSE.BAT*

```
REM This file is named RESPONSE.BAT
REM
ECHO You'll never say goodbye.
```

Figure 5.24   *RESPONSE.BAT file*

When the command GREETING is entered, the following two messages will appear on the screen:

```
Hello.
You'll never say goodbye.
```

These messages appear because when GREETING passes control to RESPONSE, it gives up control altogether. There is no way for the ECHO Goodbye command to ever execute.

If you want control to return to a calling file, you must execute the second batch file with a CALL command. When the second batch file finishes executing, control returns to the first batch file, at the line immediately following the CALL command. The batch files in Figures 5.25 and 5.26 illustrate this process:

```
@ECHO OFF
REM This file is named GREETING.BAT
REM
ECHO Hello.
CALL RESPONSE
ECHO Want to bet?
ECHO Goodbye!
```

Figure 5.25   *GREETING.BAT file with returnable call to RESPONSE.BAT*

```
REM This file is named RESPONSE.BAT
REM
ECHO You'll never say goodbye.
```

Figure 5.26   *RESPONSE.BAT file*

Now when the command GREETING is entered, the following messages appear
on the screen:

```
Hello.
You'll never say goodbye.
Want to bet?
Goodbye!
```

As you can see, the CALL command causes control to return to the calling file.
Note that there is no ECHO OFF command at the beginning of
RESPONSE.BAT. The ECHO state is passed from one batch file to another and
is restored when control returns. This means that when GREETING.BAT sets
ECHO OFF, it remains off in RESPONSE.BAT unless an ECHO ON command
is encountered. If RESPONSE.BAT sets ECHO ON, it will be restored to its off
status when control returns to GREETING.BAT.

You can pass parameters from one batch file to another. For example, the batch
files in Figures 5.27 and 5.28 both accept parameters. The file in Figure 5.27 calls
the file in Figure 5.28 and passes its parameter number 2 to the Figure 5.28 batch
file's parameter number 1:

```
@ECHO OFF
REM This file is named BATCH1.BAT
COPY %1 %2
BATCH2 %2
```

Figure 5.27   Passing parameters from one batch file to another

```
REM This file is named BATCH2.BAT
DIR %1
```

Figure 5.28   A batch file that receives parameters from the file in Figure 5.27

The first file, BATCH1, can be called with the command **BATCH1 FILENAME C:\DOS**. This command will copy the file named FILENAME to the DOS directory. FILENAME will become parameter %1 in this file and C:\DOS will become parameter %2. The second batch file will then be called with the command BATCH2 C:\DOS, which will result in the C:\DOS directory being displayed.

Batch files that call each other can be nested as deep as you want; there is no limit to how many you can have. You can even have a batch file that calls itself, or two batch files that call each other. However, there are a few important considerations to keep in mind.

Each time a batch file calls another batch file, the first file must be stored in memory until control returns to it so that DOS will know what command to execute at that time. If the second batch file calls a third batch file, the second batch file as well must be stored in memory. Eventually, all of the available memory could be used up and the computer will "lock up" (i.e., stop responding to the keyboard). You will have to reboot in order to get started again. Consequently, if you are going to use the CALL command, you must think through its logic very carefully to make sure that control will eventually be passed back to the first execution of the first file in the calling sequence so the whole process can terminate.

If you suspect that a batch file sequence has gone into an endless loop or is in danger of running out of memory, you can always stop it with a [Ctrl/Break] keystroke.

Note that this situation is much different from the batch file in Figure 5.6, which is used for copying disks from drive A to drive B. That batch file contained the following commands:

```
@ECHO OFF
ECHO Place source disk in drive A and target disk in drive B
PAUSE
COPY A: B:
%0
```

This file does call itself, but in this case it is done with the %0 command, not a CALL command. Because no CALL is involved, DOS does not save the calling file in memory in order to return control to it. The calling file is discarded when the %0 command is encountered, so there is no danger of running out of memory.

CALLING THE SHELL FROM BATCH FILES
AND CALLING BATCH FILES FROM THE SHELL

Batch files can call the Shell in the same ways that they call each other. If the command DOSSHELL is executed in a batch file, the Shell takes over and control does not return to the batch file. If the Shell is called with the command CALL DOSSHELL, when you choose the Exit command (or press F3) from the Shell, control returns to the batch file. This works because the command DOSSHELL is actually a call to a batch file named DOSSHELL.BAT. DOSSHELL.BAT contains all of the commands for setting up and entering the Shell.

Control will not return to the batch file when you choose Command Prompt or press [Shift/F9] to leave the Shell because the Shell is still in control. Entering the Exit command at the command prompt will return you to the Shell. To work at the command prompt, you can use the Command Prompt option as often as you want. When you eventually choose the Exit option from within the Shell, the batch file will regain control.

Shell programs can also call batch files. Shell programs are actually passed through the same batch processor that is used for executing batch programs, so the calling mechanisms are similar. A batch file can be called from a Shell program simply by referring to it by name, but then control is given up by the Shell when the batch file starts executing.

Often, when one batch file calls another this giving up of control is the desired effect; you may not want control to return to the calling batch file. But in the Shell it is unlikely that this will ever be the desired effect. Exiting the Shell should be done using the Command Prompt or Exit choices provided with the Shell. Consequently, batch files should only be called from Shell programs, using the CALL command. Just as this command returns control to a calling batch file when the second batch file finishes executing, it also returns control to the Shell.

These techniques are all discussed further in Chapter 6, which describes a password system that uses calls from batch files to the Shell and calls from the Shell to batch files. The password system described in Chapter 6 will effectively prevent unauthorized persons from gaining access to your computer.

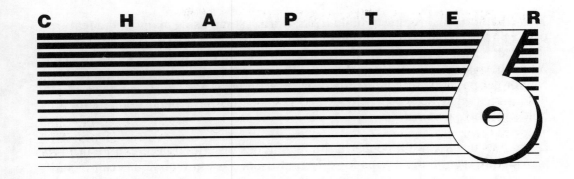

PUTTING IT ALL TOGETHER: A COMPLETE PASSWORD SYSTEM

This chapter explains how to build a password system, using many of the features of the Shell and of DOS 4.0 discussed in previous chapters. The password system uses batch files to call the Shell with a configuration that only allows users to log on to the system with their password. The user who enters an illegal password cannot get past this screen. If the user enters a legal password, the system then determines what access privileges and color setup have been defined for the holder of the password.

Even if security is not a concern, the techniques described here can be used to provide different Shell setups for different users. These techniques can include different menus, different colors, and different access privileges. While the password system does not use every single aspect of DOS 4.0 that has been discussed, it uses a great many of them. If you understand how this password system works, you will have a solid grasp of the DOS 4.0 Shell and how to customize it to meet your own needs.

This chapter assumes you have read through the previous chapters and are already familiar with Shell programs and how to create them. You should already understand how to specify startup options for the Shell. You should be familiar with the AUTOEXEC.BAT file and batch files, and know the difference between calling a batch file with just the name of the file and calling it with the CALL command.

Throughout this chapter, the phrase **nonreturnable call** refers to a call made to a batch file without the CALL command. The phrase **returnable call** refers to a call made to a batch file with the CALL command. For example, if a batch file is named START.BAT, the command START is a nonreturnable call because control will not return to the file that called START. The command CALL START is a returnable call because control will return to the batch file that called START when START terminates.

AN OVERVIEW OF HOW THE PASSWORD SYSTEM WORKS

When you boot your computer, the AUTOEXEC.BAT file executes automatically. Your computer will bring up the Shell when it is booted if the command DOS-SHELL is in your AUTOEXEC.BAT file. This is the last command in the AUTOEXEC.BAT file because it is a nonreturnable call to the DOSSHELL.BAT file.

The password system described here removes the DOSSHELL command from the AUTOEXEC.BAT file and replaces it with two commands. The first command copies a file named CYCLE.FIL to a file named PROCEED.BAT. (CYCLE.FIL contains one command—a nonreturnable call to a file named GETPW.BAT.) The second command is a nonreturnable call to a batch file named GETPW.BAT.

GETPW.BAT contains four commands. The first command copies a file named LOGON.SHL to the file named DOSSHELL.BAT. (When setting up the password system, you should copy the original DOSSHELL.BAT file to a file named DOSSHELL.ORG; this will allow you to recover it at any time.) LOGON.SHL is a Shell setup that only permits the user to select one option: to log on to the computer. This procedure is described in detail later in this chapter. The next command in GETPW.BAT is a CD C:\DOS command, which assures that the current directory is C:\DOS. If you have the DOS files in another directory, you will need to change this command to make that directory current.

The third command in GETPW.BAT is a returnable call to DOSSHELL. This command brings up the Shell, but the only option available is "Log on to the computer" as defined in the LOGON.SHL file. Remember that this file was copied to DOSSHELL.BAT, so the command DOSSHELL starts the Shell with the LOGON.SHL configuration. Because the call to DOSSHELL is returnable, control will return to GETPW.BAT when the Shell is exited.

The last command in the GETPW.BAT file is a nonreturnable call to a file named PROCEED.BAT. The contents of PROCEED.BAT will depend on whether a valid password was entered when the Shell was called up in the previous command.

If a valid password was entered, then PROCEED.BAT will contain a Shell COPY command that copies to DOSSHELL.BAT the Shell startup options that have been specified for the owner of this password. These options will specify the menus and functions that this person will have access to. The Shell Logon program assures that these commands exist in PROCEED.BAT only if a valid password was used to log on.

If a valid password was not used to log on in the Shell, then PROCEED.BAT contains one command, a nonreturnable call to GETPW.BAT, which cycles back through the process of bringing up the Shell with only the logon option available. Until a valid password is entered, that is the only screen the user will see.

The key to this system is the Shell program that executes when the logon option is selected. This program prompts the user for his or her password. The passwords used here are not only passwords; they are also the names of files, though users do not know they are. The Parameter dialogue box that captures the password is set up to make sure the file identified by the password exists before DOS proceeds. If the file does not exist, the dialogue box beeps and displays an error message.

If the file identified by the password does exist, the Shell program proceeds to copy that file into the file PROCEED.BAT. The file that is copied to PROCEED.BAT contains a COPY command. This COPY command copies to DOSSHELL.BAT a file that indicates the Shell configuration specified for the owner of the password. The file copied to PROCEED.BAT also contains a Shell startup command that provides the color setup and access privileges defined for this person.

HOW THE PASSWORD SYSTEM WORKS—IN DETAIL

Walking through this process will help to clarify how the system works. Suppose that the password ABC has been assigned to one user, and the password XYZ has been assigned to another user. The owner of the ABC password has full access rights to the Shell. The owner of the XYZ password, on the other hand, cannot use the File System or DOS Utilities, modify the Shell, leave the Shell for the command prompt, or exit the Shell.

The files needed for this system are shown in Figures 6.1 through 6.9. The AUTOEXEC.BAT file in Figure 6.1 contains a typical set of commands. The actual commands you use will vary depending on how you have configured your computer. The only commands the password system requires are the last two: the COPY command and the GETPW command.

```
@REM filename: AUTOEXEC.BAT
@REM
@ECHO OFF
SET COMSPEC=C:\DOS\COMMAND.COM
VERIFY OFF
PATH C:\DOS;C:\UTILITY;C:\;C:\SPRINT;C:\WP
APPEND /E
APPEND C:\DOS
PROMPT $P$G
C:\DOS\GRAFTABL 437
VER
@COPY CYCLE.FIL PROCEED.BAT
@GETPW
```

Figure 6.1   *AUTOEXEC.BAT file for the Password System*

```
@REM filename: CYCLE.FIL
@REM
@GETPW
```

Figure 6.2   *CYCLE.FIL file for the Password System*

```
@REM filename: GETPW.BAT
@REM
@copy c:\dos\logon.shl c:\dos\dosshell.bat
@c:
@cd c:\dos
@call DOSSHELL
@PROCEED
```

Figure 6.3   *GETPW.BAT file for the Password System*

```
@REM filename: LOGON.SHL
@REM
@c:
@CD C:\DOS
@SHELLB DOSSHELL
@IF ERRORLEVEL 255 GOTO END
:COMMON
@SHELLC /TRAN/MENU/SND/MEU:LOGON.MEU/CLR:SHELL.CLR/EXIT/SWAP/DATE
:END
@BREAK=ON
```

Figure 6.4   *LOGON.SHL file for the Password System*

```
@REM filename: PROCEED.BAT
@REM
@REM This file contains either the command GETPW or the
@REM Shell configuration definition and startup commands
@REM for the owner of the last password used to log on.
@REM When the computer is booted the command GETPW is placed
@REM in this file during AUTOEXEC.BAT execution.  Shell
@REM configuration and startup commands are placed in it by
@REM the Shell program that is used for logging on to the
@REM computer.
```

Figure 6.5   *PROCEED.BAT file for the Password System*

```
@REM filename: ABC
@REM This file sets up the DOSSHELL.BAT file to grant
@REM full access privileges to the DOS Shell, as defined
@REM in the file DOSSHELL.ORG
@REM
@COPY C:\DOS\DOSSHELL.ORG C:\DOS\DOSSHELL.BAT
@DOSSHELL
```

Figure 6.6   *ABC file for the Password System*

```
@REM filename: XYZ
@REM This file sets up the DOSSHELL.BAT file to grant only
@REM limited access to the DOS Shell, as defined in the file
@REM XYZ.SHL.
@REM
@ COPY C:\DOS\XYZ.SHL C:\DOS\DOSSHELL.BAT
@DOSSHELL
```

Figure 6.7   *XYZ file for the Password System*

```
@REM filename: DOSSHELL.ORG
@REM This file starts the Shell with the original Shell
@REM configuration, along with all user-added menus and
@REM programs.  It does this by calling the Shell with the
@REM original Shell menu defined in SHELL.MEU and providing
@REM all options available on the Shell startup command line.
@REM
@C:
@CD C:\DOS
@SHELLB DOSSHELL
@IF ERRORLEVEL 255 GOTO END
:COMMON
@SHELLC
/TRAN/COLOR/DOS/MENU/MUL/SND/MEU:SHELL.MEU/CLR:SHELL.CLR/PROMPT/MAINT
/EXIT/SWAP/DATE
:END
@BREAK=ON
```

Figure 6.8   *DOSSHELL.ORG file for the Password System*

```
@REM filename: XYZ.SHL
@REM
@REM This file grants limited access to the DOS Shell for the
@REM owner(s) of the password XYZ.  Privileges are restricted
@REM to only those programs defined in the menu definition in
@REM the file XYZ.MEU.  The Shell startup command uses XYZ.MEU
@REM for the startup menu, and prevents access to the File
@REM File System, the Change Colors option, the Command Prompt,
@REM and the Exit option.  The user is also prevented from
@REM modifying the Shell.
@REM
@C:
@CD C:\DOS
@SHELLB DOSSHELL
@IF ERRORLEVEL 255 GOTO END
:COMMON
@SHELLC /TRAN/MENU/MUL/SND/MEU:XYZ.MEU/CLR:SHELL.CLR/SWAP/DATE
:END
@BREAK=ON
```

Figure 6.9   *XYZ.SHL file for the Password System*

To begin, suppose the holder of the ABC password boots the computer. The
AUTOEXEC.BAT file copies the contents of CYCLE.FIL (Figure 6.2) into the
file named PROCEED.BAT. PROCEED.BAT now contains one command, a
nonreturnable call to GETPW.BAT.

Now AUTOEXEC.BAT executes a nonreturnable call to GETPW.BAT (Figure
6.3). The first thing GETPW.BAT does is copy the file LOGON.SHL into the
file DOSSHELL.BAT. LOGON.SHL appears in Figure 6.4 and contains a
modified version of the original DOSSHELL.BAT file. The LOGON.SHL version has removed all of the functions of the Shell except for one user-defined menu
option for logging on to the computer.

After GETPW.BAT has copied LOGON.SHL into DOSSHELL.BAT, it executes
a returnable call to DOSSHELL.BAT. The Shell Start Programs screen will appear as in Figure 6.10.

```
01-24-89                       Start Programs                    2:03 pm
Program   Group   Exit                                    |     F1=Help
                              Main Group
               To select an item, use the up and down arrows.
             To start a program or display a new group, press Enter.

Log on; press F3 when menu returns
Command  Prompt
File System
Change Colors












F10=Actions                    Shift+F9=Command Prompt
```

Figure 6.10   Start Programs Screen

The Command Prompt, File System, and Change Colors options cannot be removed from the menu, but they can be shut off by the STARTUP command in the DOSSHELL.BAT file. Remember that DOSSHELL.BAT now contains a copy of LOGON.SHL. If you examine the SHELLC line in Figure 6.4 (LOGON.SHL), you will see that the /DOS, /PROMPT, /COLOR, and /MAINT options have all been removed. These options provide access to the File System, the Command Prompt function, the Change Colors function, and the Shell-modification functions, respectively. You will also see the /MEU:LOGON.MEU specification, which tells the Shell to use the menu defined in a file named LOGON.MEU as the startup menu. The Startup menu is the one that appears in Figure 6.10. The technique for defining and saving this menu is discussed later in this chapter.

There are several keystrokes the user could attempt to enter at this time. The user could attempt to choose one of the unavailable menu options, such as File System. Each of those options will result in the dialogue box that appears in Figure 6.11.

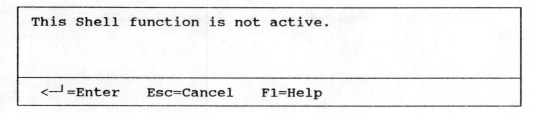

Figure 6.11   *Dialogue box for inactivated Shell functions*

The user could press the [Shift/F9] combination, but that too will result in the dialogue box in Figure 6.11. The user could press F3 to exit the Shell without logging on. If this is done, the user will exit the Shell, but control will be returned to the file GETPW.BAT because it started the Shell with a returnable call to DOS-SHELL.BAT.

The next command in GETPW.BAT is a nonreturnable call to PROCEED.BAT. Recall that one of the last commands in AUTOEXEC.BAT (Figure 6.1) was to copy the contents of CYCLE.FIL into PROCEED.BAT. PROCEED.BAT therefore contains one command: a nonreturnable call to GETPW.BAT. Consequently, when a user presses F3 to exit the Shell without first choosing the logon option, he or she exits the Shell only to be returned to it still displaying the screen in Figure 6.10.

The only option in Figure 6.10 that will get anywhere is the first one on the menu — "Log on; Press F3 when menu returns." When this option is selected, the dialogue box in Figure 6.12 appears.

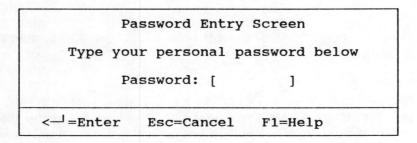

Figure 6.12   *Password Logon Screen*

If an illegal password is entered, the computer beeps and the dialogue box in Figure 6.13 appears.

```
┌─────────────────────────────────────────────────────────────┐
│                                                             │
│    File not found.                                          │
│                                                             │
│                                                             │
│ ├────────────────────────────────────────────────────────── │
│    <─┘=Enter     Esc=Cancel     F1=Help                     │
└─────────────────────────────────────────────────────────────┘
```

Figure 6.13   Result of entering an illegal password

Pressing either the Return key or the Esc key will restore the Main Group menu shown in Figure 6.10 where the logon option can be chosen again.

If a legal password is entered, the Shell option copies the file associated with this password into the file PROCEED.BAT. In this example, the file is named ABC because ABC is the password. The filename and the password are the same. The screen clears momentarily while the file is being copied, and then the Main Group menu returns.

The logon option instructs the user to Press F3 when the menu returns. If the user now presses F3, he or she will exit from the Shell, and control will be returned to the GETPW.BAT file. The next command in GETPW.BAT is a nonreturnable call to PROCEED.BAT. Because the SHELL copied the file ABC to PROCEED.BAT, PROCEED.BAT now contains the following two commands:

```
@COPY C:\DOS\DOSSHELL.ORG C:\DOS\DOSSHELL.BAT
@DOSSHELL
```

First, PROCEED.BAT copies DOSSHELL.ORG into the file DOSSHELL.BAT. DOSSHELL.ORG (Figure 6.8) contains a Shell startup command (SHELLC) that provides the user with access to all of the Shell features. It uses the menu in SHELL.MEU for its Main Group. That menu contains all of the options that come with the DOS 4.0 Shell as well as any that have been added.

The second command in PROCEED.BAT is a nonreturnable call to DOS-SHELL.BAT. The user is therefore returned to the Shell with all of the access privileges and setup options that have been assigned to him or her.

If the user with password XYZ had logged on, the file that the Shell would have copied into PROCEED.BAT would have been XYZ. File XYZ (Figure 6.7) contains the following two commands:

```
@COPY C:\DOS\XYZ.SHL C:\DOS\DOSSHELL.BAT
@DOSSHELL
```

Consequently, when PROCEED.BAT executes, it first copies the file XYZ.SHL (Figure 6.9) into DOSSHELL.BAT. XYZ.SHL was created by copying DOS-SHELL.ORG, which contains the original Shell startup options, and editing it to contain options that provide the user with access to a limited set of Shell features. If you examine the Shell startup command (SHELLC) in Figure 6.9, you will see that the /COLOR, /MAINT, /DOS, /PROMPT, and /EXIT options have been removed. The /MENU option specifies that the Main Group menu will be found in a file named XYZ.MEU. This menu contains only the programs that this user has been granted access to. If the user wanted a particular color setup, that setup could also be specified here, using the /CLR command. In Figure 6.9 /CLR specifies the colors defined in the file SHELL.CLR.

FILES REQUIRED FOR THE PASSWORD SYSTEM

AUTOEXEC.BAT

The AUTOEXEC.BAT file is created by modifying the file used for starting the Shell without the password system. The only change is to remove the DOSSHELL command and replace it with the following two commands:

```
@COPY CYCLE.FIL PROCEED.BAT
@GETPW
```

CYCLE.FIL

CYCLE.FIL is created with any text editor or with the COPY CON: command. Its only purpose is to store the GETPW command so that PROCEED.BAT can be initialized when AUTOEXEC.BAT copies CYCLE.FIL into PROCEED.BAT.

GETPW.BAT

GETPW.BAT is created with any text editor or with the COPY CON: command. It first intializes the file DOSSHELL.BAT by copying into it the contents of the file LOGON.SHL. This defines a Shell that only provides the user with one option: option 2, logging on. Because the DOSSHELL command is returnable, after the user has logged on and exited the Shell, GETPW.BAT continues with a non-returnable call to the PROCEED.BAT.

PROCEED.BAT

There are two mechanisms from which PROCEED.BAT is created and both are taken care of automatically by the password system. The first, in the AUTOEXEC.BAT file, initializes PROCEED.BAT to return the user to the Shell (via a nonreturnable call to GETPW.BAT). The effect is that if the user exits the Shell without having logged on, he or she is immediately returned to the Shell, still with the only available option being to log on.

The second mechanism from which PROCEED.BAT is created is the Shell program that executes when a user logs on. For each legal password, there is a corresponding file that contains a Shell definition for that user. When the user logs on, that file is copied into PROCEED.BAT. The effect is that after logging on and exiting the Shell, the user is returned to the Shell with the definition specified by his or her password.

DOSSHELL.ORG

When the Select program is used to install the DOS 4.0 Shell on your computer, it creates a file named DOSSHELL.BAT. This file contains a Shell startup command that provides full access to all features of the Shell. It uses the SHELL.MEU file to define the Start Programs menu and the SHELL.CLR file to define the Shell colors. The DOSSHELL.ORG file is a duplicate of this original DOS-SHELL.BAT file. It is created for two reasons: to preserve the original setup so that it can easily be restored at any time, and to provide full access to the owners of full-access passwords. The example discussed earlier uses it to provide full access to the owner of the password ABC.

LOGON.SHL

LOGON.SHL is created by making a copy of DOSSHELL.ORG and editing the SHELLC command to remove access to the Command Prompt, File System, and Change Colors options of the Main Group menu. The SHELLC command is also edited to specify the LOGON.MEU file as the source of the Start Programs menu.

LOGON.MEU

LOGON.MEU is a Shell menu file. Before creating the file, you should copy SHELL.MEU to a new file — for example, SHELL.ORG — so that you can restore the original Start Programs menu.

LOGON.MEU is created by starting the Shell and removing the DOS Utilities choice from the Main Group menu. The option "Log on; press F3 when menu returns" is added by selecting the Program choice on the Menu Bar, then selecting Add from the pull-down menu. This brings up the Add Program dialogue box. Enter "Log on; press F3 when menu returns" on the Title line and enter the following commands on the Commands line:

```
COPY [/T"Password Entry Screen"/I"Type your personal
password below"/P"Password: "/L"8"/M"e"] PROCEED.BAT
```

These commands define the Password Entry Screen shown in Figure 6.12. The /M "e" option stipulates that whatever the user enters as a password must also be the name of a file that exists in the current directory (presumably C:\DOS on a fixed disk and A:\ on a floppy disk system). When an invalid password is entered, the "File not found" message appears in the dialogue box shown in Figure 6.13.

The effect of these commands is that the password entered in the Password Entry Screen is inserted into the COPY command. If the password ABC is entered, the final command looks like the following:

```
COPY ABC PROCEED.BAT
```

After DOS Utilities has been removed from the menu and the Logon option has been defined and saved, you should exit the Shell (using the F3 key or the Exit option from the Menu Bar). This will save the new Start Programs menu in the file SHELL.MEU (which is why you should have copied the original SHELL.MEU to another file before creating this one). Now the file SHELL.MEU is renamed LOGON.MEU, and the file SHELL.ORG is copied into SHELL.MEU. This leaves you with two menu files to choose from for the Start Programs Main Group menu. The original SHELL.MEU can be used to provide all of the Main Group menu options, and the LOGON.MEU menu can be used to provide only the Logon option.

Password-Specific Files

There are at least two files that are created for each password. The name of the first file matches the password. For password XYZ, the filename is XYZ; for ABC, the filename is ABC; and so on. The name of the second file is the password with the extension .SHL. For password XYZ, the second file is named XYZ.SHL. In the previous example, the DOSSHELL.ORG file is used in place of the ABC.SHL file because the holder of the ABC password is granted full access to the Shell.

The first password file, without the extension, contains two commands. The first command copies the second file (with the .SHL extension) into the file DOS-SHELL.BAT. The second command in the first file is a nonreturnable call to DOSSHELL.BAT.

The second password file, with the .SHL extension, contains a copy of the DOS-SHELL.ORG file that has been modified to provide only those access rights granted to the holder of this password.

Special menu definitions can be defined for a particular password in the same manner as the LOGON.SHL file was created. Enter the Shell, make the additions and deletions you want to make, and exit the Shell. This will save the new menu setup in the SHELL.MEU file, which can then be copied to a menu file that reflects the password (e.g., XYZ.MEU). This menu can then be specified with the /MEU parameter in the SHELLC command in the password-specific .SHL file.

Special color setups can be created for each password in the same way. Enter the Shell, modify the colors, and exit the Shell. This will leave the color setup definition in the SHELL.CLR file, which can be renamed to a password-specific file name such as XYZ.CLR. This file can then be specified with the /CLR parameter in the SHELLC command in the password-specific .SHL file.

ENHANCING THE PASSWORD SYSTEM

There are two modifications that can improve the password system, depending on your needs. The first modification will remove the Command Prompt, Change Colors, and File System options from the Logon menu. The second will use the File System password facility to hide the logon passwords when they are typed in.

To create a logon menu that does not contain the Command Prompt, Change Colors, and File System choices, select Add Group from the Group option in the Main Group menu bar. Use this option to create a new group called Logon (or whatever you want to call it). Select this new group and give it one choice: Logon. Now exit the Shell. The new group will be saved in a .MEU file with the name you gave it in the Add Group dialogue box. You can make this menu file the Start Programs Main Group by specifying it with the /MEU option.

The second modification, using the password system that is built into the Shell, can be implemented by providing a menu option on this new menu for each user who will log on. Use the Shell Password option to define the password for each user. Now when the user enters his or her password, it will not appear on the screen.

There are two drawbacks to the technique described for using the built-in Shell password system. First, there is a maximum of 16 options that can occur on one menu, so you can only define passwords for 16 users. The second drawback is that each user occupies one menu option, and the number of total menu options in the Shell is limited. However, the limit is large, so unless you are developing a very large Shell setup this should not be a problem.

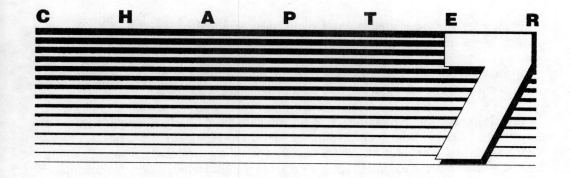

COMMAND DICTIONARY

This chapter provides a command dictionary of all commonly used DOS commands. A statement of each command's purpose and its syntax are given. A Shell setup (with a suggested title), the Shell commands needed for defining an appropriate Parameters dialogue box, and text for the Help screen are described for each command. You can add your own password if you want.

In the Help text, the use of an & symbol will cause the text following it to start on a new line. Because the amount of information in Help screens is limited to 478 characters, if you are not at least somewhat familiar with the commands, it may be necessary to refer to this chapter or a DOS manual when using the commands from within the Shell.

Some of these commands are discussed in greater detail in other chapters in this book. You can locate these discussions by checking the index.

A **location** is also specified for each command. The location will be one of the following:

- Internal
- External
- External-Internal
- CONFIG.SYS

Commands labeled Internal are loaded into memory when you boot your computer. It is not necessary to have a DOS disk or directory available when you invoke these commands.

Commands labeled External are not loaded into memory when the computer is booted. Consequently, you must have a DOS disk available on a floppy-disk system or have the DOS directory available (via a PATH or APPEND command if the directory is not the current directory) to use the command.

Commands labeled External-Internal are external the first time they are invoked. The DOS disk or directory must therefore be available when they are used for the first time. After the first use, they become internal commands (i.e., they are then retained in memory and can be used without access to a disk). When you reboot your computer, they become external until they are invoked again.

Commands labeled CONFIG.SYS must be specified in the CONFIG.SYS file. In general, these commands cannot be entered at the command prompt, although there are some exceptions to this rule. If they can be entered at the command prompt as well, they will have two labels (e.g., Internal and CONFIG.SYS).

@

Location:	Internal
Purpose:	Used in batch files to suppress the echoing of a command, even if ECHO is set ON. Has no effect if ECHO is set OFF.
Syntax:	*@ command*
Parameters:	*command* is any legal batch file command
Comments:	Useful if you do not want to set ECHO OFF but do want to suppress the display of a batch file command.

Adding @ to a Shell menu:

@ is only used in batch files.

APPEND

Location:	External-Internal
Purpose:	Sets a path of directories that DOS will search when it cannot locate a file in the current directory. The /X parameter can be specified to instruct DOS whether or not to use the APPENDed directories when searching for executable files (files with a .COM, .EXE, or .BAT extension). The APPENDed directories will always be used when searching for nonexecutable files. The /PATH parameter can be used to instruct DOS whether to search APPENDed directories for files that include a drive or path specification.

Syntax: APPEND *path1*; *path2* ... /X:OFF /PATH:OFF
                                            ON   ON

APPEND /E /X:OFF /PATH:OFF
                ON   ON

APPEND ;

APPEND

Parameters: /X same as /X:ON.

/X:ON turns on the use of APPENDed directories when searching for executable files.

/X:OFF turns off the use of APPENDed directories when searching for executable files. The default is /X:OFF.

/PATH:ON tells DOS to search APPENDed directories even if a drive and/or path is specified with the filename. The default is /PATH:ON.

/PATH:OFF tells DOS not to search APPENDed directories when a drive and/or path is specified with the filename.

/E tells DOS to keep the APPEND paths in the DOS environment, which permits the APPEND paths to be viewed and changed with the SET command as well as with the APPEND command. /E can only be used the first time APPEND is invoked; if /E is used, you cannot specify any paths to be APPENDed the first time it is invoked. You can specify paths to be APPENDed on subsequent calls to APPEND.

; (a semicolon) is used to separate paths being APPENDed. If the APPEND command is entered with just the semicolon, the previous APPEND command is cancelled.

Comments: Each time you enter a new APPEND command, the preceding one is cancelled; consequently, only the most recent APPEND command is in effect at any time. If APPEND is entered with no parameters the first time, it is loaded into memory and becomes an internal command. If APPEND is entered with no parameters after the first time, a list of APPENDed paths is displayed.

If a file is found in an APPENDed path by a program and is then saved, it will be saved in the current directory, which can lead to multiple versions of the same file existing in different directories.

If the ASSIGN command is to be used as well as the APPEND command, the first APPEND command must be entered before the ASSIGN command.

If a path that does not exist is included in a list of APPEND paths, DOS will ignore that path and go on to the next path; however, if a path cannot be found because the drive on which the path exists is not ready, DOS terminates the APPEND search.

Shell setup for APPEND:

Title: Define appended directories

Commands: **APPEND [/T"APPEND Parameters"/I"Leave blank to display current status"/P"Enter parameters: "]**

Help text: This program instructs DOS to search the specified directories if a requested file is not found in the current directory. Parameters are as follows: &drive1:\directory1;drive2:\directory2 &Example: C:\WP; A:\

ASSIGN

Location: External

Purpose: Causes a reference to a drive to access a different drive.

Syntax: ASSIGN *drive1* = *drive2* *drive3* = *drive4* ...
            ASSIGN

Parameters: *drive1* and *drive3* refer to drives being reassigned;
                drive2 and *drive4* refer to drives that *drive1* and *drive3* are
                being reassigned to.

Comments: You should not use the JOIN or SUBST commands if ASSIGN
                is in effect. Some programs will ignore the effect of ASSIGN
                and use the drive specified, even if it has been reassigned.

                ASSIGN commands are cumulative. If you assign drive A to
                drive B and then later assign drive C to drive B, drive A will
                continue to be assigned to drive B. You can reset all drive
                assignments to their normal setting by entering the command
                ASSIGN with no parameters.

                It is recommended that you not use ASSIGN unless it is
                absolutely necessary.

Shell setup for ASSIGN:

Title: Assign one drive letter to another

Commands: **ASSIGN [/T"ASSIGN Parameters"/I"Leave blank to restore
                original assignments"/P"Enter assignments:"]**

Help text: This program is used to make DOS refer to one drive when
                another drive is specified. Parameters of A = B will turn all
                references to drive A into drive B references. Pressing Return
                without entering parameters will restore the original meanings
                of drive letters.

ATTRIB

Location: External

Purpose: Used to switch the read-only and archive attributes on and off.
                Can be used on one or multiple files using * and ? wild cards.
                Can also be used to locate all occurrences of a file on a disk or
                to display a file's read-only and archive attribute settings.

Syntax:	ATTRIB + /- R + /- A *filespec* /S
	ATTRIB *filespec*

Parameters: + R turns on the read-only attribute
-R turns off the read-only attribute
+A turns on the archive attribute
-A turns off the archive attribute

filespec specifies the file or files whose attributes should be set. Wild card symbols * and ? can be used to change attributes in sets of files. Drive and path specifiers can be included.

/S causes all files in a specified directory and its subdirectories to be affected by the R and A settings. For example,

ATTRIB +A C:\WP*.* /S

will turn on all the archive attributes for all files in the **directory** WP and all its subdirectories.

Comments: When the only parameter is a filename, DOS displays the attribute settings for that file. For example, entering

ATTRIB MYFILE.LET

will result in a message similar to "R C:\MYFILE.LET," which indicates that MYFILE.LET has the read-only attribute set on and the archive attribute set off.

If you attempt to delete a file that has the R attribute set on, DOS will display the message "Access denied." You can use the ATTRIB command to turn off the R attribute.

The /S parameter can be used to locate all occurrences of a file on a disk. For example, the command

ATTRIB C:\MYFILE.LET /S

will cause DOS to display all occurrences of the file MYFILE.LET on drive C.

The Shell File System provides more powerful facilities for locating files and changing their attributes.

Shell setup for ATTRIB:

Title: Set file attributes

Commands: **ATTRIB [/T"ATTRIB Parameters"/I"Enter filename only to show its attribs"/P"Enter parameters: "]**

Help text: This program is used to display or modify a file's read-only and archive attributes. +/- R filename will turn on and off the read-only attribute; +/-A filename will turn on and off the archive attribute. /S will affect all files with the given name in the specified directory and its subdirectories. Just a filename will display the attributes for the file.

BACKUP

Location: External

Purpose: Used to back up files from one disk to another disk. The files can be restored with the RESTORE command.

Syntax: BACKUP *source-filespec target-drive* /S /M /A /D:*mm-dd-yy* /T:*hh:mm:ss* /L:*filename*

Parameters: *source-filespec* specifies the file(s) to be backed up; a drive and path can be included. If only a drive is specified, all files in the current directory of that drive will be backed up. If a drive and path are specified, all files in the specified directory will be backed up. If a filename is specified, only the file(s) specified by the filename will be backed up. The handling of subdirectories is determined by the /S parameter.

/S backs up all files that match the *filename* specification in the current directory and its subdirectories.

/M backs up files that have been modified since the last backup. This is determined by checking the archive attribute of the file(s).

/A adds the files being backed up to files that already exist on the target disk. If /A is not specified, all existing files on the target disk will be erased by the BACKUP command.

/D:*mm-dd-yy* backs up files that were modified on or after the date specified. The format of the date depends on the Country setting, which is determined during the installation of DOS 4.0; it can be modified with the COUNTRY command.

/T:*hh:mm:ss* backs up files that were changed at or after the time specified on the date indicated with the /D parameter. If /D is not used with /T, all files changed at or after the time specified on any date are backed up. Whether the time is interpreted as 12-hour format or 24-hour format depends on the Country setting, which is determined during the installation of DOS 4.0. The setting can be modified with the COUNTRY command.

/L:*filename* creates a log file. If the /L parameter is used without a filename, the name BACKUP.LOG is used. If the specified log file already exists, the new information is appended to it. The first line in the log file indicates the date and time of the backup. Subsequent lines contain the backup disk number, path, and filename of each backup file.

Comments: BACKUP will automatically format a floppy disk if it is not already formatted. For it to do this, the FORMAT program must be in the current directory or in a directory specified by the path. If the FORMAT program cannot be located, the BACKUP command will display an error message and terminate the backup process.

Files can be backed up from a fixed disk to a floppy disk, from one floppy disk to another floppy disk, from a floppy disk to a fixed disk, and from one fixed disk to another fixed disk.

When one floppy disk is filled, BACKUP automatically prompts you to insert the next disk. The disks are labelled by BACKUP to indicate the order in which they occur.

Files created with the BACKUP command are not ordinary files, which means they cannot be accessed directly by DOS or by your programs. You must use the RESTORE command to make them accessible.

The BACKUP command sets an Exit code that can be accessed by the Batch command IF ERRORLEVEL.... The Exit code is set according to the following table:

Exit code	Meaning
0	The BACKUP completed normally.
1	There were no files found to back up.
2	Some of the specified files were not backed up due to file-sharing conflicts on a network.
3	The BACKUP operation was terminated by the user pressing [Ctrl/Break].
4	The BACKUP operation terminated due to an error.

The DOS Utilities group that comes with the Shell includes Backup and Restore options that use these two DOS commands. If you want to have the BACKUP command available on another menu, you could use the following setup.

Shell setup for BACKUP:

Title: Backup a disk

Commands: BACKUP [/T"BACKUP Parameters"/I"Enter the BACKUP parameters"/P"Enter parameters: "]

Help text: This program is used to back up one disk to another disk. The parameters are as follows: &SOURCE TARGET filename /S /M /A /D:mm:dd:yy /T:hh:mm:ss /L:filespec. &/S backs up subdirectories; /M specifies only files changed since the last backup; /A adds files to the target without deleting other target disk files. /D and /T back up only files modified on or after the specified date and time. /L specifies a log file to record the backup activity.

BREAK

Location: Internal and CONFIG.SYS

Purpose: Tells DOS whether to check for a [Ctrl/Break] keystroke whenever a program requests any DOS function.

Syntax: At the command line:

BREAK ON
BREAK OFF

In the CONFIG.SYS file:

BREAK = ON
BREAK = OFF

Parameters: ON instructs DOS that whenever a DOS function is requested from an application program, DOS should check to see if the user has pressed the [Ctrl/Break] key combination. If the user has pressed [Ctrl/Break], DOS will terminate the program and return the user to the DOS prompt.

OFF instructs DOS to check for a [Ctrl/Break] combination only when one of the following operations is occurring:

standard input operations
standard output operations
standard print device operations
standard auxiliary device operations

OFF is the default condition; if no BREAK command is entered, BREAK is set to OFF.

Comments: Setting BREAK ON allows you to terminate programs that use few or no standard device operations.

You can enter BREAK at the command prompt to see the current BREAK setting.

Adding BREAK to a Shell menu:

Title: Set Ctrl/Break checking

Commands: **BREAK [/T"BREAK Parameters"/I"Leave blank to display current status"/P"Enter ON or OFF: "]**

Help text: This program is used to tell DOS whether it should check for a user-requested program termination during any requests for a DOS operation or only during standard device operations. ON specifies checking during all DOS operations, and OFF specifies checking only during standard device operations.

BUFFERS

Location: CONFIG.SYS

Purpose: Specifies the number of internal disk buffers that DOS should allocate.

Syntax: BUFFERS = *num1,num2*/X

Parameters: *num1* specifies the number of disk buffers to be used. The minimum is 1 and the maximum is 99, unless the /X paramter is used.

num2 specifies the number of look-ahead buffers to be used. The minimum is 1 and the maximum is 8.

/X indicates that expanded memory is available and should be used for the disk buffers.

Comments: The default number of buffers is set to the greatest number determined according to the following specifications: if a floppy disk drive greater than 360K is installed, the default number of buffers is 3; if there is more than 128K of memory, the default number of buffers is 5; if there is more than 256K of memory, the default number of buffers is 10; if there is more than 512K of memory, the default number of buffers is 15. If none of these conditions are met, the default number of buffers is 2.

Look-ahead buffers are used to read into memory not only the disk sector that contains the requested information but also the specified number of sectors that follow that sector on the disk. If an application reads many data elements that are in consecutive order on the disk, this can enhance disk performance. If the look-ahead buffers parameter is not specified, none are used.

Each regular buffer increases the amount of memory required for DOS by 532 bytes, and each look-ahead buffer increases the amount of memory by 512 bytes.

Adding BUFFERS to a Shell menu:

BUFFERS is a configuration command; it can only be executed from within the CONFIG.SYS file and, therefore, cannot be included in a Shell menu.

CALL

Location: Internal — only used in Batch files and Shell programs

Purpose: Used in a batch file to execute another batch file and return control to the first batch file when the second is finished executing.

Syntax: CALL *filespec*

Parameters: Drive and path specifiers can be included in the *filespec*. However, they are not necessary if the batch file being called is in the current directory or in a directory specified in the current path.

Comments: Shell programs are passed to the DOS batch processor after their parameter dialogue boxes have been processed. They therefore appear to DOS as batch files, so you can use the CALL command to execute a batch file from a Shell program and then return control to the Shell program. If you execute a batch file from a Shell program without using the CALL command, control will not return to the Shell program.

When one batch file calls another, the first can pass parameters to the second. For example, if the line CALL BATCH2 %2 %4 appeared in a batch file, the %2 parameter in the first file would become the %1 parameter in the second file, and the %4 parameter in the first file would become the %2 parameter in the second file.

The ECHO mode is passed to the CALLed batch file. If that batch file changes the ECHO mode, the mode is restored when control returns to the first batch file. Thus, if the first file sets ECHO OFF and the second file sets ECHO ON, when the second file is called, ECHO is initially OFF, and when control returns to the first file, ECHO is reset to OFF even though the second file set ECHO ON.

Two or more batch files can repetitively CALL each other, or one batch file can CALL itself. It is essential, however, that eventually the cycle ends, control returns to the command following the first occurrence of a CALL command, and the first batch file finishes executing.

If a batch file has the same name as an internal command (e.g., COPY), attempting to CALL the COPY batch file will result instead in the internal COPY command executing. It is recommended that batch files be given unique names.

If you have an established set of batch files that you would like to execute from within the Shell, it can be useful to add a generic Call option to a menu.

Adding CALL to a Shell menu:

Title: Call a batch file

Commands: CALL [/T"CALL Batch File Screen"/I"Enter name of the batch
file to call"/P"Batch File: "].BAT

Help text: This program executes a batch file and returns control to the Shell.
Enter the name of the batch file you want to execute (do not
include the .BAT ending) and press the Return key.

CD or CHDIR

Location: Internal

Purpose: Changes or displays the current directory of the specified drive.

Syntax: CHDIR *drive:path*
CD *drive:path*
CHDIR *drive*:
CD *drive*:

Parameters: *drive* specifies the drive for which the current directory should
be changed; if no drive is specified, the current drive is used.
When only a drive is specified, the current directory for that
drive is displayed without being changed.

path is the path to which the current directory for the specified
drive should be changed. *path* cannot be more than 63
characters long, starting from the root directory.

Comments: Each drive has its own current directory. Thus, the commands
CD C:\DOS and CD A:\WP will cause the current directory of
drive C to be C:\DOS and the current directory of drive A to
be A:\WP. When you change drives, the current directory is
the one you are automatically in.

If your prompt does not show the current directory, you can use
the CD command to determine the current directory.

A leading backslash instructs DOS to start at the root directory.

Adding CHDIR to a Shell menu:

Title: Change current directory

Commands:	**CHDIR [/T"Change Directory Screen"/I"Drive only to see current directory"/P"New directory: "]**
Help text:	This command changes the current directory. If you specify a drive, as in: &A:\wp & the current directory for the specified drive is changed. If that drive is different from the current drive, the current directory for the current drive is unchanged. If no drive is specified, the current drive is used. Entering the parameter &C: &will display the current directory of drive C without changing it.

CHKDSK

Location:	External
Purpose:	Displays the current status of the specified directory, the total amount of memory on the computer, and the amount of memory that is available for programs.
Syntax:	CHKDSK *drive:path\filename* /F /N
	drive indicates the drive to be checked
Parameters:	*path\filename* instructs DOS to give additional reports about the specified files (wild cards can be used to specify more than one file). For example, if a file named MYFILE.LET existed in the WP directory of drive C, the command

CHKDSK C:\WP\MYFILE.LET

would result in a report similar to the following:

```
Volume Serial Number is 2X5B-32BC

21309440 bytes total disk space
  133120 bytes in 10 hidden files
55296 bytes in 20 directories
11771904 bytes in 641 user files
9349120 bytes available on disk

 2048 bytes in each allocation unit
10405 total allocation units on disk
 4565 available allocation units on disk

 655360 total bytes memory
 302656 bytes free

C:\WP\MYFILE.LET Contains 3 non-contiguous
blocks
```

/F tells DOS to correct any errors it finds in the directory and file allocation table and to write the corrections on the disk. If you do not specify /F, /FDOS will go through the motions of correcting the errors, which gives you an indication of what effects the correction might have without actually writing the correction to disk. If CHKDSK reports that there are "lost allocation units" or "lost clusters" on the disk, the /F parameter will cause CHKDSK to ask you if you want to recover them. Lost allocation units are sections of files that have become "orphaned" on a disk—DOS can no longer identify what file they belong to. Consequently, the space they occupy is no longer available for other purposes. They may also contain valuable information. There are several possible causes of lost allocation units. A power failure during operation is a common cause. If you respond with Y(Yes) to indicate that you want DOS to recover them, it will convert them to ASCII text files with FILE*nnn*.CHK, where *nnn* represents a number. You can then examine the files to determine whether the data in them is valuable. In any case, this will free up the disk space occupied by these files.

/V instructs DOS to display the names of all files on the specified drive. The pathname for each file is displayed as well as the filename. DOS does not pause when the screen fills, but pressing Ctrl/S will stop the screen from scrolling until you press another key.

Comments: The disk status information includes the total disk space; the number of hidden files on the disk and the number of bytes they occupy; the number of directories on the disk and the number of bytes they occupy; the number of user files on the disk and the number of bytes they occupy; the number of bad sectors on the disk; the number of bytes of available space on the disk; the size of the allocation units on the disk; the total number of allocation units on the disk; and the number of available allocation units on the disk.

When you use CHKDSK to check a floppy drive, DOS assumes the drive is ready, so you must be sure to have a disk in the drive before executing this command.

It is a good idea to run CHKDSK periodically on any disks in regular use; this will alert you to problems that may be developing in your files before you lose valuable information.

If a file is badly fragmented (i.e., it contains a large number of noncontiguous blocks), it can cause the computer to take longer than necessary to access the file. This situation can be remedied by copying the file to another disk, erasing it from the first disk, and then copying it back to the first disk. This procedure results in the file occupying one contiguous area of the disk.

Adding CHKDSK to a Shell menu:

Title: Run disk and memory status check

Commands: **CHKDSK [/T"DOS Check Disk Screen"/I"Enter the parameters you want to use"/P"Enter parameters: "]**

Help text: This program will run a status check on a disk. It will also produce a status report on the memory in the computer. The status report indicates how disk space is allocated and will recover allocation units that have become lost. It will also attempt to recover the data in those allocation units. /F turns on file recovery; /V displays all files and their paths.

CLS

Location: Internal

Purpose: Clears the screen.

Syntax: CLS

Parameters: none

Comments: This command is used to clear the screen. After the command executes, the cursor and prompt appear at the top left corner of the screen. This command is useful in batch files to avoid having clutter that will obscure messages generated by the batch file.

Adding CLS to a Shell menu:

CLS is not useful as a Shell menu feature because it will simply clear the screen and then restore it when the Shell returns.

COMP

Location: External

Purpose: Compares the contents of one set of files to the contents of a second set of files.

Syntax: COMP *filespec1 filespec2*

Parameters: *filespec1* specifies the first set of files to compare. It can include wild cards and a drive and path specification. If you specify a drive and path with no filename, DOS assumes a *.* filename.

filespec2 specifies the second set of files against which the first is compared. It can include wild cards and a drive and path specification. If you specify a drive and path with no filename, DOS assumes a *.* filename.

Comments: This command compares the contents of files to determine whether or not they are identical. If *filespec1* and *filespec2* are individual filenames containing no wild cards, the contents of the two files are compared. If *filespec1* contains wild card symbols and *filespec2* does not, each file specified in *filespec1* is compared with the file named in *filespec2* that meets the criteria specified below. If both *filespec1* and *filespec2* contain wild cards, only files with the same name are compared.

COMP will not compare two files if their sizes are different because they could not possibly be identical. In this case, DOS displays an error message and asks if you want to compare more files.

If a parameter is missing or does not adequately specify a set of files, DOS will prompt you for the missing information.

If you specify a floppy disk drive in one of the filespecs, DOS assumes the drive is ready. Be sure the drive has the necessary disk in it before entering this command.

If two files that are being compared do not match, DOS displays an error message in the following format:

```
Compare error at OFFSET xxx
File1 = yy
File2 = zz
```

xxx indicates the number of bytes (in hexadecimal) into the files at which a mismatch occurred; *yy* indicates the hexadecimal value of the first mismatched byte in *file1*, and *zz* indicates the hexadecimal value of the first mismatched byte in *file2*. If COMP encounters 10 files that do not match, it terminates and displays a message.

If the message "EOF mark not found" appears, it means that the files may be identical even if they produced "Compare error" messages. This situation occurs because some types of files have directory entries that indicate they are a multiple of 128 bytes in length when, in fact, they terminate before the end of the last 128-byte block. COMP still attempts to compare these files out to the end of the last 128-byte block, and it may be that the Compare error occurred beyond the true end of the file. In that case, the files would be identical but still produce an error message.

Note that this command is distinctly different from the DISKCOMP command, which is used in the Shell DOS Utilities Disk Compare option. DISKCOMP compares two complete disks to see if they are identical in all respects, while COMP compares the contents of two files.

Adding COMP to a Shell menu:

Title: Compare two disk files

Commands: **COMP [/T"File Comparison"/I"Enter two file specifiers for comparison"/P"File Specifiers: "]**

Help text: This program compares the contents of two sets of files. Files are only compared if their sizes are identical. If wild cards are used in both file specifiers, only files with matching names are compared. &Example:&C:\WP*.* A:\WP*.* & will compare each file in C:\WP with a file of the same name in A:\WP.

COPY

Location: Internal

Purpose: Used to copy one or more files from one location to another. Also used to combine two or more files into one file.

Syntax: COPY *filespec1* /B *filespec2* /B /V
                                  /A   /A

             COPY *f1* + *f2* + ... + *fn* /A *target* /A /V
                                           /B   /B

Parameters: *filespec1* specifies the file or files to be copied. Wild card
             symbols can be used.

             filespec2 specifies the destination of the new copies. Wild card
             symbols can be used.

             /A and /B are optional parameters used to inform DOS
             where in the source file to stop copying and how to specify the
             end of the destination file.

             When /A is specified for the source file, DOS expects the source
             file to be an ASCII text file and copies everything up to the
             first Ctrl/Z character it encounters. Ctrl/Z is the ASCII
             end-of-file character. The Ctrl/Z charcter itself is not copied. If
             neither /A nor /B is specified, /A is taken as the default if two
             or more files are being combined.

             When /B is specified for the source file, DOS determines the
             size of the file by the number of bytes specified for it in the
             directory. If neither /A nor /B is specified, /B is taken as the
             default unless two or more files are being combined (see the
             following "Comments" section).

             When /A is specified for the target file, DOS adds a Ctrl/Z
             character to the end of the file.

             When /B is specified for the target file, DOS does not add a
             Ctrl/Z character to the end of the file.

             /V is used to make absolutely certain that the new file is written
             to the disk without any errors. The V stands for "Verify." This
             option considerably slows the copying process because DOS must
             read and check each sector after it is written. In most cases, it is
             unnecessary because errors rarely occur during a copy process,
             but if an error will result in a serious loss, it is worth the extra
             time.

f1, *f2*, and *fn* represent files that will be combined to create one new file, specified by *target*.

Comments:　All file specifications (indicated in the syntax by *filespec1*, *filespec2*, *f1*, *f2*, *fn*, and *target*) can include a drive and path specification. COPY copies only files in the specified directory or in the current directory if no directory is specified. Files in subdirectories are not copied. If you want to copy files in subdirectories, you should use the BACKUP or XCOPY command.

If the target directory (*filespec2* and *target* in the syntax) is not the same as the source directory, the files will be copied with the same names unless new names are specified. If the target directory is the same as the source directory, the new names must be specified because a file cannot be copied to itself.

If the target filename already exists, the old file is replaced by the new one. DOS does not issue a warning before replacing the old file, so you must be careful not to overwrite a file you want to keep.

The target file will never be created with the read-only attribute set on, even if the source file has read-only set on.

You can use COPY to transfer information between devices. For example, the command

COPY CON: filename

will copy whatever you type at the keyboard into the file named *filename*. Copying will end when you hold down the Ctrl key, press Z, and then press the Return key. This sequence will create a file named *filename* that contains whatever you typed at the keyboard, up to the Ctrl/Z. The command

COPY filename PRN:

will copy the file *filename* to the printer, causing it to be printed.

When combining files, if you do not specify a target file, all files following the first one named are appended to the first one named. For example, the command

COPY file1 + file2 + file3

will result in the files *file2* and *file3* being appended to *file1*.

The Shell File System provides faster and more powerful facilities for making copies of files; however, the COPY command is useful for copying between devices and for combining one or more files.

Adding COPY to a Shell menu:

Title: Copy or combine files

Commands: **COPY [/T"Copy or combine files screen"/I"Enter filenames; use + to combine"/P"Filenames: "]**

Help text: This program will copy information from one location (the source) to another (the target). The source and target can be files (the most common use) or devices. To make a copy of a file, enter filename1 filename2 as the parameters; to copy between devices, enter device1 device 2 as the parameters.

COUNTRY

Location: CONFIG.SYS

Purpose: Specifies the country for which country-specific formats are used. Formats include date and time formats, collating sequence, capitalization, folding format, currency symbol, and decimal separator.

Syntax: COUNTRY=*code, codepage, filespec*

Parameters: *code* refers to a three-digit number that specifies a particular country, as specified in the following table.

codepage refers to the three-digit code page to use with the specific country. Code pages determine how the ASCII codes will be translated into characters. Some country codes support more than one code page. The code pages for each country are specified in the following table. The code page is optional in the COUNTRY command; if it is not used, DOS will use the primary code page for the specified country. The primary code page is the first one listed in the following table (e.g., the primary code page for the U.S. is 437).

filespec indicates the file that contains the country-specific information; this file is named COUNTRY.SYS. If the *filespec* parameter is omitted, DOS assumes that COUNTRY.SYS is located in the root directory of the boot disk. If DOS cannot locate the file, it produces an error message when it encounters the COUNTRY command.

Comments: If you specify the *filespec* parameter, you must use the *codepage* parameter or replace it with a comma so that DOS will know not to interpret the *filespec* as a *codepage*, for example,

COUNTRY=001,,C:\DOS\COUNTRY.SYS

Notice that two commas are used; one replaces the *codepage*, and the other is the command that follows the *codepage* parameter.

If no COUNTRY command in included in the CONFIG.SYS file, the default country code that DOS uses is 001, which is the U.S. country code and code page 437.

It is important to understand that the COUNTRY command does not translate DOS messages or other information into another language; it simply defines the format for such information as date and time.

Country	Code	Available Code Pages
Arabic-speaking	785	864, 850
Australia	061	437, 850
Belgium	032	850, 437
Canada (French-speaking)	002	863, 850
Denmark	045	850, 865
Finland	358	850, 437
France	033	437, 850
Germany	049	437, 850
Hebrew-speaking	972	86, 850
Italy	039	437, 850
Japan	081	932, 437
Korea	082	934, 437
Latin America	003	437, 850
Netherlands	031	437, 850
Norway	047	850, 865
Portugal	351	850, 860
Simplified Chinese	086	936, 437
Spain	034	437, 850
Sweden	046	437, 850
Switzerland	041	850, 437
Traditional Chinese	088	938, 437
United Kingdom	044	437, 850
United States	001	437, 850

Adding COUNTRY to a Shell menu:

COUNTRY is a configuration command, so it can only be executed from within the CONFIG.SYS file. Therefore, it cannot be included in a Shell menu.

DATE

Location: Internal

Purpose: Sets the date stored in the internal clock.

Syntax:	DATE *mm-dd-yy*
	DATE *dd-mm-yy*
	DATE *yy-mm-dd*
	DATE

Parameters: *mm* stands for the numeric month (1-12).

dd stands for the day of the month (1-31).

yy stands for the year and can be entered as a two-digit or four-digit year. If entered as a four-digit year, the century digits must be 19 or 20.

Comments: If you type an incorrect date, DOS will display the message

```
Invalid date
Enter new date (mm-dd-yy)
```

If you press the Return key at this point, the date will be left unchanged.

You can use the forward slash (/) in place of the hyphens to separate the month, day, and year.

Entering DATE with no parameters causes DOS to display the current date. A three-day abbreviation of the day of the week will also be displayed, e.g.,

```
Sun 10-16-1988
```

The Shell DOS Utilities group provides a menu selection for setting the date and time.

Adding DATE to a Shell menu:

Title: Set the computer's internal date

Commands: DATE [/T"Set the computer's date"/I"Leave blank to display current date"/P"Enter mm-dd-yy "]

Help text: This choice will set the computer's date, which appears in the upper left corner of the Shell screen. It is also used for date-stamping the creation or modification of files.

DEL

Location: Internal

Purpose: Deletes one or more files from a disk.

Syntax: DEL *filespec* /P

Parameters: *filespec* is the name of the file(s) you want to delete. Wild cards can be used. A drive and path specifier can be included.

/P causes DOS to display each filename and pause with a prompt that asks whether or not you want to delete the file, before it deletes it from the disk.

Comments: The DEL command is functionally identical to the ERASE command.

DEL will not remove files whose hidden attribute is set ON.

If the DEL command is entered with a drive and path specifier but no filename, the command assumes *.* for the filename.

If you enter a DEL command to delete all files in a directory or all files on a disk and do not use the /P parameter, DOS will pause and display the message,

```
All files in directory will be deleted!
Are you sure (Y/N)?
```

This is to prevent you from accidentally deleting a large number of files by accident. Press Y for (Yes) or N for (No), and then press the Return key.

The DEL command cannot be used to delete a subdirectory; you must use the RMDIR (Remove Directory) command for that purpose.

The Shell File System provides much more convenient and powerful features for removing files and subdirectories than does the DEL command.

Adding DEL to a Shell menu:

Title: Delete files from a disk

Commands: **DEL [/T"File deletion screen"/I"Enter the file to delete"/P"Filename: "]**

Help text: This program is used to delete files from a disk. Enter the filename to be deleted; you can use wild cards (* and ?) and drive and path specifiers. If you use wild cards, it is advisable to use the /P parameter as well, which will cause DOS to verify that you want to delete each file before it is removed. /P should be entered after the filename.

DEVICE

Location: CONFIG.SYS

Purpose: DEVICE is used to install a device driver when you boot your computer.

Syntax: DEVICE=*filespec parameters*

Parameters: *filespec* is the filename of the device to be installed. It can include a drive and path specification.

parameters represents any parameters required by the device driver.

Comments: A separate DEVICE= command is required for each device driver you want to install. The following device drivers are included with DOS 4.0:

ANSI.SYS allows you to modify the handling of the screen and keyboard.

DISPLAY.SYS can be used to provide code page switching for CON.

DRIVER.SYS allows you to access a disk device by referencing a logical drive letter.

PRINTER.SYS provides code page switching support for printers PRN, LPT1, LPT2, and LPT3.

VDISK.SYS can be used to set up a virtual, or memory, disk.

XMAEM.SYS emulates the IBM PS/2 80286 Expanded Memory Adapter/A to provide expanded memory support above 1 megabyte. This driver can only be used with 80386-based systems.

XMA2EMS.SYS supports the Lotus-Intel-Microsoft (LIM) Expanded Memory Specification 4.0.

Adding DEVICE to a Shell menu:

DEVICE is a configuration command. It can only be executed from within the CONFIG.SYS file and, therefore, cannot be included in a Shell menu.

DIR

Location:	Internal
Purpose:	Displays a directory listing for a specified directory.
Syntax:	DIR *filespec* /P /W
Parameters:	*filespec* specifies the directory to be displayed. A drive and path can be included. A filename and wild cards can be used to display only selected files. If no filespec is provided, the current drive is assumed, and the filename *.* is assumed.

/P, which stands for "pause," is an optional parameter. When it is used, after one screenful is displayed, DOS pauses with the message "Press any key to continue ..." and waits for a key to be pressed before displaying the next screenful of information.

/W, which stands for "wide," is an optional parameter. When it is used, it eliminates the size, date, and time information from the display and places the filenames in columns across the screen, thereby allowing many more filenames to be displayed on one screen. /W should only be used with 80-column monitors.

Comments: Files with the hidden attribute set on are not displayed in DIR listings.

Subdirectories are shown as well as files. Subdirectories are labeled with <DIR> in the file size area.

If a filename does not include a period, and you want to specify the name in the DIR command, you should terminate it with a period. For example, if a file were named MYFILE, the following command would be used to display its directory entry:

DIR MFYILE.

In addition to the files contained in the specified directory, the DIR command displays the volume label and serial number, if one exists. The number of bytes free on the specified drive is shown at the end of the file listing.

The Shell File System provides much more power and flexibility for viewing files than does the DIR command; however, the DIR command displays the date and time a file was created or last modified, while the Shell File System displays only the date.

Adding DIR to a Shell menu:

Title: List the files in a directory

Commands: **DIR [/T"Directory Listing Program"/I"Leave blank to display all files "/P"Enter directory: "]**

Help text: This program will list all of the files in the specified directory. File size, date of creation or last modification, and time of creation or last modification are also displayed. Subdirectories are displayed with the symbol <DIR> in the size field. You can specify /P to pause the display after each screenful of information, and you can specify /W to display filenames only in multiple columns, and across the screen.

DISKCOMP

Location: External

Purpose: Compares two floppy disks to determine whether they are identical in all respects.

Syntax: DISKCOMP *source target* /1 /8

Parameters: *source* is the source drive to compare to *target*.

target is the target drive against which *source* is compared.

/1 instructs DOS to compare only the first side of the disks even if they are double-sided.

/8 instructs DOS to compare only 8 sectors per track, even if the source disk has 9 or 15 sectors per track.

Comments: DISKCOMP compares two floppy disks sector by sector. Two disks can contain identical sets of files (as determined by the COMP command), but the files cannot occupy identical sectors on each disk. For example, on the source disk *file1* may occupy sectors 1, 2, and 3 of track 1, while on the target disk, *file1* may occupy sectors 4, 5, and 6 of track 2. These two disks will not compare as identical with the DISKCOMP program.

If two disks do not compare, DOS will display a message indicating the track and side at which they first differed.

If you have only one floppy drive, the DISKCOMP command can be used by omitting the target drive specification. DISKCOMP will then compare two disks on the same drive, prompting you to change disks at the appropriate times.

If you do not use the /1 and /8 parameters, DISKCOMP will automatically determine the maximum number of sides and sectors per track supported by the source drive and use those values.

The Shell DOS Utilities menu includes a Disk Compare program that uses DISKCOMP. This is the easiest way to access DISKCOMP.

Adding DISKCOMP to a Shell menu:

Title: Compare two floppy disks

Commands: **DISKCOMP [/T"Disk Comparison Utility"/I"Enter the drives to compare"/P"Drives: "]**

Help text: This program is used to compare two floppy disks on a sector-by-sector basis. For them to compare properly, the disks must contain identical files, and the files must occur in the same physical locations on the two disks. Use /1 to compare only side 1 of the disks. Use /8 to compare only 8 sectors per track.

DISKCOPY

Location: External

Purpose: Used to create an exact duplicate of a floppy disk.

Syntax: DISKCOPY *source target* /1

Parameters: *source* is the drive to be copied from.

                 target is the drive to be copied to.

                 /1 copies only side 1 of the source disk, even if it is a two-sided disk.

Comments: DISKCOPY creates a copy of a disk that is identical in all respects. A disk that has been created with DISKCOPY will compare properly with the original disk when the two disks are compared with DISKCOMP.

If the target disk is not formatted, DISKCOPY will format it during the copy process.

Any files on the target disk will be erased during a DISKCOPY.

If you have only one floppy drive, omit the target drive. DOS will then perform the copy, using a single drive. You will be prompted to change disks.

If an error occurs during the copy, DOS displays a warning message indicating the drive, side, and track on which the error occurred, and then proceeds to complete the copy.

DISKCOPY will ignore any ASSIGN commands in effect.

In general, it is better to use the COPY command because it will defragment files and will not erase any additional files on the target disk.

Adding DISKCOPY to a Shell menu:

Title: Create exact duplicate of a floppy disk

Commands: **DISKCOPY[/T"Create duplicate floppy disk"/I"Enter the drives to copy"/P"Drives: "]**

Help text: This program produces an exact replica of a disk. The source disk is copied sector by sector to the target disk. Use /1 to copy only side 1. The File System Copy utility is usually a better way to accomplish this task.

DOSSHELL

Location: External

Purpose: Starts the DOS 4.0 Shell from the command line.

Syntax: DOSSHELL

Parameters: None

Comments: The DOSSHELL.BAT file must in the current directory or in a directory specified in the current path.

Adding DOSSHELL to a Shell menu:

This command is used at the DOS prompt to start the Shell. It has no use once you are in the Shell.

ECHO

Location: Internal

Purpose: Turns on and off the screen display of batch file commands. Also used to force the display of a message in a batch file or Shell program.

Syntax: ECHO ON
ECHO OFF
ECHO *message*
ECHO

Parameters: ON turns on ECHO mode. ON is the default mode.

OFF turns off ECHO mode.

message is a message that you want displayed, even if ECHO is set OFF.

Comments: When the ECHO command is entered with no parameters, the current ECHO state is displayed.

ECHO ON and ECHO OFF are useful in batch files for causing or suppressing the display of batch file commands. They have no effect in Shell programs because the Shell automatically suppresses all Shell commands.

ECHO *message* displays the specified message. This command is useful in both batch files and Shell programs.

Adding ECHO to a Shell menu:

ECHO is intended for use in batch files and Shell programs. It has no use as a Shell menu option.

ERASE

Location: Internal

Purpose: Deletes one or more files from a disk.

Syntax: ERASE *filespec* /P

Parameters: *filespec* is the name of the file(s) you want to delete. Wild cards can be used. A drive and path specifier can be included.

/P causes DOS to display each filename and pause with a prompt that asks whether you want to delete the file, before it is actually deleted from the disk.

Comments: The ERASE command is functionally identical to the DEL command.

ERASE will not remove files whose hidden attribute is set on.

If the ERASE command is entered with a drive and path specifier, but no filename, it assumes *.* for the filename.

If you enter an ERASE command to delete all files in a directory or all files on a disk, and do not use the /P parameter, DOS will pause and display the message,

```
All files in directory will be deleted!
Are you sure (Y/N)?
```

This is to prevent you from accidentally deleting a large number of files by accident. Press either Y (for Yes) or N (for No) and press the Return key.

The ERASE command cannot be used to delete a subdirectory; you must use the RMDIR (Remove Directory) command for that purpose.

The Shell File System provides much more convenient and powerful features for removing files and subdirectories than the ERASE command.

Adding ERASE to a Shell menu:

Title: Delete files from a disk

Commands: **ERASE [/T"File deletion screen"/I"Enter the file to delete"/P"Filename: "]**

Help text: This program is used to delete files from a disk. Enter the filename to be deleted; you can use wild cards (* and ?) and drive and path specifiers. If you use wild cards, it is advisable to use the /P parameter as well. This will cause DOS to verify that you want to delete each file before it is removed. /P should be entered after the filename.

FASTOPEN

Location: External and CONFIG.SYS

Purpose: Increases the speed with which you can access disk files when the same files are repeatedly used.

Syntax: FASTOPEN *drive1 = buffers drive2 = buffers ...*/X
                  FASTOPEN *drive1 = (buffers,continuous-buffers)...* /X
                  FASTOPEN *drive = (buffers,)...* /X
                  FASTOPEN *drive = (,continuous-buffers)...* /X
                  INSTALL = FASTOPEN.EXE ...

Parameters: *drive* is the drive on which the files to be made quickly accessible reside.

buffers specifies the number of buffers to be used for the specified drive. The minimum number is 10, and the maximum is 999 for all drives specified. If buffers is not specifed with FASTOPEN, the default value is 34.

continuous-buffers is the number of continuous space buffers to be used for the specified drive. Continuous-space buffers record information related to the way a file's contents are distributed on the disk. The minimum number is 1, and the maximum number is 999 for all drives specified. If only a drive letter is specified with FASTOPEN, the default value is 34. If buffers is specified but continous-buffers is not, the continous-buffers feature is not activated.

/X causes DOS to use expanded memory for the FASTOPEN buffers. This saves conventional memory space for use by application programs.

Comments: FASTOPEN works by setting up buffers in memory that contain the directory information for recently opened files. This information includes the location of the directory information and continous space information. Retaining this information in a memory buffer allows it to be retrieved much faster than if it is read from the disk.

There is one drawback to using FASTOPEN; it reduces the amount of memory available to applications, unless you have expanded memory and specify the /X parameter. Each buffer takes 35 bytes of memory, and each continuous-buffer takes 16 bytes of memory.

The INSTALL= version of the command is used if you want to execute FASTOPEN from the CONFIG.SYS file when you boot your computer. You must include the extension (.EXE) if this version is used.

All drives for which you want to specify FASTOPEN buffers must be specified the first time you use FASTOPEN.

The number of buffers specified should be larger than the greatest number of subdirectories that share a common path. For example, if the path to your deepest subdirectory contained ten directories, there should be at least 10 buffers.

Example: FASTOPEN C: = (100,200) specifies 100 buffers for file and directory information and 200 buffers for continous space information.

Adding FASTOPEN to a Shell menu:

Title: Configure fast opening of files

Commands: FASTOPEN [/T"Fast File Opening"/I"This command can only be entered once"/P"Enter parameters: "]

Help text: This program can only be executed once for each disk on the system. Enter (x,y) for parameters, where x represents the number of buffers to set up, and y represents the number of continous-space buffers to set up.

FILES

Location: CONFIG.SYS

Purpose: Sets the maximum number of files that can be open at any one time.

Syntax: FILES = *num*

Parameters: *num* specifies the maximum number of files that can be open at any one time. The minimum is 8 and the maximum is 255.

Comments: If no FILES = command is included in your CONFIG.SYS file, the default value of 8 is used.

Each time a program is run, the file that contains the program is opened. Each data file that must be accessed by a program must be opened. If a program uses overlay files, they also must opened. It is becoming common for applications to require more than eight files to be open at once. FILES is used when more than eight files must be open at one time.

Adding FILES to a Shell menu:

FILES is a configuration command; it can only be executed from within the CONFIG.SYS file and, therefore, cannot be included in a Shell menu.

FIND

Location:	External
Purpose:	Locates text strings in files.
Syntax:	FIND /C /N /V *"string" filespec1 filespec2 ...*
Parameters:	/C displays a count of the lines that were found to contain the string.
	/N displays the line number and the line that was found to contain the string.
	/V displays all lines that do not contain the string.
	filespec1, filespec2, etc. specify the files to be searched for the string. They may not contain wild cards, but drive and path specifiers are allowed.
Comments:	Files are assumed to be ASCII text files, so they are searched up to the first Ctrl/Z character encountered.
	The string to be searched for must be enclosed in double quotation marks.

Adding FIND to a Shell menu:

Title:	Search files for a text string

Commands: FIND [/T"File search utility"/I"Enter the file search criteria:"/P"Search: "]

Help text: This program is used to search text files for particular character "strings." Enter the string in double quotation marks followed by a list of filenames to search. Wild cards are not allowed in filenames. The following parameters can be entered before the string:

&/C to display a count of lines containing the string.

&/N to display the line number and the line in which the string is found.

&/V to display all lines that do not contain the string.

FOR

Location: Internal

Purpose: Used in batch files and at the command line for repetitively executing a command.

Syntax: FOR *%variable* IN (*set*) DO *command*
FOR *%%variable* IN (*set*) DO *command*

Parameters: *%variable* is the % sign followed by any single character, including 0 through 9. %variable is used in batch files to indicate a variable name that will take on each value in (*set*), one at a time, and execute a command for each value.

%%variable is the same as *%variable*, except it is used at the command line instead of in a batch file.

(*set*) contains one or more values that the variable takes on, each for one execution of the command.

command represents the DOS command that will be executed once for each value in (*set*).

Comments: FOR is useful when a single command must be executed several times, with one value in the command changing. The following command entered at the command prompt will display the directory listing of DIR1, DIR2, and DIR3:

FOR %D IN (DIR1, DIR2, DIR3) DO DIR %D

The same command could be executed at the command prompt as follows:

FOR %%D IN (DIR1, DIR2, DIR3) DO DIR %%D

Adding FOR to a Shell menu:

Title: Repetitive execution of a DOS command

Commands: **FOR %D IN ([/T"Repeat values screen"/I"Enter repeat values "/P"Values: "]) DO [/T"Repeat command screen"/I"Enter command to repeat"/P"Command: "] %D**

Help text: The first parameter screen, "Repeat values screen," is used to enter the set of values that should be repeated for each execution of the command. The second screen, "Repeat command screen," is used to enter the command that should be repeated for each value entered in the previous screen.

FORMAT

Location: External

Purpose: Prepares a new floppy or fixed disk for use.

Syntax: FORMAT *drive:* /S /B /V:*label* /8 /4 /1 /N:*xx* /T:*yy* /F:*size*

Parameters: *drive* is the drive on which the disk will be formatted.

/S copies the operating system files to the disk so that the computer can be booted from the disk.

/B formats a floppy disk and reserves space for the system files so that even if files are copied to the disk, the system files can still be transferred to it, using the SYS command.

/V:*label* specifies a volume label for the disk. If /V is not specified, you will be prompted to enter a label after the format is complete. If you press the Return key, no label will be created.

/8 is used to format a 5.25 inch floppy disk with 8 sectors per track (as opposed to the default of 9).

/4 is used to format a 360KB or 180KB 5.25-inch floppy disk in a high-capacity (1.2 Meg) drive. This does not produce a disk that can be reliably read or written in a 360KB drive.

/1 formats side one only on a 5.25-inch floppy disk.

/N:*xx* /T:*yy* specifies the number of sectors per track and the number of tracks per disk. If either parameter is used, then both parameters must be specified or DOS will terminate the command with an error message.

/F:*size* allows you to specify an alternate media size for a floppy disk. For example, a 360KB floppy disk can be formatted to 320KB, 180KB, or 160KB.

Comments: If you use FORMAT on a disk that contains files, all files will be destroyed.

The FORMAT command is available on the Shell DOS Utilities menu.

Adding FORMAT to a Shell menu:

Title: Format a disk

Commands: **FORMAT [/T"Disk format program"/I"Enter the drive you want to format"/P"Drive: "]**

Help text: The /S parameter will make the disk bootable. The /B parameter will reserve space for system files. The /V: *label* parameter
assigns a volume label. The /8 parameter formats a 5.25-inch
disk to 8 sectors per track. The /4 parameter formats a 360KB
or 180KB disk in a high-capacity drive. The /1 parameter formats only one side of a disk. /N:*xx*/T:*yy* formats *xx* sectors per
track and *yy* tracks per disk.

GOTO

Location: Internal

Purpose: Used in batch files to create a branching flow of control.

Syntax: GOTO *label*

Parameters: *label* refers to a line in the file that contains a colon followed by
the label. When the GOTO command executes, control jumps
to the line following the label.

Comments: Only the first eight characters of a label are examined, so if
more than one label is used in a batch file, they must not contain
the same first eight characters.

Labels are never displayed, even if ECHO is set ON, so you can
use the colon to add comments to a batch file instead of using
the REM command, which is echoed unless ECHO is set OFF. If
you use the colon in this way, make sure the first eight characters
of the comments do not match the first eight characters of a
legitimate label.

Adding GOTO to a Shell menu:

GOTO has no use outside of batch files, so it cannot be added
to a Shell menu.

GRAPHICS

Location:	External
Purpose:	Used to print graphic images.
Syntax:	GRAPHICS *printer-type drive:path\profile* /R /B /LCD/PB:*identifier*

Parameters: *printer-type* indicates the type of printer you have. If you do not specify a printer type, the default value is graphics.

profile refers to the file that contains information on all printers that are supported by the GRAPHICS command. If the profile parameter is omitted, the default value is GRAPHICS.PRO.

/R specifies that black and white should not be reversed. Normally, everything that appears black on the screen is not printed, and everything that appears white is printed in black. /R is used to turn off this reversal.

/B causes the background color to print if you have a color printer specified. If /B is not included in the GRAPHICS command, then the background color is not printed.

/LCD is used if you have a liquid crystal display (LCD) and want to print the graphics image exactly as it appears on the display. This parameter has the same effect as specifying /PB:LCD.

/PB: *identifier* is used if you have a laptop computer. It specifies how to print screen images when different displays are used on the computer. *Identifier* can be either STD, which specifies a standard full-size screen, or LCD, which specifies a liquid crystal display. The aspect, or ratio of width to height, is different on an LCD display.

Comments: Your printer must have the ability to print graphic images for this command to work.

Adding GRAPHICS to a Shell menu:

Title: Set up graphics printing capability

Commands: **GRAPHICS [/T"Graphics print setup"/I"Enter parameters:"/P"Parameters: "]**

Help text: Parameters can be as follows: &/R — do not reverse black and white &/B — print background color (color printers only) &/LCD — print image exactly as it appears on LCD display &/PB:identifier — identifier is either STD for standard screen or LCD for LCD screen &/PB:LCD is identical to /LCD.

IF

Location: Internal

Purpose: Used in batch files to cause a command to execute only if certain conditions are met.

Syntax: IF (NOT) *condition command*

Parameters: NOT is used to cause the command to execute only if the condition is not met.

condition can be one of the following:

1)   the existence of a file that is named in the batch file
2)   the existence of a file passed as a parameter
3)   a parameter matching a value that is specified in the batch file
4)   whether the previous command in the batch file terminated normally

command is any DOS command.

Comments: The IF command is discussed in detail in Chapter 5.

The IF command cannot be used in Shell programs.

Adding IF to a Shell menu:

The IF command can only be used in batch files. It has no purpose as a Shell menu choice.

KEYB

Location:	External and CONFIG.SYS
Purpose:	Defines a keyboard layout that corresponds to that used in a country other than the U.S.
Syntax:	KEYB *layout codepage filename* /ID: *identifier* KEYB *identifier* KEYB INSTALL = KEYB.COM ...
Parameters:	*layout* specifies the layout as defined in the following table.

codepage specifies the code page to use. Two code pages are available for each country. If *codepage* is not specified, the first code page listed in the following table is used.

filename is the name of the file that contains the keyboard definitions. If *filename* is omitted, KEYB looks in the root directory of the current drive for the file named KEYBOARD.SYS.

ID:*identifier* specifies an alternate keyboard for the country specified. In the following table, some countries have two keyboards available, and the first listed is used by default. Specifying the second with the ID:*identifier* will cause that keyboard to be used instead.

The following table specifies the values the various parameters can take for each country.

Country	Keyboard Layout	Code Pages	Identifier
Belgium	BE	850, 437	120
Canada (French speaking)	CF	863, 850	058
Denmark	DK	850, 865	159
Finland	SU	850, 437	153
France	FR	437, 850	120, 189
Germany	GR	437, 850	129
Italy	IT	437, 850	141, 142
Latin America	LA	437, 850	171
Netherlands	NL	437, 850	143
Norway	NO	850, 865	155
Portugal	PO	850, 860	163
Spain	SP	437, 850	172
Sweden	SV	437, 850	153
Switzerland (French speaking)	SF	850, 437	150
Switzerland (German speaking)	SG	850, 437	000
United Kingdom	UK	437, 850	168, 166
United States	US	437, 850	103

Comments: The INSTALL version of the command is used when the KEYB command is included in the CONFIG.SYS file.

When KEYB is entered without any parameters, the current alternate keyboard is displayed.

You can change the alternate keyboard by entering the KEYB command. When the alternate keyboard is in effect, pressing [Ctrl/F1] will switch to the U.S. keyboard; pressing [Ctrl/F2] will switch back to the alternate keyboard.

Example: KEYB FR,437 /ID:189 specifies the French keyboard layout, using code page 437 and keyboard ID 189.

Adding KEYB to a Shell menu:

Title: Change country keyboard layout

Commands: KEYB [/T"Keyboard Layout Change Screen"/I"Leave blank to display current country"/P"Enter country code: "]

Help text: Press the Return key to display the current alternate keyboard layout. The alternate keyboard layout can be installed or modified using the following parameters &layout codepage ID:identifier& Refer to a DOS reference manual for the various country codes.

LABEL

Location: External

Purpose: Defines a disk volume label. If a disk does not have a label, the LABEL command adds one. If the disk has a label, the LABEL command is used to change or delete the label.

Syntax: LABEL *drive label*

Parameters: *drive* is the drive containing the disk whose label will be defined. If the drive is not specified, the current drive is assumed.

label is the label that will be placed on the disk. The label can be from 1 to 11 characters. The same characters as used for file names can be used, but no period should be used to separate an extension. Spaces can also be used.

Comments: If no label is specified, a message similar to one of the following will appear:

```
Volume label in drive C is label
Volume Serial Number is 5A32-21E3
Volume label (11 characters, ENTER for none)?
Volume label in drive C has no label
Volume label (11 characters, ENTER for none)?
```

Adding LABEL to a Shell menu:

Title: Define a label for a disk

Commands: **LABEL [/T"Disk labelling screen"/I"Enter drive and up to 11 characters"/P"Drive and label: "]**

Help text: This program will create or change the label on a disk. The label can be up to 11 characters, and it can contain spaces but should not contain periods. The parameters should be as follows: &drive label.

LASTDRIVE

Location: CONFIG.SYS

Purpose: Defines the maximum number of drives that can be accessed.

Syntax: LASTDRIVE = *driveletter*

Parameters: *driveletter* is any alphabetic character from A to Z. Uppercase and lowercase letters are treated identically. This is the last drive letter that DOS will allow you to reference.

Comments: If no LASTDRIVE command is included in your CONFIG.SYS file, the default letter E is used.

  LASTDRIVE is helpful when you use the SUBST command; it determines the largest drive letter you can use when SUBST is in effect.

  The minimum drive letter you can specify is the last drive letter on your computer. If you specify a drive letter less than the last drive letter on your computer, the command will be ignored when CONFIG.SYS commands are executed.

Adding LASTDRIVE to a Shell menu:

Title: Set the maximum drive letter

Commands: **LASTDRIVE [/T"Set maximum drive letter"/I"Enter maximum drive letter"/P"Drive letter: "]**

Help text: This command program will define the maximum drive letter that DOS will allow you to reference. The letter can be anything from A to Z. It must be at least the largest letter on your computer.

MEM

Location: External

Purpose: Displays a report of the amount of memory used by the system, the contents of memory in use, and the amount of memory available for programs.

Syntax: MEM /PROGRAM /DEBUG

Parameters: /PROGRAM is used to list all programs currently in memory and the total amounts of memory in use and available in the system.

/DEBUG is used to list much more detailed information regarding the current contents of the system memory. This includes system device drivers, installed device drivers, all programs currently in memory, and the total amounts of memory in use and available in the computer.

Comments: Entering the MEM command without any parameters produces just a report of used and unused memory, as follows:

```
655360 bytes total memory
655360 bytes available
569504 largest executable program size

1703936 bytes total EMS memory
1703936 bytes free EMS memory

524288 bytes total extended memory
524288 bytes available extended memory
```

Following is an example of the result of entering the MEM command with either the /PROGRAM or /DEBUG parameter:

```
Address Name      Size      Type

000000            000400        InterruptVector
000400            000100        ROM Communication Area
000500            000200        DOS Communication Area

000700  IBMBIO    002130        System Program

002830  IBMDOS    008890        System Program

00B0C0  IBMBIO    006A00    System Data
        ANSI      001190      DEVICE=
                  0000C0      FILES=
                  0004B0      FCBS=
                  004410      BUFFERS=
                  0001C0      LASTDRIVE=
                  000CD0    STACKS=
011AD0  IBMDOS    000030      -- Free --
011B10  KBDRIV    000040      Environment
011B60  IBMDOS    000030      -- Free --
011B60  IBMDOS    000030      -- Free --
011BA0  FASTOPEN  0041B0      Program

655360 bytes total memory
655360 bytes available
302656 largest executable program size

      TIME = 18:43:14.23 DATE = Sun 10-16-1988
```

The MEM command with the /DEBUG parameter produces a report similar to that produced with /PROGRAM, only with a finer breakdown of the use of memory.

/PROGRAM and /DEBUG should not be used together.

Adding MEM to a Shell menu:

Title: Produce report of memory usage

Commands: **MEM [/T"Memory report screen"/I"Leave blank for brief report "/P"Memory parameters: "]**

Help text: This program produces a report of all memory usage. Use the /PROGRAM parameter for a more detailed report and /DEBUG for a highly detailed report.

MKDIR or MD

Location: Internal

Purpose: Creates a new subdirectory on the specified drive, under the specified directory.

Syntax: MKDIR *drive:path*
                   MD *drive:path*

Parameters: *drive* indicates the drive on which the new subdirectory should be created. If omitted, the current drive is used.

                   path is the complete path specification for the new subdirectory, including the new subdirectory name. If only the new subdirectory name is specified, the current directory is used.

Comments: The commands MKDIR and MD are functionally identical.

                   Naming subdirectories follows the same rules as naming files. The convention, however, is to omit extensions from subdirectory names.

                   The number of subdirectories that can exist on a disk is limited only by disk space. Each subdirectory created requires that 2048 bytes be free.

                   The complete path specification from the root directory to the subdirectory, including the backslash characters required to separate subdirectories, must not exceed 63 characters.

                   The Shell File System contains a function for creating new directories. It is easier to see exactly what you are doing in the Shell because you have a graphical representation of the disk directory structure.

Adding MKDIR to a Shell menu:

Title: Create a new subdirectory

Commands: **MKDIR [/T"Create new directory screen"/I"Enter the complete new directory path"/P"New directory path: "]**

Help text: This program will create a new subdirectory under an existing directory. If only the new directory name is specified, it will be created in the current directory.

MORE

Location: External

Purpose: Causes the screen display to pause whenever it fills up and waits for a key to be pressed before scrolling up the next screen of information.

Syntax: MORE < *filename*
command | MORE

Parameters: < *filename* causes the contents of the file *filename* to be displayed on the screen in the same way as the TYPE command, except that when the screen fills up MORE < *filename* pauses with the message "More" at the bottom of the screen. Pressing any key will cause the next screen to be displayed.

command | MORE causes the output of the command to be processed by MORE. This results in the display pausing when the screen fills up and the message "More" appearing at the bottom of the screen. Pressing any key will cause the next screen to be displayed.

Comments: An example of the first syntax is as follows:

MORE MYFILE.LET

This command will cause the contents of MYFILE.LET to appear on the screen. MYFILE.LET should be an ASCII text file.

An example of the second syntax is as follows:

DIR | MORE

This command will cause the screen to pause scrolling each time it fills up with directory information. The effect is similar to the /P parameter in the DIR command.

Adding MORE to a Shell menu with the first syntax:

Title: Display a file's contents:

Commands: **MORE < [/T"File viewing program"/I"Enter file name to display. "/P"Filename: "]**

Help text: This program will display the contents of a file on the screen, one screen at a time. If the file is not in the current directory, specify a complete path.

Adding MORE to a Shell menu with the second syntax:

Title: Pause command output between screens

Commands: **[/T"Command scrolling program"/I"Enter command to scroll."/P"Command:] | MORE**

Help text: This program will display the output from a DOS command one screen at a time, pausing between screens to wait for you to press a key.

PATH

Location: Internal

Purpose: Defines a set of directories in which DOS will search for executable files if they are not found in the current directory. Executable files are those that have extensions of .COM, .EXE, and .BAT. Also used to display the current path setting.

Syntax: PATH *path1*; *path2*; ....
PATH ;

Parameters: *path1*, *path2*, etc. are the directories to be searched. They should include the complete path starting from the root directory.

; (semicolon) removes all subdirectories from the path. DOS will only search the current directory for executable files.

Comments: PATH entered with no parameters will display the current path without changing it.

Each time a new path is specified, the previous path is removed, so to define multiple subdirectories as part of the path, you must include all of them in one PATH command.

If there is an error in a subdirectory specification, DOS will not detect the error until it attempts to access the directory.

If a subdirectory specified in the PATH command does not exist, DOS will ignore that directory and go on to the next one.

Adding PATH to a Shell menu:

Title: Set the current path

Commands: **PATH [/T"Set Current Path Program"/I"Leave blank to display current path"/P"Enter new path: "]**

Help text: The PATH is a set of subdirectories in which DOS will search for executable files if it does not find them in the current directory. Entering a semicolon for the parameter will remove all subdirectories from the path. Pressing the Return key with no parameters specified will display the current path.

PAUSE

Location: Internal

Purpose: The PAUSE command is used in batch files and Shell programs to suspend execution of the batch file or Shell program until a key is pressed.

Syntax: PAUSE *message*

Parameters: *message* is an optional message that will display when the program pauses. The message will only display if ECHO is ON and the PAUSE command itself is also displayed.

Comments: PAUSE is useful in batch files and Shell programs, especially in conjunction with the ECHO command when it is used to display a message instructing the user to perform some action. PAUSE allows the user to read the message before the program continues executing.

When the PAUSE command executes, it suspends the execution of the batch file or Shell program and displays the "Press any key to continue..." message.

Adding PAUSE to a Shell menu:

The PAUSE command is useful only in batch files and Shell programs. It would serve no purpose as a Shell menu option.

PRINT

Location: External

Purpose: Used to establish and manipulate a print queue for printing one or more files while you continue to use the computer for other purposes.

Syntax: PRINT /D:*device* /Q:*num* /B:*size* /S:*timeslice* /U:*busy* /M:*max filespec1* /C /T /P *filespec2* /C /T /P ...

Parameters: These parameters are described in detail in Chapter 4.

Comments: The PRINT command is discussed in detail in Chapter 4.

Adding PRINT to a Shell menu:

Adding a PRINT option to the Shell menu is discussed in Chapter 4.

PROMPT

Location: Internal

Purpose: Defines the format of the DOS prompt.

Syntax: PROMPT *text*
PROMPT

Parameters: *text* can be constructed of regular text and parameters. The text and parameters can be intermixed as much as you want, though the entire command cannot exceed the DOS limit of 128 characters.

Comments: When PROMPT is entered with no parameters, the DOS prompt is reset to its default, which shows the current drive followed by a greater than sign (>).

The prompt is what appears on the DOS command line when you exit the Shell either via a permanent exit (exiting from the Main Group Menu Bar or pressing F3 to exit the Shell) or a temporary exit (exiting from the Command Prompt in the Main Group or pressing [Shift/F9] to go to the Command Prompt).

The parameters that can be interspersed with text are as follows:

$$	includes a $ in the prompt
$t	includes the current time in the prompt
$d	includes the current date in the prompt
$p	includes the current directory of the current drive in the prompt
$v	includes the DOS version number in the prompt
$n	includes the default drive letter in the prompt
$g	includes the greater than sign (>) in the prompt
$l	includes the less than sign (<) in the prompt
$b	includes the bar symbol (	) in the prompt
$q	includes the equal sign (=) in the prompt
$h	inserts a backspace into the prompt, deleting the character immediately preceding the backspace
$e	includes the Escape character in the prompt; this can be used to send commands to the ANSI.SYS device driver
$_	includes a Carriage Return/Line Feed sequence in the prompt, allowing you to develop multi-line prompts

The PROMPT command is discussed in detail in Chapter 4.

Adding PROMPT to a Shell menu:

Title: Define Command Prompt

Commands: **PROMPT [/T"Command Prompt Definition"/I"Leave blank to set to default"/P"Enter new prompt: "]**

Help text: This program is used to define the format of the Command Prompt, which is what prompts you to enter commands when you exit the Shell. If you are not familiar with the PROMPT parameters, refer to a DOS reference manual.

RECOVER

Location: External

Purpose: Helps in recovering files that occupy a bad disk sector. Also useful in recovering all the files on a disk that has a damaged directory.

Syntax:　　　RECOVER *filespec*
　　　　　　　　RECOVER *drive*

Parameters:　*filespec* is a file identifier that indicates which file to attempt to recover; it can include a drive and path specification. If no drive or path is specified, the default drive and path are assumed.

　　　　　　　　drive is a drive that contains a disk with a damaged directory.

Comments:　If a file contains a bad disk sector, using RECOVER on the file will recover all of the data in the file except that which occurs in the bad sector. For this reason, nontext files (e.g., program files) are not good candidates for using RECOVER because you have no means of restoring the missing part of the file.

The same is true of spreadsheet files and database files because the missing data will probably make at least the last part of the file unreadable by the database or spreadsheet program. However, you may be able to see what the data is and reenter it.

When a file is recovered, DOS often includes some extra information at the end of the file because DOS recovers complete allocation units, even if the end of the file does not occupy a complete allocation unit.

You cannot recover in one operation more files than will fit in the root directory of the disk. On double-sided floppy disks, this limit is 112 files. If the total number of files being recovered exceeds 112, you must enter multiple RECOVER commands. After the first RECOVER operation, copy the files you want to keep to a new disk and delete them from the damaged disk. Then issue the next RECOVER command, until all damaged files have been recovered.

The form RECOVER *drive* should only be used if the disk directory has become unusable. DOS will then ignore all information in the directory and attempt to recover everything on the disk. This is done by determining what allocation units belong together to make a file and then copying those allocation units into a file named FILE*xxxx*.REC, where *xxxx* is a sequential number starting with 00001. Each .REC file represents one recovered file.

RECOVER is not a "miracle program," and it will not necessarily produce useful files. It should be used only in extreme situations where there is no other choice for recovering files.

Adding RECOVER to a Shell menu:

Title:	File and disk recovery
Commands:	**RECOVER [/T"Recover a damaged file or disk"/I"Enter the filename or drive to recover"/P"File or drive: "]**
Help text:	This program is used to recover data from a file that has a bad disk sector in it or from a disk that has a bad directory. Enter a filename, which can include a drive and path, to recover an individual file. Enter a drive designator to recover all the files on a disk with a bad directory.

REM

Location:	Batch files and CONFIG.SYS
Purpose:	Used to include lines in batch files and in the CONFIG.SYS file that DOS does not attempt to execute but that contain information helpful to someone reading the file.
Syntax:	REM *comment* REM
Parameters:	*comment* is any text message up to 123 characters long that explains some aspect of the commands in the file.
Comments:	Using REM by itself helps to space out the lines in a batch file or CONFIG.SYS file, making them easier to read. If ECHO is ON, the entire REM line, including the letters REM, will be displayed when DOS encounters the line in a batch file. If ECHO is OFF, the REM lines do not appear on the screen.

Adding REM to a Shell menu:

REM only has meaning in the context of a batch file or a CONFIG.SYS file; it is therefore not useful as a Shell menu option.

RENAME or REN

Location: Internal

Purpose: Changes the name(s) of one or more files.

Syntax: RENAME *oldname newname*
REN *oldname newname*

Parameters: *oldname* is the name of the file being renamed.

newname is the new name of the file being renamed.

Comments: If a file named *newname* already exists, DOS will display a message and terminate the command without changing the filename.

There are two ways in which wild card symbols can be used. The first is to change only the name or only the extension of a file. For example, the command

REN TEST.BAT *.TMP

will rename the file TEST.BAT to TEST.TMP.

The second way in which wild cards can be used is to rename a set of files by replacing only certain letters of their names. For example, the files TEST1.BAT, TEST2.BAT, and TEMPEST.BAT could be renamed with the command

REN T*.BAT XY*.BAT.

This command renames the three files as XYST1.BAT, XYST2.BAT, and XYMPEST.BAT. In other words, the number of letters replaced is defined by the number of letters in the new filename.

The Shell File System provides better methods for renaming files.

Adding RENAME to a Shell menu:

Title: Rename one or more disk files

Commands: **REN [/T"Rename files program"/I"Enter old name followed by new name"/P"Old and new names: "]**

Help text: This program is used to rename one or more files. Wild cards are allowed but must be used carefully to achieve the desired results.

REPLACE

Location: External

Purpose: Used to copy files from one disk to another, choosing files based on one or more of several selection criteria as discussed next.

Syntax: REPLACE *source target* /P /R /W /S /U /A

Parameters: *source* is the file specifier of the files to be copied; it can include the * wild card. A drive and path specifier can also be included.

target is the target drive to copy to. Target filenames are not allowed because the files will be given the same name as they have on the source drive.

/P causes DOS to prompt you before copying any files that match the specified criteria. This allows you to perform a file-by-file replacement of old files or addition of new files.

/R causes DOS to replace files on the target that have the read-only attribute set on. If /R is not specified, read-only files will not be replaced.

/W causes DOS to wait for you to insert a floppy disk into the source drive before it starts to search for the files.

/S causes DOS to search subdirectories of the target disk, as well as the current directory, to locate files that match the source file-name.

/U causes DOS to replace files on the target disk if the date and time on the source disk are more current.

/A causes DOS to copy all specified files on the source that do not exist on the target. This parameter is used to add files to the target without overwriting existing files. /A cannot be used if /S or /U is used.

Comments: If /W is not specified, the REPLACE operation will begin as soon as you press the Return key.

Hidden and system files will not be found on the source and therefore will not be copied to the target.

The REPLACE command returns an error code when it has finished executing. The most common codes are as follows:

Return Code	Cause	Description
2	File not found	No source files exist
3	Path not found	The source path does not exist
5	Access denied	/R should be specified
8	Insufficient memory	REPLACE requires more memory than is available
11	Invalid format	REPLACE command was not entered correctly
15	Invalid drive	A specified drive does not exist
22	Unknown command	The version of DOS being used does not support REPLACE

Adding REPLACE to a Shell menu:

Title: Selectively copy files

Commands: **REPLACE [/T"Selective copy program"/I"Enter the file specifiers and parameters"/P"Enter parameters: "]**

Help text: This program is used to selectively replace files, based on whether the source files already exist on the target and which copy of the files is most current. If you are not familiar with the DOS REPLACE command, refer to a DOS manual for legal parameters.

RESTORE

Location: External

Purpose: Restores files that have been backed up with the BACKUP command.

Syntax: RESTORE *source target filename* /P /M /S /B:*mm-dd-yy*/A:*mm-dd-yy* /E:*hh:mm.s* /L:*hh:mm:.s* /N

Parameters: *source* is the drive that contains the disk that was backed up with the BACKUP command.

target is the drive that the backed up file(s) should be restored to.

filename is used to restore only certain files. A drive and path specifier, as well as wild cards, can be included. If no filename is used, the default *.* is used.

When /P is used, the computer pauses before restoring a file that has been modified since the last backup or has the read-only attribute set on. This protects against replacing a recent version of a file with an older version.

/M is used to restore files that have been modified or deleted since they were last backed up. This allows you to recover an earlier version of a file if the current version has been modified in a way that you don't like.

/S restores files in the subdirectories as well as in the current directory.

/B:*mm-dd-yy* restores all files modified on or before the date specified by *mm-dd-yy*.

/A:*mm-dd-yy* restores all files modified on or after the date specified by *mm-dd-yy*.

/E:*hh:mm.s* restores all files modified at or after the time specified by *hh:mm.s.* If /E is used with/B, then files are restored only if they were modified at or before the specified time on or before the specified date.

/L:*hh:mm.s* restores all files modified at or later than the time specified by *hh:mm.s* If /L is used with /A, then only files modified at or later than the time specified and on or after the date specified are restored.

/N is used to restore only files that do not exist on the target. This situation could result when you are restoring to a disk other than the one that was backed up or when the file has been deleted from the disk.

Comments:　　RESTORE only works with files created with the BACKUP command. The system files cannot be restored, so RESTORE cannot be used to create a system disk. If you want to create a boot disk, you should use the SYS command to transfer the system files, or format the disk with the /S parameter before using RESTORE. RESTORE will then transfer the rest of the files, and you will have a boot disk that contains the files you want.

The filename can contain drive and path specifiers. If a path is specified, a filename must also be specified.

You must RESTORE files to the same directory from which they were backed up. Attempting to restore to a different directory will result in an error message.

When you start RESTORE, you will be prompted to put the disk containing the file(s) to be restored in the source drive. If you are restoring all of the files that were backed up, this disk should be disk 1. RESTORE will prompt you to insert subsequent disks. If you are restoring only one file or a set of files and know which disk they start with, you can immediately put that disk in the source drive. If you are not sure which disk they start with, put disk 1 in the drive. RESTORE will let you know if the file(s) requested is not there, and you can then put in disk 2, and so on.

The RESTORE command sets an Exit code that can be accessed by the Batch command IF ERROR LEVEL .... The Exit code is set according to the following table:

Exit code   **Meaning**

Exit code	Meaning
0	The RESTORE completed normally.
1	There were no files found to restore.
2	Some of the specified files were not restored due to file-sharing conflicts on a network.
3	The RESTORE operation was terminated by the user pressing the [Ctrl/Break] keys.
4	The RESTORE operation terminated due to an error.

The DOS Utilities group that comes with the Shell includes Backup and Restore options that use these two DOS commands. If you want to have the RESTORE command available on another menu, you could use the following setup.

Shell setup for RESTORE:

Title: Restore files that were backed up with BACKUP

Commands: RESTORE [/T"RESTORE parameters"/I"Enter the RESTORE parameters"/P"Enter parameters: "]

Help text: This program is used to restore files created with the BACKUP command. The parameters are as follows: &SOURCETARGET filename /P /M /S /A /B:mm-dd-yy /A:hh:mm.s/E:hh:mm.s /L:hh:mm.s. /N &If you are not familiar with the RESTORE command, refer to a DOS reference manual.

RMDIR or RD

Location: Internal

Purpose: Removes directories from a disk. Only directories that contain no files can be removed.

Syntax: RMDIR *drive:path*
             RD *drive:path*

Parameters: *drive* is the drive that contains the directory to be removed.

             path is the path from the current directory or from the root directory to the directory being removed.

Comments: The root directory cannot be removed. A directory cannot be removed if it is the current directory.

             The Shell File System includes the ability to remove directories.

Adding RMDIR to a Shell menu:

Title: Remove a directory

Commands: **RD [/T"Remove Directory Program"/I"Only empty directories may be removed."/P"Directory: "]**

Help text: This program is used to delete directories. Only empty directories can be removed, and the directory being removed must not be the current directory.

SELECT

Location: External

Purpose: Used to install DOS 4.0 on a computer.

Syntax: Should not be used from the command line. SELECT should only be used by booting the computer with the DOS 4.0 startup disk.

Parameters: none

Comments: Refer to Chapter 1 for more information.

Adding SELECT to a Shell menu:

You should not attempt to execute SELECT from within the Shell.

SET

Location: Internal

Purpose: Creates variables that contain text strings. These variables are stored in the DOS environment and are therefore available to all programs, including batch files.

Syntax: SET *variable* = *value*
SET *variable* =
SET

Parameters: *variable* is the variable being created.

value is the string that is assigned to the variable.

Comments: Variables defined with the SET command can be accessed by batch files in the same manner as %*x* parameters. For example, the command SET PW=XYZ will cause the characters XYZ to be substituted for %PW% in a batch file.

There is only a limited amount of memory reserved for the DOS environment. If there is not enough environment memory available for the variables you are defining, DOS will display an error message.

Entering SET *variable* = with no value will remove the variable from memory. This will free up memory for other variables.

Entering SET with no parameters will display all of the current environment variables.

Adding SET to a Shell menu:

Title: Create an environment variable

Commands: **SET [/T"Create environment variable "/I"Leave blank
to display current variables"/P"Enter parameters: "]**

Help text: The SET command is used to place a variable that contains a
text string in the DOS environment. These variables are then
available to programs and batch files. The parameters should
consist of a variable name and a value, as follows:
&variable=value &Entering just a variable name will remove the
variable from the environment. Entering no parameters will
display the current variables.

SHIFT

Location: Internal

Purpose: Used in batch files to access more than ten parameters.

Syntax: SHIFT

Parameters: None

Comments: Each time a SHIFT command is encountered, the number of each parameter in a batch file is decreased by 1. The first parameter (%0) is dropped and an additional parameter can then be used. The following command demonstrates this concept. TEST is the name of the batch file being executed, and *parm1, parm2*, etc. are the parameters being passed to the file:

TEST *parm1 parm2 parm3 parm4 parm5 parm6 parm7 parm8 parm9 parm10*

Within the file TEST, %0 refers to the batch filename (TEST), %1 refers to *parm1*, and so on. The largest parameter reference is %9, which refers to *parm9*. To reference *parm10*, the SHIFT command is used once. It will cause %0 to reference *parm1*, %1 to reference *parm2*, and so on. %9 will therefore reference *parm10*.

SHIFT can be used as many times as you want within a batch file. The only drawback to it is that each time it is used, the lowest parameter is lost.

SHIFT can only be used in batch files. There is no need for it in Shell programs because the limit on the number of parameters is set only by the number of characters that can be included in a Shell program.

Adding SHIFT to a Shell menu:

SHIFT is for use in batch files only. It does not function as a Shell menu option.

SORT

Location: External

Purpose: Used to sort lines in files and the output of DOS commands.

Syntax: SORT /R / +*col* < *filename*
command | SORT /R / +*col*

Parameters: /R is an optional parameter that causes sorting to occur in reverse order.

/+*col* is an optional parameter that causes sorting to be done based on the characters starting in the column *col*.

<*filename* is a file whose contents will be sorted. It is preceded by a less than sign. The filename can include drive and path specifiers. The output will appear on the screen.

command is a DOS command whose output will be sorted. For example, the command DIR | SORT will create a directory listing that is sorted alphabetically.

Comments: Only ASCII text files should be sorted.

For characters in the first half of the ASCII table (characters 0 through 127), all sorting is done in the order in which characters appear in the ASCII table, except that the sorting is not case sensitive — the letter a is equivalent to the letter A.

For characters greater than 127 in the ASCII table, the sort order is determined by the country code currently in use.

If you want the output to go somewhere other than the screen, you can specify the output device with a greater than sign and the destination following the SORT command. For example,

SORT /R /+*col* <*filename* >*outfile*

will create a sorted copy of *filename* in *outfile*. *Outfile* refers to a device or filename that will receive the output. For example, if *outfile* is PRN:, then the output will appear on the printer. If *outfile* is NEWFILE.TST, then the output will be placed in a file named NEWFILE.TST.

Adding SORT to a Shell menu (for sorting a file's contents):

Title: SORT a file's contents

Commands: SORT < [/T"Sort program"/I"Use /R to sort in reverse order"/P"Enter filename: "]

Help text: This program produces a sorted copy of the file specified. If
you want the sort to be reversed, specify /R after the filename.
If you want the sort to start in a column other than the first
column, specify /+*col* after the filename. Uppercase and
lowercase letters are treated equally.

Adding SORT to a Shell menu (for sorting the output of a DOS command):

Title: SORT a DOS command's output

Commands: [/T"DOS command for sorted output"/I"Enter the DOS
command"/P"Command: "] | SORT [/T"Sorted output
parameters screen"/I"Enter parameters"/P"Parameters: "]

Help text: This program uses two dialogue boxes: the first is for a DOS
command whose output will be sorted, and the second is for the
sort parameters. Parameters can be /R for a reverse order sort
and +*col* to start the sort with column number *col*.

SUBST

Location: External

Purpose: Used to substitute a drive letter for a path. It is useful for
programs that do not recognize paths but do recognize drive
letters.

Syntax: SUBST *newdrive olddrive:path*
SUBST *drive* /D

Parameters: *newdrive* is the drive letter that will be used to refer to the
old drive and path.

olddrive:path is the path being substituted with the *newdrive*
letter. You can use just a path if /D is used to delete the
substituted drive letter specified by *drive*.

Comments: Entering SUBST with no parameters will display all current
substitutions.

You can only specify drive letters less than or equal to the drive letter specified in CONFIG.SYS with the LASTDRIVE command. If LASTDRIVE is not included in CONFIG.SYS, then the largest drive letter you can use is E. The new drive letter cannot be the current drive.

The substituted drive letter can be used in place of the drive and path that it is replacing.

You should not use any of the following commands when a substitution is in place:

ASSIGN, BACKUP, DISKCOMP, DISKCOPY, FDISK, FORMAT, LABEL, and RESTORE

Be very careful and test the effects before using the following commands when a substitution is in place:

CHDIR, MKDIR, RMDIR, and PATH

If you have a very long subdirectory path that you reference frequently, using SUBST to substitute a drive letter for the path can save a lot of typing.

If you want to replace an entire drive letter with another drive letter, you should use the ASSIGN command. SUBST is intended for substituting drive letters for subdirectory references.

Adding SUBST to a Shell menu:

Title: Substitute drive letter for path

Commands: **SUBST [/T"Path reference substitution"/I"Leave blank to see substitutions"/P"Enter parameters: "]**

Help text: This program is used to substitute a drive letter for a path. It provides a shorthand notation for a long path and for programs that do not recognize paths but do recognize drive letters. Enter the new drive letter first, followed by the old drive letter.

SWITCHES

Location:	CONFIG.SYS
Purpose:	Causes an enhanced keyboard to behave like a conventional keyboard.
Syntax:	SWITCHES = /K
Parameters:	Causes DOS to behave as though a conventional keyboard is installed when an enhanced keyboard is actually installed.
Comments:	Some applications do not run properly when an enhanced keyboard is installed. SWITCHES will allow you to run these applications with an enhanced keyboard.

Adding SWITCHES to a Shell menu:

SWITCHES is a configuration command. It can only be executed from within the CONFIG.SYS file and therefore cannot be included in a Shell menu.

SYS

Location:	External
Purpose:	Used to transfer the hidden system files to a disk.
Syntax:	SYS *drive*
Parameters:	*drive* is the drive that the files will be transferred to.
Comments:	Transferring the hidden system files to a disk, as well as to the COMMAND.COM file, makes the disk a bootable disk.

SYS can move files that already exist on your disk. To be safe, back up your disk before transferring the system files.

SYS can be used on a disk that has been formatted without the /S or /B parameters, as long as the disk is blank. It can be used to transfer files to a disk that has been formatted with the /B parameter at any time because /B reserves the space for the system files and does not let other files occupy that space.

Adding SYS to a Shell menu:

Title: Transfer hidden system files to a disk

Commands: **SYS [/T"System file transfer"/I"Enter the drive to transfer files to"/P"Drive: "]**

Help text: This program transfers the hidden system files to a disk to make it a bootable disk. The disk must not have any files on it unless it was formatted with the /B parameter.

TIME

Location: Internal

Purpose: Sets the time that is stored in the internal clock.

Syntax: TIME *hh:mm:ss.hs*
                    TIME

Parameters: *hh* stands for the hour (1-12 or 1-24)
                    mm stands for the minute (1-59)
                    ss stands for the second (1-59)
                    hs stands for the hundredth second (1-99)

Comments: You can specify only as much of the time as you feel is important. Entering TIME 9 will set the time to 9:00.

If you type an incorrect time, DOS will display the message

```
Invalid time
Enter new time
```

If you press the Return key at this point, the time will be left unchanged.

Entering TIME with no parameters causes DOS to display the current time.

The Shell DOS Utilities group provides a menu selection for setting the date and time.

Adding TIME to a Shell menu:

Title: Set the computer's internal time

Commands: **TIME [/T"Set the computer's time"/I"Leave blank to display current time"/P"Enter hh:mm:ss.hs:"]**

Help text: This choice will set the computer's time, which appears in the upper right corner of the Shell screen. It is also used for time stamping the creation or modification of files.

TREE

Location: External

Purpose: Used to display a directory, its subdirectories, and the files contained in them.

Syntax: TREE *drive:path* /F /A

Parameters: *drive* is the drive on which the directory exists.

                 path is the path to the subdirectory to be displayed.

                 /F causes the files as well as subdirectories to be displayed.

                 /A uses graphics characters when displaying the tree.

Comments: To show the complete directory of the entire disk, specify the root directory.

                 Directory trees almost always fill up more than one screen. To cause the display to pause, you can use the MORE command or press [Ctrl/S].

The Shell File System is more powerful and useful for viewing and manipulating directories and files.

Adding TREE to a Shell menu:

Title: Display a directory tree

Commands: **TREE [/T"Directory tree program"/I"Leave blank for current directory tree"/P"Enter directory: "]**

Help text: This program is used for displaying a directory tree, similar to the one in the Shell File System. Enter the drive and path specifier for the directory you would like to see. /F will display filenames as well as subdirectories. /A will cause a graphics character set to be used.

TYPE

Location: Internal

Purpose: Prints the contents of a file on the screen.

Syntax: TYPE *filename*

Parameters: *filename* is the name of the file to be typed on the screen. It can contain a drive and path specifier but cannot contain wild card symbols.

Comments: TYPE is useful for reviewing the contents of text files. It is similar to the Shell File System View option. It is not useful for nontext files because it interprets them as ASCII codes and does not have a Hex mode, as does the Shell File System View option.

Adding TYPE to a Shell menu:

Title: Print a text file on the screen

Commands: **TYPE [/T"Print a text file on the screen"/I"Enter the file name to display"/P"Filename: "]**

Help text: This program will display the contents of a text file on the screen. Enter the filename. You can use a drive and path specifier but wild cards cannot be used.

VER

Location: Internal

Purpose: Displays the version of DOS that is being used.

Syntax: VER

Parameters: None

Comments: The version is displayed as a single digit before a period and two digits after, indicating major and minor versions.

Adding VER to a Shell menu:

Title: Display DOS Version

Commands: VER

Help text: This program displays the version of DOS that you are using.

VERIFY

Location: Internal

Purpose: Causes DOS to verify all disk write operations.

Syntax: VERIFY ON
VERIFY OFF
VERIFY

Parameters: ON causes DOS to perform a verification after every disk write operation.

OFF causes DOS to not verify disk write operations. The default value is OFF.

Comments: Entering VERIFY with no parameters displays the current status of VERIFY.

Disk write errors are rare, so generally it is unnecessary to have VERIFY set ON. VERIFY will significantly slow down your computer's performance because verification is a slow process; however, if highly critical data is being written, it may be worth the extra time.

Adding VERIFY to a Shell menu:

Title: Turn on Write Verification

Commands: VERIFY [/T"Turn on Write Verification"/I"Enter ON or Off; default is OFF"/P"On or off: "]

Help text: This program will instruct DOS to verify all information written to disks, which will slow down the computer and is usually unnecessary, but for highly critical data you may want to turn it on. Entering no parameters will display the current status of VERIFY.

VOL

Location: Internal

Purpose: Displays the volume label and serial number (if there is one) of the specified disk.

Syntax: VOL *drive*

Parameters: *drive* is the drive that contains the disk whose label will be displayed.

Comments: If no drive is entered, the volume label of the current drive is displayed.

Adding VOL to a Shell menu:

Title: Display a disk volume label

Commands:	VOL [/T"Display a disk volume label"/I"Enter the drive "/P"Drive: "]

Help text:	This program displays the volume label and serial number, if there is one, of the disk in the specified drive. If no parameter is entered, the volume label of the current drive is shown.

VDISK.SYS

Location:	CONFIG.SYS
Purpose:	Creates a virtual disk drive in memory.
Syntax:	DEVICE = VDISK.SYS KB *sector-size files* /E:*m* /X:*m*
Parameters:	KB is the size of the virtual disk.

sector-size is the number of bytes per sector on the virtual disk. It must be one of the following: 128, 256, or 512. If no sector-size is specified, the default of 128 is used.

files specifies the maximum number of files that can be stored on the virtual disk. The number can be anywhere from 2 through 512. If no file number is specified, the default of 64 is used.

/E:*m* is used to put the virtual disk in extended memory. This leaves low memory available for conventional applications. The *m* parameter specifies the maximum number of sectors that VDISK will transfer at one time.

/X:*m* is used to put the virtual disk in expanded memory. This leaves low memory available for conventional applications. The *m* parameter specifies the maximum number of sectors that VDISK will transfer at one time.

Comments: Virtual disks are used to speed up system performance. Because they exist entirely in memory, they eliminate physical disk accesses. They are best used for overlay files, spelling and thesaurus dictionaries, and other such files that programs must access during routine operations. It is not a good idea to use them for data files because they are lost if a power failure occurs or if you reboot your computer.

Adding VDISK to a Shell menu:

VDISK is a configuration command. It can only be executed from within the CONFIG.SYS file and therefore cannot be included in a Shell menu.

XCOPY

Location: External

Purpose: Used to copy groups of files, including those in subdirectories.

Syntax: XCOPY *source target* /P /D:*mm-dd-yy* /W /S /E /V /M /A

Parameters: *source* is the set of files to copy. It can contain a drive and path specifier and wild cards.

target is the path to copy to. It can contain a drive and path specifier and wild cards.

/P causes XCOPY to prompt you with a "(Y/N)?" before copying each file.

/D:*mm-dd-yy* copies files whose creation or last modification date is on or after the date specified. The date format will depend on the country code; the format shown above is for the U.S.

/W causes XCOPY to wait while you insert disks into the source drive.

/S specifies that subdirectories should be copied in addition to the specified or current directory. If /S is not included, only the files in the specified or current directory are copied. If /S is included, any subdirectories that do not exist on the target will be created, as long as they are not empty subdirectories on the source.

/E tells XCOPY to create subdirectories on the target even if they are empty.

/V turns on write verification for the XCOPY operation. This will slow down the copy process considerably due to the extra work involved in verifying that each file is written properly to the disk. Because write errors are rare, /V is usually unnecessary. However, if your data is highly critical, you may want to use it as a safeguard.

/M is used to copy only those files that have the archive attribute set on. These are files that have been created or modified since the last BACKUP command or XCOPY /M command. /M is useful if XCOPY is used for backing up files. When /M is specified, XCOPY sets the archive attribute off after the copy is completed.

/A is used to copy only those files that have the archive attribute set on. These are files that have been created or modified since the last BACKUP command or XCOPY /M command. /A is useful if XCOPY is used for backing up files. When /A is specified, XCOPY does not change the archive attribute of the file.

Comments: If no drive is specified, XCOPY starts with the current directory. If no filename is specified, XCOPY assumes the *.* specification. XCOPY does not copy hidden files.

You can rename files with the XCOPY command in the same ways you can rename them with the COPY command.

XCOPY cannot copy a file larger than the target disk. If you need to do this, you should use the BACKUP command. However, files created with XCOPY are standard DOS files so they can be used without a RESTORE operation.

The Shell File System has options that perform the same function as XCOPY and are easier to use.

Adding XCOPY to a Shell menu:

Title: Copy multiple files and directories

Commands: **XCOPY [/T"Copy multiple files and directories"/I"Enter the source path and parameters"/P"Enter parameters: "]**

Help text: This program is used to copy sets of files, including subdirectories. If you are not familiar with the XCOPY command, refer to the DOS reference manual.

DOS COMMANDS THAT RETURN EXIT CODES

BACKUP

Exit Code	Meaning
0	BACKUP ended normally.
1	There were no files that matched the file specification on the BACKUP command line.
2	The BACKUP was on networked files, and some of them could not be backed up due to file-sharing conflicts.
3	BACKUP was interrupted by the user pressing [Ctrl/Break].
4	An error caused BACKUP to terminate.

FORMAT

Exit Code	Meaning
0	FORMAT ended normally.
1	Undefined
2	Undefined
3	FORMAT was interrupted by the user pressing [Ctrl/Break].
4	An error caused FORMAT to terminate.
5	Disk specified for formatting was a fixed disk, and user responded with "N" when DOS asked whether user wanted to format the fixed disk.

REPLACE

Exit Code	Meaning
2	There were no files that matched the file specification on the REPLACE command line.
3	REPLACE could not locate either the source path or target path.
5	The read-only attribute on the files is set on; this can be corrected by running REPLACE with the /R parameter.
8	There is not enough memory available to run REPLACE.
11	There was an error in the syntax of the REPLACE command line.
15	Either the source and target drives were the same or one of the specified drives does not exist.

22   The version of DOS that is running on the computer is not the same as the REPLACE program version.

RESTORE

Exit Code	Meaning
0	Restore ended normally.
1	There were no files that matched the file specification on the RESTORE command line.
2	The RESTORE was on networked files, and some of them could not be restored due to file-sharing conflicts.
3	RESTORE was interrupted by the user pressing [Ctrl/Break].
4	An error caused RESTORE to terminate.

/ (forward slash), 140
/# command, 124
/@ command, 124
& (ampersand), 274
\ (backslash), 38
$ (dollar sign), 161, 188
% (percent sign), 119-122, 230
@ command, 275
@@ sign in ECHO commands, 242
[] (square brackets), 111, 126

A

action bar. *See* menu bar
Add Group dialogue box, 133
Add Group option (Group menu),
    132-135
  using to restore deleted group, 136
Add Program dialogue box, 104
Add Program option (Program menu),
    102-127
  Command line, 108-110
  Help screens, 106
  Password line, 106-107
  Title line, 105
Alt/F1, 33
American Standard Code for Information
    Interchange. *See* ASCII
ampersand (&), 274
ANSI.SYS device driver, 8, 171
APPEND command, 16, 203-205, 275-277
Archive attribute, 61
Arrange menu, 39, 72-75
  Multiple File List option, 73
  Single File List option, 72
  System File List option, 74-75
arrow keys, 30. *See also* scrolling
ASCII format, 62, 179-187
  vs. hexadecimal format, 64-65
ASSIGN command, 205-206, 277-278
Associate option (File menu), 44-47
asterisk (*) as wild card symbol, 39, 40, 67
ATTRIB command, 278-280
attributes, 59-61
AUTOEXEC.BAT file, 20-22, 156, 256,
    258-259, 263, 267
  customizing PRINT command in, 51

AUTOEXEC.4xx file, 16, 20-21

B

/B: option, 146-147
Back Up Fixed Disk utility, 84-85
backslash (\), 38
BACKUP command, 280-283, 358
backwards compatibility, 3
base driver, 145
.BAT filename extension, 5, 6, 222
batch files, 6, 125, 222-223
  calling from the Shell, 254
  calling from within, 232-248
  calling the Shell from, 254
  conditional execution of, 234-239
  creating, 224-227
  displaying messages in, 227-228
  ECHO commands in, 124, 227-228, 242
  FOR statements in, 244-248
  GOTO statements in, 242-243
  halting execution of, 234
  IF statements in, 234-239
  making transparent, 242
  passing parameters to, 229-231
  PAUSE commands in, 124, 227-229
  in Program Startup Command lists, 125
  suspending execution of, 227-229
  that call other batch files, 249-253
  that call themselves, 232-248
  vs. .MEU files, 125-126
  vs. Shell programs, 223
batch programs. *See* batch files
bits, 3
bootable disks, creating, 91, 94
booting DOS 4.0
  from fixed disk, 4, 21
  with floppy boot disk, 13, 21-22
brackets, square ([]), 111, 126
branching. *See* GOTO command
BREAK command, 283-284
buffers, 143, 146-147, 209-211. *See also*
    print queue
BUFFERS command, 210-211, 284-285
  modifying, 211-213
bytes, 3

C

CALL command, 250-251, 256, 285-287
capacity of disks, 4-5
CD command, 287-288
central processor unit (CPU), 2-3
CGA adapter, 151
Change Attribute option (File Menu), 59-61
Change Colors option (Main Group menu), 75-76, 144, 152
Change Group option (Group menu), 135
Change Program option (Program menu), 129
CHDIR command, 287-288
chips, 2-3
CHKDSK command, 288-291
CLS command, 291
/COLOR option, 144
color setups, 75-76, 144, 152
.COM filename extension, 5, 6
Command line, 108-110. *See also* Program Startup Commands
Command Prompt (Main Group menu), 23, 24, 34, 35, 207, 254.
    See also DOS prompt
    activating (/PROMPT), 142
    Help screen for, 31-32
COMMAND.COM file, 206-208
commands
    configuration commands, 208-219
    DOS commands, 274-359
    DOS environment commands, 155-206
    Program Startup Commands, 108-127
COMP command, 291-293
comparing disks using Diskcomp utility, 82-84
compatibility, 3
computer files. *See* files
computers, parts of, 2-5
conditional processing, 223, 234-239
CONFIG.SYS file, 20-22, 156, 208, 213, 215, 217-219, 274-275
configuration commands, 208-219
Configuration Parameters screen, 79
CONFIG.4xx file, 20-21
confirmation boxes, eliminating, 68-69

Control/Break, 234
Control/Z, 224, 225
COPY command, 293-296
COPY CON: command, 224-225
Copy File option (File menu), 54-56, 79
Copy Program option (Program menu), 130-131
copying
    disks using Diskcopy utility, 79-81
    files
        using File menu, 54-56
        using Program menu, 130-131
    groups to other computers, 136-137
    programs between menus, 130-131
country, 213-216
    selecting, 11
COUNTRY command, 213-214, 296-298
CPU, 2-3
Create Directory option (File menu), 65
creating bootable disks, 91, 94
creating directories using File Menu, 65
current drive, 123, 165
cursor, 30
    overwrite mode vs. insert mode, 105
    positioning using escape sequences, 172-174
CYCLE.FIL file, 257, 259, 263, 268

D

data files, 6
date, 77-78, 158-159
    in File List, 40
    including in DOS prompt, 166
DATE command, 158-159, 298-300
/DATE option, 144
default directory, 12-13
default settings, 69
default values, 116-117
    automatic clearing of (/R), 117, 127
    displaying (/D), 116-117, 127
DEL command, 300-301
Delete File option (File menu), 56-58
Delete Group option (Group menu), 135
    restoring deleted groups, 136
Delete Program option (Program menu), 130

titles for parameters (/T), 113-126
titling disks. ISeeJ volume label
tracks, 208, 209
    formatting sectors per track, 96, 97
/TRAN option, 145-146
transient mode, 10
    installing shell with /TRAN, 145-146
TREE command, 349-350
tree structure, 38
TYPE command, 350-351

U

Up Arrow key, 30, 32. *See also* scrolling

V

variables. *See* parameters
VDISK command, 353-354
VER command, 351
VERIFY command, 351-352
version. *See* DOS version number
VGA adapter, 151
View option (File menu), 61-65, 107,
        138-139
viewing files, 61-65, 107, 138-139
VOL command, 352-353
volatile memory, 4
volume label, 95
volume serial number, 95

W

wild card symbols, 39-40, 67-68
    asterisk (*) as, 39-40, 67
    in customizing File List, 67-68
    in Filename area, 39-40
    in PRINT command filenames, 201
    question mark (?) as, 39-40, 68
    using to locate files, 75

X

/X:ON/OFF parameter (APPEND
        command), 204
XCOPY command, 354-356